# Australian and Indian Literature: Studies in Mutual Response

# Australian and Indian Literature: Studies in Mutual Response

*Edited by*
**David Kerr and R.K. Dhawan**

ISCS
Indian Society for Commonwealth Studies

*Published by*
**Indian Society for Commonwealth Studies**
New Delhi
*in association with*
**Prestige Books**
3/28, East Patel Nagar, New Delhi 110 008


ISBN: 81-85218-24-2

*Phototypesetting by*
**data culture**
Lajpat Nagar IV
New Delhi 110 024

*Jacket design by*
**Three-A Corporation**
New Delhi 110 002

*Printed at*
**Mehra Offset Press**
New Delhi 110 002

# Contents

## Section I

# Contributors

**Soma Banerjee**, Ranchi

**Veronica Brady**, Australia

**Radharani Chakravarty**, Delhi

**K. Chellappan**, Tiruchi

**Ian Copland**, Clayton

**R.K. Dhawan**, Delhi

**S.C. Harrex**, Bedford Park

**David Kerr**, Dromana, Victoria

**Enrique Martinez**, Victoria

**Malati Mathur**, Alwar

**Sudesh Mishra**, Australia

**Tom Mulcaire**, Melbourne

**David Myers**, Rockhampton

**Chaman Nahal**, Delhi

**Veena Noble**, Hyderabad

**N.E. Pavithra**, Tiruchi

**Jagdish Rai**, Delhi

**M. Kumaraswamy Raju**, Anantapur

**S. Ramaswamy**, Bangalore

**Ratnakar S. Sadawarte**, Vaijapur

**Paul Sharrad**, Wollongong

**Ron Shepherd**, Perth

**S.K. Tikoo**, Imphal

**Walter Tonetto**, Elwood

**Haydn Williams**, Adelaide

# Introduction

R.K. DHAWAN

Australian literature's evolution spans over a period of two hundred years. All Australian literature of the nineteenth century, since the first settlement in 1788, relates broadly to the imagery of bush life. In Australia, it was environment that dominated; the place was unlike Europe. The landscape there was new and strange; it drew the writers's attention. For the sake of convenience, we may divide Australian literature into three periods: (a) a colonial period, extending from 1788; (b) a nationalist period terminated by World War I; and (c) a modern period following World War I.

The earliest miscellaneous writings were produced by convicts, emancipators, travellers and explorers. New South Wales of 1800 was a convict outpost, a prison romantically remote but still a prison. The first Australian novel was the disguised autobiography of a convict, Henry Savery's *Quintus Servinton* (1830). The convict was felt instinctively by writers to be the symbol on which they built their fictional world.

Australian writers responded significantly to the Depression of the 1930s. In the thirties and forties, several writers produced short stories in which the Depression figures as an ingredient in the narrative. Among the more memorable ones are Vance Palmer's "The Trap," Don Edward's "What Chance" and John Morrison's "Christ, the Devil and the Lunatic." A representative work of the Depression period is the novel *Power Without Glory*. Frank Hardy has recorded that his main intention in writing this book was "to show the face, the lived face behind the democratic facade that (he) had seen in the 30s."

There grew up a generation of "bush balladists" and narrative writers who were widely published by the *Sydney Bulletin*. The leading writers were A.B. Paterson and Henry Lawson. Lawson was the best of the writers of this group and has been regarded as one of the world's masters of short fiction.

Contemporary Australian literature is marked by great diversity. Robert FitzGerald and Kenneth Slessor have contributed significantly to the Australian poetry. The main feature of FitzGerald's work has been its consistent intellectual challenge.

There has been a phenomenal growth of activity in the theatre also. This is especially reflected in the plays of Douglas Stewart and Ray Lawlor. Stewart's work anticipates in many ways the course of Australian drama in the renaissance of the 1950s. His plays are at once a counterpart in drama of the cult of historical narrative in modern Australian verse. And, in Lawlor's *The Summer of the Seventeenth Doll*, Australian drama seems to have found a new footing.

Since the last War, the writers who have achieved world-wide prominence are: Judith Wright and A.D. Hope in poetry, and Patrick White (who died recently) in the novel. Australian writing in the recent decades has acquired great breadth and diversity. There has been a steady flow of European migrants to Australia since the War, a fast industrial development and an increase in urban population. All these charges have been reflected in recent Australian writing. Judith Wright's poetry is marked by emotion, humanity and nostalgia. She is perhaps the most womanly of the Australian women poets. Her first collection *The Moving Image* (1946) made a great impact on the contemporary literary scene. She broke away from the stock attitude of the bush-balladist and put an end to nature poetry in Wordsworth-Kendall mode.

A.D. Hope, a great intellectual and learned scholar, may be regarded as a University Wit. He has been prolific and all his work has a great complexity and richness. The appearance of Hope's *Collected Poems 1930-1965* declared the range of his output and justified his conception of poetry as a "celebration of the world," an act of joy. Amongst the modern Australian poets, it is necessary to include James McAuley and Douglas Stewart . McAuley, like Hope, is a professor of literature, and his poetry has a definite academic precision.

Patrick White is the best-known Australian novelist and is ranked among the best in the world. In India, he is extremely popular and a great deal of study and research is being conducted by scholars on his writings. His reputation dates from the appearance of *The Tree of Man* (1955), and White has won recognition as a playwright and short-story writer as well. *Voss, Riders in the Chariot, The Solid Mandala* and *A Fringe of Leaves* are all popular novels. In the development of Australian drama, White marks a conscious swing from naturalism. Indeed, he is the first significant writer to identify himself with an Australian social and intellectual outlook. His books draw their extraordinary power from his exploration of territories unchartered before.

The last two decades have witnessed a massive increase in the production of Australian fiction. Many of the works were accorded due recognition. In 1973, Patrick White won the Nobel Prize for literature. In 1982, Thomas Keneally won Britain's most prestigious award for his novel *Schindler's Ark*. In 1988, the prestigious Booker Prize was awarded to the forty-seven year old Peter Carey for his novel *Oscar and Lucinda*. This work is a romantic mystery—the story of an unlikely love-affair between a nineteenth-century priest and an heiress with gambling addiction.

It is worth-noting that, under the Commonwealth Literary Fund, several works of fiction have been published in Australia. The establishment of the Literature Board has led to a further rise in the production of creative writing. In 1979, Penguin Australia began an ambitious programme of publishing Australian literature, especially fiction, which has given it a great impetus. The scholarly journals *Australian Literary Studies, Westerly, Southerly* and *Meanjin* have contributed significantly to the enrichment of the literary scene.

## II

The first section of this project is a rich collection of papers offered by Indian academics on Australian literature. The first piece, "Australia, the Centre Pole," is an extract from Chaman Nahal's recently published novel *The Salt of Life*. The extract is prefixed by an introductory note by Chaman Nahal. Carol Schnicke, we learn, was an Australian woman who wanted to meet Gandhi before leaving for her country. She had to see Gandhi who was the prototype of her experiment in Australia. Her encounter with Gandhi finds a vivid description in the scene. *The Salt of Life* is a colossal work and covers the most dramatic phase of India's freedom movement when in 1930, Mahatma Gandhi undertook the 200-mile march on foot from his ashram in Sabarmati to Dandi, a small village near Bombay on the Arabian Sea, to protest against the continued British Raj in India.

Jagdish Rai in his paper brilliantly traces the origins of Australian poetry. He finds the birth of Australian poetry unique and peculiar in a way in which no other such literary phenomenon seems to have been. First, because the Australian poetry has gone through genuine pains of birth while coming forth under circumstances and in a geography most uncongenial for such a naissance. If we set Charles Harpur's poetry, we find that there is something qualitatively new and elemental in the former which is lacking in the latter. There is something more enduring and impressive than the emotion in his poem. Though there were some others like Gordon and Kendall who displayed occasional moods of affection fro Australia and garnered a very useful treasure of Australian symbols for the coming generations of Australian poets, it is Harpur who set the tone of the Australian poetic tradition. He was the first to express a love of the landscape itself. The most popular of his poems were those in which he tried to deal with life and landscape in terms heavily influenced by English poetry, especially Wordsworth's romantic nature-philosophy.

In her paper "Mirroring the land," Soma Banerjee explores those special characteristics of Nature poetry – Australian and Indian – that reveal the uniqueness of the land that has been the source of inspiration. She gives illustrations from several poems that bespeak of the distinctive flavour of the soil.

In her paper, "A.D. Hope's Ulysses and Kate Llewellyn's Penelope; Two Modern Voices from the Past," Malati Mathur emphasizes that it is in his imaginative and innovative use of myths that Hope's brilliance clearly reveals itself. Myths provide the most satisfactory answer, both philosophically and artistically, to the problems Hope encounters as a man and as a poet.

Poets have always been preoccupied with the problem of time and change. In her illuminating paper on Judith Wright, Radharani Chakravarty says that the poet's individualized formulations of time and change are the product of her own sensitive response to the social situation in Australia.

James McAuley is considered to be one of the major modern poets of Australia and is placed along side A.D. Hope, Judith Wright, Mary Gilmore and Douglas Stewart. S.K. Tikoo finds a close similarity between McAuley and T.S. Eliot as both these writers uphold the European tradition and in many ways McAuley has things in common with Eliot – his classicism., Catholicism, attitude towards the supernatural and an active interest in politics. Thus, despite the fact that McAuley is a modern Australian poet, he can be placed in the English poetic tradition along side T.S. Eliot, a most important exponent of that tradition which runs from Chaucer to the Metaphysicals to the beginnings of the 1920s when the vogue for the Metaphysicals began anew and critical efforts were made to reinvigorate studies in that poetry.

S. Ramaswamy in his paper "Australian Drama: Major Trends" makes a survey of the main trends of the Australian drama, namely the Documentary, Poetic Drama/Radio Play, Realistic/Naturalistic Theatre and the Revolt against it. Moreover, some of the Australian themes are connected with elements of colonial life, like bushranging, changing pattern of sexual and social behaviour in the younger generation, violence and racism.

According to K. Chellappan and N.E. Pavithra, Patrick White belongs to the great tradition of novelists such as Dostoevsky, Tolstoy, Lawrence and Joyce in his epic vision of life and his concern with man's place in the universe, though he confines his milieu to Australia. T.S. Eliot seems to have been a major influence on the early works of White, especially on his second novel *The Living and the Dead.* It is the only novel which is set outside Australia. It registers White's feelings towards England, which after the War appeared to him sterile. Indeed, the very titles *The Waste Land* and *The Living and the Dead* are similar as they embody the theme of life and death, suggesting man's struggle through a death-in-life existence. In White's novel, there are not only echoes and images from Eliot's *The Waste Land* but the overall atmosphere and the very exploration of theme shows a clear and consistent affinity with Eliot's poem.

Veena Noble in her paper on Patrick White's *The Solid Mandala* offers some fresh insights. Ratnakar Sadawarte in his paper on the same novel discusses many levels of meaning in it.

M. Kumaraswamy Raju in his article "Male Loneliness in Koch's *Double Man*" points out that the novel is a clarion call for an art free from European and trans-Atlantic literary and cultural matrix and a recognition of Australian proximity to a culture that is anything but European.

## III

In May 1988, The Library Society held a symposium at the State Library of New South Wales on "Asian Influences on Australian Literature." The symposium was one of an occasional series designed to provide not only a widening of horizons for the audience, but also to give scholars working in similar areas an opportunity to discuss each other's works. Myfanwy Gollan in his "Introduction: Widening the Horizons" declared that "Asia is no longer seen as a single entity but as a collection of different countries with rich and diverse cultures." Two papers presented at the Conference have a special relevance from our point of view. These were: (i) "Out of the Mainstream: Theosophy and Escape from Protestantism: The Cultural Connection" by Jill Roe, an historian; (ii) "Australia and India: Readings in Two Hemispheres" by Jeremy Nelson, a poet and teacher.

Jill Roe explored the Indian influence on Australian Cultural history. Her book *Beyond Belief: Theosophy in Australia 1879-1939* details the Australian search for belief at the turn of the last century. In her view, some Australians in the nineteenth century evinced a keen interest in theosophy that added Indian dimension to Australian cultural history. Theosophy thus appealed mostly to people dissatisfied with Victorian religion. Interestingly, some of these were feminists who raised a revolt against male-dominated churches. There was a significant theosophical tendency among "the thinking classes" in the last decades of the nineteenth century and early decades of the twentieth. The theosophists sought to focus "the light of the Asia" on the dilemmas thrown by Victorian religion. Incidentally, Edwin

Arnold's *The Light of Asia*, a philosophical masterpiece on the life of the Buddha, was published in 1879. The "ancient wisdom" of the India was held in the highest esteem by the Australians. For instance, Godfrey Miller, a Sydney abstractionist, extolled India as his source of inspiration and died a member of Theosophical Society. Theosophy, thus, made some contribution to the making of the literary legends and to the coming of modernism in Australia.

Jeremy Nelson's paper on the "cultural connection" was based on his personal experience as a poet. In the early 1950s while still a student at Sydney University, he went to Madras to attend a Conference and afterwards travelled widely in India. He was so drawn to the "strange, various and exciting nation of many cultures and languages" that he went back later to study at Calcutta university. During the three years that he was there, Indian people and environment made an everlasting impact on his mind. And this impact was an enduring one on the poetry that he wrote! As is evident in his poetry, he felt "the whole world as sacred both in itself and as mankind's place."

The present collection of critical articles from Australia and India indicates the growing possibilities for cross-cultural links between the two countries. Indian Society for Commonwealth Studies, since its inception, has done its best to promote Commonwealth literature and other allied disciplines. Amongst its other activities of promoting awareness, scholarship and mutual understanding, the Society organizes lectures, seminars and an annual conference. Apart from the bi-annual journal, *The Commonwealth Review*, it publishes bibliographies, monographs and scholarly books of the members.

## IV

The growing interest in Australian literature by Indian academics has led to a number of literary programmes and publications. In July 1987, a one-day seminar on "Contemporary Australian Literature" was organized at New Delhi. It was inaugurated by the then-Australian High Commissioner, Mr. G.B. Feakes. The participants included creative writers—C.J. Koch and Les Murray, Nissim Ezekiel and Chaman Nahal. In the first Commonwealth Conference held at the

University of Poona, Dr. Brady Roderigues presented a paper and read her poems. At the second Commonwealth Conference, Dr. David Kerr gave an open lecture on Aboriginal literature and Ms. Rosemary Kerr spoke on education in Australia.

It is heartening to note that *The Commonwealth Review* has been very well received, in India and abroad. The inaugural number had scholarly articles; it included a paper by A.D. Hope, entitled "Standard English: Whose Standard?" The second issue of the journal was a special number on the Bombay-born novelist Salman Rushdie. Ron Shepherd, University of Western Australia, contributed a paper on *Midnight's Children*. And the latest issue is again a special one – a double-number on "Australian and Indian Literature: Studies in Mutual Response." I am sure this will prove a useful aid to the research scholars and all those interested in this area.

It is a promising start and I am sure such joint ventures as the present one will be highly conducive to the promotion of Australian literature and culture.

# Australia, the Centre Pole

## CHAMAN NAHAL

(The following is an extract from Chaman Nahal's novel, *The Salt of Life*, which has just been released by Allied Publishers of New Delhi. This novel deals with one of Gandhi's movements against the British during India's freedom struggle. The fictional protagonists of the novel are Raja Vishal Chand, the ruler of a small princely state, and his wife Kusum, who had been living in the Gandhi ashram at Sabarmati for a number of years before marrying the Raja. An Australian woman, called Carol Schnicke visits India at that time and gets involved with the Raja and his wife. She acquires some idea of the Gandhian non-violent methods when Kusum resists a British officer who tries to bully her. Later, Carol Schnicke gets involved with a Public School that the Raja and Kusum have started in their state, Lambini. She returns to Australia and in Fremantle, a few miles out of Perth, she starts an ashram on the model of the Gandhi ashram. On a subsequent visit to India and Lambini, she joins the Raja on a mountain expedition to a monastery in the interior of his state. The Raja, unfortunately, is killed in an accident during this expedition. Kusum returns to the Gandhi ashram, which has now been shifted from Sabarmati to Sevagram. Carol Schnicke wants to sympathize with Kusum on the death of her husband and she wants to see Gandhi before leaving for Australia. In the meantime, she has also collected a few Indians, whom

> she is taking with her to her ashram in Fremantle.
> So one day, with her usual vigour and aplomb, she
> lands in Sevagaram. . . .)

It was only when the carnival arrived that Gandhi became aware of his neglect of Kusum. He had not offered her his condolences yet. Though he squirmed at the word--gaiety and fun for its sake was anathema to him--he had to call the new guests by that name only. As soon as they descended on the place, they started appropriating it. They shouted loudly for help, demanded clean living quarters, demanded clean food, and asked to be taken straight to Kusum. That anyone should arrive at Sevagram asking for anyone else but Gandhi gave Gandhi a pleasant jolt. He was strolling the grounds, thinking of how best to extoll further the virtues of continuous satyagraha in *Harijan*. The group arrived in two ghora garis, one of which was being driven by a large, sumptuous white woman, who was showering on the horse Indian words of endearment and also cracking the whip at him.

'Pooh, pooh, ruko now, beta, ruko,' she said, pulling in the reins.

She jumped off the carriage in one clear leap and said to the coachman, who sat intimidated next to her:

'See, how well I managed it!'

'Yes, memsahib,' the man acknowledged, grudgingly.

The woman was dressed in baggy trousers, which gave her an even greater dimension, and she was wearing sports shoes.

Gandhi's first reaction was she was some relation of Mirabehn, who was even larger and bigger.

'Eh, baba,' she said to Gandhi, without recognizing him.

'Can you tell us who we report to here?'

Before Gandhi could answer, she told her companions:

'Get off, now. We are at the ashram.'

She lent them a hand and out of the carriages she pulled out, as does a magician from his box, a tall, anaemic white man, who was all jitters, the way he glanced around to make sure of the ground he was stepping on, a faded and pale white young woman, a tall well-built Indian in the white habit of a priest, his curly hair neatly parted, his white whiskers pressed against his cheeks, and another Indian with three or four cameras slung around his neck.

In the like manner, she retrieved their luggage, pulling it out with a flourish, and then while the others stood around, she sat down on a suitcase and began to mop her face--it was *so* hot.

'Baba--old man, didn't you hear me?' she called after Gandhi again.

And then she had a careful look at him and almost fell off her suitcase.

'Sorry, sir. Sorry, Mr. Gandhi. I guess I was a little exhausted by the journey.'

'At seventy-one, I *am* old!'

'Please forgive me.'

Gandhi watched their luggage. There were suitcases and handbags and a violin case and a bag containing golf sticks.

'Who plays the violin?'

'I do sir, sometimes,' said the priest. 'I'm John Tree.'

'And who plays golf?'

Percy Wand raised his hand, though first nervously looking around to see if there wasn't a trap in it.

'Are you a travelling circus?'

Gandhi asked this in all seriousness. Everything about them seemed so unreal, so exaggerated, so threateningly dramatic. The priest had a comic smile on his lips and was constantly tugging at his habit, as though trying to get rid of it or pull it up around his waist. The lanky white man was wearing a monocle--it seemed only for show. Occasionally he took it off, polished the glass, and put it back on his eye, yet he remained uneasy in handling it as though he might drop it and break it (it was part of the new identity Percy Wand was acquiring). The white young woman was biting her nails, making jerky motions with her torso, and her lips were mumbling and murmuring as though rehearsing a part. The man with the cameras was ever pulling down his bowler on his head and aiming his cameras in different directions without actually shooting.

Carol Schnicke joined in the joke.

'My, we do look like a travelling circus, don't we?'

'Aren't you?'

'To the extent that we are all part of such a circus.'

'A good answer--a good answer,' Gandhi laughed. All his teeth were now gone except three of four lower incisors.

The secretaries had appeared on the .scene and the requests of the party were being attended to.

'How do you know Kusum?' Gandhi asked Carol Schnicke who seemed to be the leader of the group.

'From Lambini. We wanted to see her before setting out for Australia.'

'Ah, you are from Australia, are you?'

'Yes.'

'And you want to see Kusum?'

Carol nodded.

'And not see me?' He had an impish grin.

'You as well,' she conceded. 'To see you was the main idea actually as you are my model for what I'm doing in Australia.'

'And what are you doing there?'

'I'm running an ashram.'

Carol didn't bat an eyelid. Yes, that's what she was doing there for some years. She had a lot of property at Fremantle, a port close to Perth and she had decided to set up a model colony there--an ashram if you will. Driven by compulsions and urges she couldn't quite define, all the money she owned had brought her no peace. This barren, inhospitable land where her ancestors had been transplanted from England, where she was born and raised, this land she found as an assault on her consciousness. The natives they had subdued, but with all the power and the skill at their disposal, the whites had not been able to subdue the unfriendly peninsula. You travelled for miles upon miles without seeing anything but rocks, dry plains, and gum trees. She had gone from Perth in the west to Darwin in the north, and from Darwin to Sydney in the east, and then to Adelaide in the south. No, there was nothing there but colossal waste. Why could God have made a land that was so hot, so arid, so waterless, so hostile to life? India too was hot but they had at least the Himalayas. In Australia, they had nothing. She had done it by road, by train, by air, by steamer. She did arrive at habitations, after long deserted journeys, but they seemed hardly like places on a map, those habitations, with no tint, no colour, no specific personality, they seemed more like outposts, exploratory camps for something more tangible to come into existence one day but which never did. That Alice Springs, right in the middle of the wide, denuded continent, did give you a wrench when you arrived there after dusty safaris. What were those couple of houses doing there thousands of miles from anywhere? And those few humans? Were they that mad to have dug up and settled in that waterhole--

there being no waterhole nearby either! The notion came to her that Alice Springs was the Centre Pole of the universe, the absolute dead centre, seemingly unproductive and sterile, these few homes, these few people, pasted down on that land rather than growing up from it. If there was a North Pole and a South Pole, how could you go up and down without interacting at a middle point? And Alice Springs was that middle point of the world where humanity intersected all the time. Humanity did not constitute of men alone; it was an amalgam of the living and the dead, the spirit and the body, and the waves upon magnetic waves generated by the two. These waves, these powers, filled all space, roamed and migrated thousands of miles like the arctic tern, paused to take breath before they took off again, humanity was an amalgam of all that existed and could possibly exist, and Alice Springs, way out from factional pulls, way out from lust and greed, stood as that pivot, that Centre Pole, where things congregated, rested, intersected, invisible to the eye, inaudible to the ear, yet seeable, touchable, feelable to those who had the grace. In the Orient, especially in India, Carol Schnicke had found everything ever mutating against everything else, that amalgam she fancied and talked about, where in spite of the economic poverty, in spite of the class walls, so many people met and intersected with each other at so many levels, and where the dead too, the cumulative dead and the individual dead, were so pronouncedly present along with the living. When John Tree watched her from his room having her bath under the tap of the Ugoki school--yes, she was aware of it all the time--it was not a voyeur looking at a naked woman, it was one spirit connecting with another on an ascending, vertical plane. How else to climb the ladder to heaven except by holding each other's hand? How else to fly the dark continents except by leaning on each other? The Occidental races would never reach that level of interdependence, that amalgam, they were too fixated on their individual egos. John Tree had no individual ego, as she believed she, Carol Schnicke, and none--as most Australians had none. Now weren't his countrymen missing the great chance of living in an amalgam, in a unity of the body and the spirit, positioned as they were in the Orient and the South Pacific. Go to any of the islands in the South Pacific and what do you come across there? Amalgam upon amalgam, harmony upon harmony. That experiment should be continued, should be enlarged, to widen the world's spheres of unities. The Europeans who came to Australia had only tried to duplicate Europe there. Large cities such as Sydney, Melbourne, Adelaide, Brishbane--what were they if not a replica of Europe! The hot, barren but beautiful Australia needed its own identity, such as it was, whatever it was. Couldn't she revive the old spirit of Australia that was going to seed at the hands of the settlers? The aborigines had lived in Australia close to three hundred thousand years and survived--in spite of the inclement climate. Yes, at Alice Springs, even the whites and the aborigines met. And she would create more spaces from them to come together, for all humanity to come together. In this her millionaire husband Rudolf Schnicke, who was thirty years older than she, and who had arrived here a broken man from Germany after the first war, leaving behind a dead wife and dead children, had invested in the opals and grown rich, and whom she had married on the rebound when she was recovering from a jilted affair, who had such a sense of humour (Rudolf: 'One should never live close enough to one's place of work; there are constant interruptions in your private life.' Carol: 'I know you live in Perth. Where do you work, Rudolf?' Rudolf: 'In Brisbane--ha!'--which was three thousands miles away and where most of his opal mines were), and such a twinkle in his eye (catching Carol by the hip, 'Come sit on my lap, dearie, you may still find something good there!'), who assured her he won't keep her for long, he would soon proceed to the grave freeing her again (which he did three years later, leaving her all his wealth), who would be content so long as he could hold her next to him just for one night (such an incorrigible romantic he was!)--in this, in her philanthropy, her quest for philanthropy, Rudolf Schnicke encouraged her. And at Fremantle, ten miles out of Perth, where she had some property, she had started that hermitage, that ashram of hers, which she simply called Crisis Centre. Yes, the Centre Pole was at Alice Springs, but the road from her Crisis Centre led towards that direction only. Gandhi's ashrams at Sabarmati and then at Sevagram, they too were similar crisis centres where humanity ruled supreme. The idea of her own centre had fastened upon her only after her repeated visits to India. She had, for some years, been dumping money into that country: funding charitable projects, sending out teachers to that public school a local prince had started in his state, accommodating odd visiting Indians at her home in Perth. Whenever Carol Schnicke visited any Asian country she went native. In Indonesia,

she wore the sarong. In Malaya, she covered her head with a stole. In India, she put on saris and applied a bindi, the pink dot mark, to her forehead. If they bathed in public, she bathed in public, if they got on their bicycle by over-the-carrier swing, she did the same, even though in the process she exposed herself right up to her undies. If they ate with their fingers, she ate with fingers as well. All right my Indian brothers, we will set up crisis centres of our own in Australia, beginning with Fremantle. And to the Fremantle Crisis Centre, which she founded in 1939, the year the war began, she had gathered together castaways and down-at-heels from Australia no doubt, but also from lonely islands such as Tonga, Fiji, Tahiti and Samoa. Come, whosoever would like to come, she announced. We will live together, we will share things, we will be human. Come, announced Carol Schnicke, we will live in peace, whatever may be happening elsewhere. And on her recent trip to India, she had picked up two castaways, Percy and Jennifer Wand, whom their own people were bent on disowning. Churchill's orders were yet to come but acting on his own, the
Viceroy, Lord Linlithgow, had already dismissed Percy Wand from service, allowing him no concession whatever, and Army & Navy Store had dispensed with the services of Jennifer Wand. Carol Schnicke had found the brother and sister in tears one day in Lambini, where they were momentarily living after their disgrace. Death is better than such life, she found them saying to each other at the Bhawani Maidan rock bluff, contemplating the deep plunge before them. How ridiculous, she found herself telling them. Come with me to Fremantle and live--*live*. Oddly enough, Carol wrote to John Tree, asking him if he would like to join her at Fremantle? It's a free town, she wrote, as its very name suggests, though this was where the convicts from England had first landed on the West coast. That first West coast prison of Australia had become its first free city, open to everyone, whoever he might be, whatever he might be. While bathing under the tap, Carol had watched the sad face of John Tree, as he sat in his room fiddling with his violin. What incoherent, woeful notes did he strike on that instrument. In spite of the adulation his flock showed him, his eyes constantly searched the distant horizons. I'll find you a better flock at Fremantle with wider reaches of the sky than you have here, she wrote to him. You can even have free love at Fremantle, she had cryptically added. (What's free love, John had innocently queried!) And

John Tree had at once accepted, drawn more to Carol Schnicke than Australia. It was with this small shipwrecked band of people that Carol Schnicke was journeying back to Australia to provide them with a new beginning. And she had to see Gandhi who was the prototype of her experiment. And she had to see Kusum--to speak to her about Raja Vishal Chand's death.

# Male Loneliness in Koch's *Double Man*

M. KUMARASWAMY RAJU

*The Double Man*, the latest of Christopher J. Koch's published novels, is, to say the least, a typical Australian novel. Winner of the 1985 Miles Franklin Literary Award, the novel establishes conclusively the novelist's reputation for a mode of realism that is distinctly South Pacific. After expeditions to the South-East Asia and the East, the novelist's imagination now explores the local and the native, the Australian landscape forming the quarry for the copplestones of his fictional discourse. In a sense his latest work is at once a clarion call for an art free from European and trans-Atlantic literary and cultural matrix and a recognition of Australian proximity to a culture that is anything but European. Chris Tiffin's observation is instructive:

> Perhaps because of the increasing ambivalence of its relationship with Britain, Australia has turned towards Asia in the last twenty years, economically, politically and culturally, and this is reflected in the creative writing.[1]

*Across the Sea Wall* and *The Year of Living Dangerously* not only have South-East Asia for dramatizing Koch's experiences but also freely refer to Wayang Kulit or Kali-myth. And now in *The Double Man* the novelist evokes the predicament of the Australian aborigines, of the convict immigrants of the 1840s and of the generation of nineteen sixties with the keenness of a historian, the penetrating insight of a psychologist and the aesthetic ordering of an artist. Therefore it may not be illegitimate to claim that with *The Double Man* Australian literature comes to self-reference as it has all the central motifs that make Australian history and culture.

In "Standards in Australian Literature," A.D. Hope has said that Australian literature has been largely concerned with life on the land since "the country and the country towers have a character quite of its own, parochial perhaps, but genuinely and recognizably Australian, and it has been the ambition of nine-tenths of the poets and novelists of the country to depict and record the typical and authentic Australia in something like its own terms."[2] Although for A.D. Hope this is natural to all colonial literatures, he disapproves of this prolonged adolescence. The story of pioneering the land therefore has been an obsession with most Australian novelists including Patrick White. Interestingly, Chris Koch's *The Double Man* instead of pioneering the land, chooses to pioneer the Australian fiction not by pushing away the stopcock ingredients but by going with and beyond the cliches. The cosmopolitan and the industrial culture, long disregarded as alien, is presented here. The transition from bush culture to pop culture and the travails of a convict generation find their symbolic expression in the novelist's experiment with the theme. It is a novel which tries to grapple with immediate realities leaving the obsessive past.

The preoccupation with the realities of Australia, the landlocked island south of latitude forty, is an obsession with Koch. References to "the landlocked island" as also the futility of Australian attempt at duplication of England recur in several of his interviews. He asserts that the duplication is only on the surface and there is a troubling strangeness about the island's landscapes:

> And beyond Port Davey's last little lights of settlement, in the extreme south-west, all normality ended. Beyond Port Davey there was nothing--there was Antarctica. In the Gothic wilderness of the south-west stretched 5000 square miles of impenetrable rain-forest, entirely unsettled, where men had walked in and never walked out and rivers ran underground. A writer who is a native of such an island comes quite soon to the problem of trying to match its spirit with the spirit of the ancestral land in his head--the lost northern hemisphere. It's possible to love both, but matching them up isn't easy: the task of a lifetime . . . that this situation, to a great or lesser degree, may be typical of many Australian writers, and it is this tension--produced by the consciousness of another lost landscape and society--that produces a quality in Australian literature that is peculiar to it.[3]

Much like Prospero, who is alienated from his landscape and society and who tries in vain to stick nurture on nature, the Australian artist nostalgically looks back at the lost landscape and society. This is for a time and finally he finds the island, like Miranda, a brave new world. So it seems that the Australian writer finds himself caught in a tension between the Prosperonian pessimism and Mirandesque optimism.

On the face of it *The Double Man* is a hopeless novel peopled by cursed men and women. They are ciphers at large, literal and metaphorical. Either one is a born cripple or ends up as a cripple. The unfortunate condition in which they find themselves is that they have a dual existence--physically, they are bound to the inimical and intransigent land and spiritually they are in their homeland. One is hard reality and other is a dream and the two don't coalesce, in fact they negate each other. One generation has been made to wear the scarlet letter and the next generation attempts to redeem the past only to fail. This truth about the predicament of Australians is dramatized pedantically in *The Double Man*.

First the physical reality, the soil and the hard matter that makes Australian land. Michael Brady who arrives on this island as a convict soon realizes that the land is not friendly. He "wasn't a man who loved the land: the land had betrayed him and the animals enslaved him. He kicked the cows into the bails with a personal animosity, menacing in his hat, his stubby figure, electric with rage."[4] (72) If this is Michael's analysis of the land, Richard Miller's is no different. His stay at Greystones is described in the following account:

> Before things began to happen, I was already in a curious state of mind. I found myself thinking of demons, as I moved about the property; and this was partly because I had demons of my own to resist. I had always seen the countryside as sexless; but now I saw that the land was not innocent, any more than the island itself was innocent. Half-seen shapes of lust and fear lurked in the sulking green bush, where, I wandered about alone, and at times I caught the land looking at me out of the corner of its eyes. Or perhaps something else did, while the bush seemed to sulk, its viscous gum-leaves gleaming like metal, the grey hair of its she oaks trailing to the ground in what looked like sorrow.

> Then I would remember that we were in Van Diemen's Land, where crimes and monotonous misery had made their indelible traces a hundred years ago; where transported pick-pockets from the rookeries and thieves' kitchens of Giles and Camden Town had yearned for a London they could never see again; where the stealers and shepherds and convicts, out of reach of the Government in Hobart, had made slaves and victims of the doomed Aborigines, hanging the heads of the husbands about the necks of the wives, using the amputated fingers to tap their pipes. And I wondered at times if the spirits that vanished race believed in, as well as their own reproachful spirits, still lingered here in the gullies or among the dunes."[5] (74)

Driven out of the native soil, desperate and disillusioned, the convict brings no love but hatred to the landlocked island. Moreover, he is determined to be unsympathetic to the aborigines. He is no Prospero, who is a victim, not a criminal. And again unlike Prospero whose magic wand of nurture attempts to neutralize nature, the convict from the Christian world has no evangelical mission. Bringing no peace, he cannot give any peace to himself or others. This idea woven into the theme of *The Double Man* makes it gloomy and sad.

What is more horrifying is that added to the criminal past there is the haunting sense of guilt which does not free even the successive generations. Richard Miller, Brian Brady, Darcy Burr, Richard Frederick, Mrs. Dillon, Katrin, all young men and women (of the sixties) try to wipe off the past and visualize a happy future unknown to an earlier generation. They dream of "territories beyond the island," plan to escape to the mainland and get into the country music circuit. So they do not seek redemption here as their goal is Europe. The Rymers club started by them is as quick to rise as it is to fall. Towards the end of the novel the harmony is broken, the members disintegrate and Europe is never reached. The guitar, the symbol of Europe, is abandoned and there is a return to the reality of the island. The world of illusion is shattered.

In spite of its unrelieved gloominess and the mood of pessimism *The Double Man's* philosophical, moral, ethical and spiritual concerns make it a compelling work. Stating that the novelist "has a duty to certain, to tell comprehensible stories to his reader . . . that a serious novelist must present his moral and social views through character and dramatic momentum," Koch asserts that "fiction must assert the general work of human beings."[6] True to his belief Koch does assert the general worth of human beings through character and dramatic momentum in *The Double Man.* At the centre of the novel is Richard Miller whose journey through life forms the story and whose consciousness of his doubleness makes the theme. Born a cripple, this polio-affected paralytic, realizes very early the doubleness in his life. His interest in the Otherworld begins when he discovers his dual inheritance--the Germannees of his grandfather Karl Miller and the Englishness of his mother. What offends the young Miller about Karl Miller is that for all his claims to pride in German descent, he suppresses the fact by a clever substitution of "K" for "C" in his "Karl." There is another reason for Richard Miller's interest in the attitudes of his grandfather and mother to his crippling. Karl Miller despising and rejecting crippledom tells Richard Miller to throw away crutches whereas his mother does not. Yet another reason for Miller's interest in the Otherworld, as he himself explains, is the analogous situation he finds himself in: his mother's insistence on his being a Catholic and his grandfather's on Protestantism. This doubleness of Richard Miller is not peculiar to him alone. Only he is aware of it, sensitive that he is. Koch himself explains the notion of doubleness in his novels:

> Well, I suppose I'm preoccupied with the idea that character is something that's not always complete. I rather doubt that any human beings have a feeling of completeness; we all want to be someone other than ourselves. If you're a man of action, if you are basically extroverted type, you perhaps yearn to be somebody more interned or inward, and it's notorious, of course, that introverted people and people who live for the imagination have some yearning to be people whose life is outward and positive and more dynamic. So I think that we tend to be incomplete; and I am perhaps particularly preoccupied with that theme.[7]

The foregoing probably explains every complex character in fiction as it does Richard Miller's doubleness. The need for completeness, rather the awareness of incompleteness, is more acute in a cripple.

The physical handicap is a constant reminder of incompleteness which is sought to be overcome in a life of fantasy and of dreams. *The Double Man* adopts this technique of substitution.

Denied social life like any cripple, Miller creates a fantasy world peopled by a witch, an Elf Queen, a black-cloaked man and himself, all of whom regularly appear in his dreams. Shutting himself in an undisturbed upstairs room, he enacts plays with figures cut from fairy tale books and sometimes reads the house's aged books. But this exchange of the real world for the fantasy world, he realizes, only leads him "to long for something else; something maddeningly vague; some absolute escape, some icy ecstasy found in far, pure reaches of the air." (31)

When Richard Miller grows into an adult he finds the erstwhile fantasy world turning into a reality. The black cloaked figure of his childhood card games appears now in the person of Broderick, the mysterious man descending into his life occasionally but who nevertheless initiates him only indirectly into a life characterized by astral travel, seances and communion with spirits. Also it is Clive Broderick who disenchants him about the Franciscan discipline (and Brother Kinsella), and later disillusions him of the value of university learning.

The witch of boy Richard Miller's fantasy world comes in the form of Deidre Dillon, a seductive young woman married to a rich old man. Young Miller, younger than Mrs. Dillon, is attracted by her physical charm and in course of time falls in love with her. But the relationship is broken after a sexual encounter because the woman leaves for Sydney to live with her husband. Richard Miller's life takes a new turn after he has met Mrs. Dillon since it only doubles his interest and fascination for the world of illusion, manifested in acting and filming. Mrs. Dillon had often told him that he would become a great actor and this severs him from university and the necessary world. From now on all his energies are directed to reach the one goal--the world of entertainment. So Richard Miller leaves for Melbourne, becomes an actor and finally ends up as a producer for ABS in Sydney. For nine years Deidre Dillon remains at the subconscious only to surface at a time when Richard Miller has developed a deep passion for Katrin, the Elf Queen of boy Richard's world. Now Mrs. Dillon has become a widow and having been raped by her stepson dies.

The association with Mrs. Dillon proves fatal for Miller as she seeks to disabuse him of his ideas about morality, ethics and spirituality. Miller himself admits that "certain things she said stayed in my mind to disturb me":

> "You're such a beautiful boy--I love to kiss you--I hate my husband making love to me--grunting and panting."
>
> "A boy is so pure. What we're doing isn't adultery, darling, is it? Only we know that."
>
> "Being crippled refined you spiritually, Richard. Don't be hurt. You're normal, of course--and that is why I love you. Neither of us is normal, darling, admit it. I can't bear bloody normal people."
>
> "I must go and feed Fiona now. My breasts are aching."

From the above it is clear that while pretending to disapprove of Miller's libertinism she makes him do those very things. The impact of her influence may be measured against Miller's emotional failure for nine long years. His bruised and atrophied soul is not to recover its crippledom until it meets the Elf Queen of his boyhood fantasy in the person of Katrin Vilde. However the witch does not disappear from his life forever. It reappears again when Miller is happily married to Katrin and tempts him with pathetic appeals to join her. But Miller is now able to distinguish between the illusion and reality and he prefers the latter.

To continue with the allegory, the correspondence between fantasy and reality, the Elf Queen of boy Richard Miller's world comes in the person of Katrin. When Richard is hard up for work in Sydney seeking job with ABS, he meets Katrin, a musical prodigy with an unhappy past. This Estonian woman was a victim of betrayal and had a crippled son through her lover. Richard Miller falls for her and subsequently marries her. Katrin, in the process of realizing her potentialities in music, which she achieves without much compromise, does make Richard jealous of her relationship with Brian Brady. Richard hears the town gossip about Katrin and Brian and is afraid of losing her. In the end, however, Katrin refuses to go to Europe and the USA with the musical group which suggests her devotion to Richard.

To suggest that Katrin Vilde belongs to the fantasy world of Miller is not a misreading of the narrative. She is a "prototype," "a figure from another time." Miller recognizes her as the prototype and truly falls in love:

> Perhaps it was when one met and recognized the descendant of a prototype that one truly fell in love; and the experience was all the more intense when the loved one was superficially different from oneself. Opposites did attract, but only when commonality was hidden underneath. This was the paradox that made for fatal poignancy and force; the long beloved face beneath the new beloved's mask; the marvellous sub-soil of the familiar, recognized with joy, shared like childhood. Potent as ancestry; the prototype whom our own prototype had known.

There is an element of Platonism in Richard Miller's love for Katrin Vilde. With Deidre Dilla Dillon dead and misgivings about Katrin and Brian Brady cleared, Richard is now a happy man. The partial man that he has appeared all through gains completeness by the reassuring love of his wife, and by returning to Catholic faith which he had rejected.

Koch's importance to Australian fiction consists, it has been suggested, in his conscious revolt against the so-called drab-fifties realism. Like his contemporaries Patrick White and Randolph Stow he was not interested in the realistic novel. Koch has said:

> Back in the 50's I reacted against the flat, dreary naturalism of most Australian fiction, just as Stow did. It's hard to convey now what a desert it was. Most Australian fiction then was everything I detested. Like Stow, my concerns were essentially poetic. That is, I was interested in myth, metaphor, and use of symbol, which was rigidly fenced off as the domain of the verse-writer in those days.[8]

Koch while disapproving the work of his predecessors, attempts a fiction which seeks to probe "beneath the surface of social everyday living and explore the realms of the spirit, a concern with the sensitive, alienated character and a common preoccupation with consciously crafted prose and made use of poetic, symbolic imagery."[9] Unfortunately there was hostility to this kind of writing and Koch was faulted as one who berated the regionalist nationalism of a young country. It is difficult to agree with criticism which calls Koch a betrayer because in his novel *The Double Man* he is concerned as much with Australian landscape as the Australian spirit. In this novel the novelist begins with a description of Tasmania, its people, its geography, its richness and moves on to give an account of metroplitan culture, of Sydney, of Hobart etc. The crisis in the life of a cripple and a series of crises which follows are but the common experience of Koch's generation. The enduring element in Koch's novel is not only the Australian landscape but also the spiritual landscape of the people. *The Double Man* measures upto the novelist's claim that he has always aimed at poetic effect. The landscape itself is symbolic. The description of Richard Miller's ascent up a hill in the beginning of the novel has a poetic quality. Even the characters, mysterious and mystical, are raised to the level of symbols.

## NOTES

1. Chris Tiffin, "Australian Literature and Film," *Dhvanyaloka*, Mysore, 1987, p. 1.
2. A.D. Hope, "Standards in Australian Literature," *The Oxford Anthology of Australian Literature*, ed. Leonie Kramer and Adrian Mitchell (Melbourne: OUP, 1985), p. 274.
3. C.J. Koch, "An Australian Writer Speaks," *Westerly*, No. 3, Sept. 1980, p. 71.
4. Chris Koch, *The Double Man* (London: Grafton Books, 1986), p. 72.
5. *Ibid.*, p.74.
6. Susan Mc Kernan, "C.J. Koch's Two-Faced, Vision," *Kunapipi*, 1986, p. 433.
7. John Thieme, "Christopher J. Koch," *Kunapipi*, 1986, p. 20.
8. Paul Sharrad, "Pour Mieux sauter: Christopher Koch's Novels in Relation to White, Stow and the Quest for a Post-Colonial Fiction," *World Literature Written in English*, Volume 23, Number 1 (1984), p. 209.
9. *Ibid.*

# A Study of the Hermaphroditic Element in Patrick White's *The Solid Mandala*

VEENA NOBLE

In an article entitled "The Prodigal Son" (Australian letters, 1, 3, April, 1958), Patrick White tells that on his return to Australia the thing that made him panic most "was the exaltation of the average."[1] It is in suburbia more than anywhere else that one finds this exaltation and it is Australian suburbia, its narrowness, its hypocrisy, its materialism, its reluctance to explore, that has been the object of White's sharpest criticism. But White was not contented with criticism alone. For he believed that behind this facade of mediocrity there was a brilliance. "I wanted," he said, "to discover the extraordinary behind the ordinary, the mystery and the poetry which alone could make bearable the lives of such people and incidentally, my own since my return."[2]

The Australia that White left and discovered to be new after his return was a country that was settled after the American War of Independence, when England needed a new colony to which to transport its criminals. The origins of Australia have haunted its literature whereas penal transportation to the older colonies is a neglected subject in American writing. While Americans see themselves as the heirs of the Puritans who supposedly fled the tyranny of the old for the paradise of the New World, Australian literature has treated its new world ambiguously.

In the nineteenth century Australian novel, it is often difficult to decide whether the country is worse than the brutalities of the colonial government and society. The early diaries, journals and other documents however give a more balanced picture of the land. The literary tradition which portrays the early settlements as horrible probably results from later attitudes and is based on a selection of historical factors. The early distinction between prisoner and government contributed towards treating the outlaw and those outside society as authentically Australian.

The literary treatment of the gentry and the middle class as British or European was strengthened in Australia by the fact that social divisions remained more obvious and sharper than in Canada. Immigration to Australia was more working clan than in other colonies and a local middle class developed less rapidly. The social establishment appealed to consist of British born officials, those connected with the government, or those wealthy enough to keep up English social ties. The identification of labourers and outcasts with Australia in contrast to the pro-English elite was strengthened by a tradition of radicalism originating in the late nineteenth century when large-scale immigration took place during an era of socialist ideology and unionization. From 1860 to 1900 the population grew from one to three million. Between the working clan dream of a new start in the colonies and the socialist ideas of the period, a radical nationalist ideology emerged which has persisted until the present.

While the legend of the 1890s and radical nationalist history has been accepted by few major Australian writers--Judith Wright being the one significant exception--even writers with no sympathy towards cultural nationalism have echoed the attack on suburbia, criticized its mass conformist society and implied that an essential Australia can be found in the desert and outback. Patrick White's *Voss*, the novels of Randolph Stow, A.D. Hope's early poem "Australia" and the first volume of Judith Wright's poetry have in the rejection of the middleclass, which is seen as foreign, and the varying degrees, the implication that whatever is uniquely Australian will be found outside the cities. Probably the most common theme of Australian literature is the lack of intensity, passion and spiritual consciousness in middle-class life.[3]

Characteristics of White's novels include an emphasis on suffering, mysticism, the use of myth and a poetic style. In a democratic immigrant culture dedicated to a rising standard of living which does not provide the artist with the status found in older hierarchial European societies, the instinct is to turn inward. Where efficiency and material accomplishment are the main social values and where the crude often succeed, failure becomes spiritual success. The lack of a usable high society means that the author will not, as in Europe, write of man in society, rather the emphasis will be on the self, especially the spiritual realization of the individual, often in opposition to convention. And as American literature often uses and parodies romance, so Australian literature with its nineteenth century heroes often parodies the romantic.

White's *The Solid Mandala*[4] is the story of the Brown twins, shambling, simple-minded Arthur and brittle, "gifted" Waldo. The movement between idea and material in the novel is vital and unbroken, and the complex theme is as intimate with the dense material as soul with body. The tension between abstract and concrete understanding, which White is so conscious of, is sustained throughout although it is not frozen in the neat antithesis which these words suggest, one side to each twin. The twins themselves, divided parts of one whole person, by their essentially complementary relationship draw the conflict into the centre of human nature. They dramatize it as a disturbance within man and within the single man. At the same time they act out that impure mixture of love and hate which is both a condition of the relationship of every human being to another and a condition of the attitude of the individual within himself to himself. The double theme makes the novel a tragedy of human incompleteness and does so in a decidedly trimmer, sparer way than is usual in the earlier novels.

*The Solid Mandala* is a novel permeated with symbolism, both in characterization and in imagery, nevertheless, the success of a novel in which mysticism is an important element depends on the believability of its human values--the value of mysticism must lie in what it has to offer to human beings, for its value to higher beings remains unassessable.

When we find ourselves not liking characters as much as the author wants us to (like Arthur and Mrs. Poulter in this novel) and liking a character more than he wants us to (like Waldo) there seem to be two factors especially at work; the author's values are too arbitrary and his presence is too obtrusive. It is the author's obligation to demonstrate to us through his portraiture and his selection of significant incidents that his values are acceptable. But White's values are too ambivalent for us to be in definite agreement or disagreement with them; and his attempts to sway us into agreement with his mood of the moment by intrusions of his personal judgement give us small credit for an ability to arrive at our own perceptions.

The extensiveness of White's ambivalence has unfortunate

consequences upon the mystical elements in the novel: without acceptable human values the mysticism has no foundation to rest upon. The characters are weighed down with too much moral significance, and the weight is harder for them to bear in that the ground is so unstable beneath their feet. One of White's less successful works, *The Solid Mandala* is a curious melange; an unhappy blend of mysticism and satire, it preaches the values of love but is prone at times to mockery. It holds up as saint figures a physically gross idiot and an unthinking suburbanite, and it damns a poor paranoid. Largely because Arthur is such an unattractive saint and Waldo such a pathetic devil, the twins become confused in the reader's mind. It is extremely difficult in discussing the novel to keep the names of the twins straight, and this confusion is itself an indication of the ambivalence that leads to White's failure to convey his moral values effectively.

White uses the device of using the twins to portray characteristics that are paired opposites. Arthur the older twin is feminine in his perception and can love, with a Christ-like love, all he comes in contact with. He has an uncanny understanding of women of all sorts, Mrs. Poulter, his neighbour whose only child had died. To her he offers himself as a child, his affection and understanding only too eagerly accepted by the lonely Mrs. Poulter. The rich young widow, Mrs. Musto, who patronizingly runs a salon for struggling poets and "local talent" and to whose house Arthur carries groceries from Allwright's departmental store where he is employed, again reveals the understanding relationship that springs up between them both. Arthur's affection for the young European Jewess, Dulcie Feinstein who visits at Mrs. Musto's reveals his ability to "see" others as Waldo is unable to understand people and is especially a failure with women.

Arthur's discovery of the "spirit" of the Mandala, the "symbol of totality" which he has discovered in the encyclopaedia in Ralph Musto's library (238) made him realize spiritual truths which he could not discuss with the carnal Mrs. Musto. Even the intellectual Mr. Brown understood the "Mandala" but inadequately. (249) However, when Arthur visited "Mount Pleasant" the home of the Jewish Feinsteins, he learnt from Mrs. Feinstein who served him some lemonade, that the *Prana* or "the vital force" must be extracted from the lemonade. Whereas Arthur understood and kept his secrets regarding people to himself, he realized that, Waldo his twin brother, in spite of "his scholastic brilliance and his knowledge of the world" was lacking in "suppleness" in his relationships with other people. Waldo at moments, Arthur feared, was "as rigid as a closed cupboard" which only he, Arthur, had learnt "the trick of jerking open." (243)

Again, Arthur Brown visits the public library where his brother Waldo works and on a rainy day "wrestles" with the many interesting books there. He had come across a passage which read, "as the shadow continually follows the body of one who walks in the sun, so our hermaphroditic Adam though he appears in the form of a male, nevertheless always carries about with him Eve, or his wife, hidden in his body." (281) Arthur's realization then arose that he was also hermaphroditic and was therefore able to "comfort" not only Mrs. Allwright since Mr. Allwright's death but also his brother and mother after Mr. Brown's death. Patrick White's interest in Jungian psychology is referred to by John Comer in his study of White's novels.[5] Jung writes "as mythology shows, one of the peculiarities of the Great Mother is that she frequently appears paired with her counterpart." This aspect of the "paired opposites" is symbolized in art through the Yoni-Lingam in India, Hermes in the West, Bes in Egypt, the Chinese *Yang*, the light warm dry masculine principle and the *Yin* (the dark, cold moist feminine principle).[6]

It is distressing that in this novel purporting to convey a spiritual message, the values are so contradictory. Instead of being an inspirational work, *The Solid Mandala* is tainted with a distance for human beings. As Arthur dances his Mandala, White refers to "people in a wooden house, groaning under the pressure of sleep their thoughts locked prudently up, safe, until their spoken thoughts or farts gave them away." (256) White's implicit equation here of thoughts with farts bespeaks a disdain for human beings, especially inappropriate at this solemn time in the novel. It would appear that as his compassion has dried up in his recent works, White has largely come to adopt Mrs. Allwright's crotchety stance, "Human beings are all very well." (217) It is sad that the profound intellect and compassion that characterize *The Aunt's Story, The Tree of Man* and *Voss*--works that give White a permanent and very high place among the great English novelists--have sunk to a shallow mysticism and an uneven, arbitrary dispensing of salvation and damnation.

Patrick White's talent is thus sad, furious, powerful. His method is the poet's, who struggles to compose--or rather to compel--glimpses of significance and shades of meaning into a solid structure of being. To help him he has his vision of man--at certain moments his dazzling vision of man--since he is a writer whose work is the application of his vision, not one who manages a plot or illustrates a period, and he has as well a gluttonous eye for details and the gift to render them fully and exactly. His art, dense and image-ridden, stained with anxiety and sometimes with loathing is, all his sumptuous fiction confirms, a substantial and a genuine thing.

## NOTES

1. Anna Rutherford, Donald Hannah, ed., *Commonwealth Short Stories* (Macmillan, 1979), p. 10.
2. *Ibid.*
3. Bruce King, *The New English Literatures* (Macmillan, 1980), p. 159.
4. Patrick White, *The Solid Mandala* (Penguin, 1966).
5. Inna Walter, *The Tiresias Motif in T.S. Eliot's "The Waste Land" and Patrick White's "The Solid Mandala"* (*unpublished*).
6. *Ibid.*

# Occult Symbolism in *The Solid Mandala*

RATNAKAR S. SADAWARTE

Patrick White, a master of the craft of fiction, has never trodden the beaten track in the choice of his themes and technique. Each of his novels takes the readers to the fresh grounds of human experience to probe the mysteries of life.

*The Solid Mandala*, like an obscure poem in prose, is a plurisign. It has many levels of meaning. The mood is sombre; melancholy permeates throughout the length of the novel. It is the story of twin brothers--Arthur and Waldo--whose abnormal psycho-physical condition forms the basis of all their actions and intentions. They are the sons of a bank employee, have contrasting personality traits and grow up with some abnormal physical secrets which even their parents, perhaps, do not know. In the first part of the novel, Mrs. Poulter gives us a hint: "There's more in the Brothers Brown than meets the eye."[1]

Arthur is physically a strong man but has feminine temperament, a talent for number and is an introvert. On the other hand Waldo is physically delicate, masculine in nature, has a flair for language and is an extrovert. Arthur works in a grocer's shop and Waldo gets a job in a library. As children, the twins learn stories from Greek mythology from their father but only the myth of Tiresias, who lived for some time as a woman, makes deep impression on their minds. Each brother identifies himself with Tiresias, and worries about his own physical secret. They are aware of their abnormal conditions and wish to overcome them. Waldo is a rationalist who just thinks over the problem, writes a tragic novel called "Tiresias a Youngish Man" and secretly puts on the mother's old dress. Arthur has four glass taws which he calls his Solid Mandalas and hopes to surmount his problem by divine help, but these are their personal secrets which they do not share with anybody.

Arthur does all the duties of a housewife as Waldo hates these chores. Meanwhile the parents die. The twins are preordained to remain bachelors throughout their lives and despite their love-hate relationship live together till ripe old age when one brother kills the other. White only suggestively hints at their bisexual existence. The quotation which Arthur pins at the back of his mind is quite eloquent:

> As the shadow continually follows the body of one who walks in the sun so our hermaphroditic Adam, though he appears in the form of a male nevertheless always carries about with him Eve, or his wife, hidden in his body. (271-72)

The bisexual personalities of these brothers place them as the forerunners of Eddie Twyborn from Patrick White's another novel *The Twyborn Affair*. Once, Arthur finds mother's old dress behind copper and asks Waldo about it. Waldo is obviously shaken by the discovery of his secret, the only way to make his worldly adjustment with abnormal situation. White suddenly gives obscure description. The dress mysteriously turns into a poem:

> To Arthur, who was holding in front of him the sheets of ice, so that Waldo might see his reflection in it. Arthur threw away the dress.
> Which turned into the sheet of paper Waldo discovered in a corner, not ferreting, but ferreted, On smoothing out the electric paper at once he began quivering. (202)

Waldo thought that Arthur has found out his secret and at the same time Arthur also was afraid that his secretly written poem would betray him to Waldo. This mysterious description shows that Arthur and Waldo had similar problems. The conversion of a dress into a poem on a crumpled paper shows that the "dress" is to Waldo as the "Poem" is to Arthur. Both the things have their roots in the myth of Tiresias. Arthur's poem speaks for his abnormality of double sex.

> My heart is bleeding for the viviseckshunist . . . all Marys in the end bleed. . . .
> They cannot have it any other way. (202)

After this Waldo burns all his papers--the novel called "Tiresias a

Youngish Man"--and wants to get rid of Arthur. He had always contemplated Arthur's death. Just then Arthur comes in. Lying on the bed Waldo holds Arthur's hand but somehow, unwittingly Arthur kills him on the very bed which he had shared with Waldo for years.

The complex web of symbolic design coupled with White's penchant for flashback technique makes the novel abstruse and obtruse. The author's interest in the occult science becomes obvious from the fact that he has laid special emphasis on Arthur's Solid Mandalas and the novel evokes critical response in the same light. The two central characters of the novel lead a completely insulated life, hardly participating in social activity, barring a couple of families and their job requirements.

The novel presents symbols within symbols that form the mosaic with three concentric circles; but before entering these circles we may consider some characters who have sufficient background in oriental metaphysics and tantric Buddhism or Hindu Shakt-tantra. We meet Mrs. Feinstein, a Jew lady, who seems to have read Upanishadas. When she offers lemonade to Arthur her advice is:

> "You should drink it slowly and concentrate. . . . Then you will extract *prana* from this lemonade."
> "The what?"
> "It is Indian . . . for "vital force"." (232)

This is not a casual remark about *prana* but it closely resembles a reference from Chandogya Upanishad (6.5.2) where the sage Uddalak Aruni tells Shwetaketu about three aspects of water we drink.

In the outer circle we also meet Mrs. Musto who is deserted by her husband. She also seems to have some esoteric knowledge. Arthur finds her performing some strange rituals before an object which she calls "Creature" and tells Arthur:

> Come to think of it . . . this other one . . . this creature . . . is the dead spirit of Ralph. (228)

Her husband, whom she now hates, was perhaps a serious student of tantric cult. He had a good collection of rare books from which, as

Mrs. Musto alleges, he learned to charm ladies. This suggests that he knew "Vashikaran" mentioned in *The Atharva-Veda.* From the same collection of books Arthur had read out the meaning and definition of a mandala:

> The mandala is a symbol of totality. It is believed to be the "dwelling of the god." Its protective circle is a pattern of order superimposed on psychic chaos. Sometimes its geometric form is seen as a vision (either waking or in a dream) or-- (229)

This leads us to the outer circle of the symbolic design. Arthur's interest in his solid mandalas and the description of a mandala which he read from Ralph's encyclopaedia make the point clear that his glass taws are not ordinary marbles of a child but meaningful objects of tantric worship of some deity who may help him overcome his abnormality, or from whom he tries to get his wishes fulfilled.

The two brothers themselves symbolize two minds of man--rational mind and emotional mind. They are two halves of one personality, existing separately, like a psychological "Jarasandh," waiting for somebody to join them in a whole. They symbolize man's quest for completeness. Waldo with his books and library job, and Arthur with his solid mandalas, Bhagwad Geeta and Upanishads, symbolize knowledge and faith respectively. They are two fundamental faculties of human soul which always conflict in their method and verdict; waiting for the discord to vanish. Since there is a clear-cut reference to mandala of "Tantra shastra" it may be said that Arthur's solid mandalas are symbolic of "Yantra" and Waldo's word power stands for "Mantra" of the tantric rituals. Yantra and mantra must be used together to get the desired result in "Tantra sadhana" because in Tantric cult "Mantra" and "Yantra" are equally important for any purpose of worship. "Mantra" is the word power and "Yantra" is special type of geometric design with divine power. Here we enter the middle circle of the symbolic mosaic which leads us to think that Arthur is a "Sadhaka" of tantric Buddhism. What is a mandala? It is an oriental art: "A systematized representation of the cosmos, chiefly characterized by a concentric organization of geometric shapes, each of which contains an image or attribute of a deity."[2]

There are various types of Mandala. Some are drawn on paper or ground. Others may be engraved on copper plates or carved on stone; but the most important Mandala is said to be the rock crystal, a substance which can be shaped to focus light at its apex. In Tantric Buddhism the terms "Mani" (Jewel) and "Vajra" (Diamond) also suggest rock crystal. There is a reference to "Pashan Mani" (Stone Bead) in the 90th Section of the 6th Canto of *The Atharva-Veda.* This section is titled "Sharir Shool Nivaran Sukta." (Formula to cure body troubles) The Pashan Mani is said to have divine power. This description also tallies with rock crystal and Arthur's Solid Mandalas. When specific words or "Mantras" inscribed on a "Yantra" are correctly recited with full concentration, the "Yantra" itself becomes infused with the actual presence of "Devata" (Deity) and the "Devata" floats up off the surface of the physical object and expands within the mind and body of the "Sadhaka." A Tantric Sadhaka gives his Mandalas to his near and dear persons when they are in critical situations, so that, by worshipping it they may become happy. When Dulcie's mother died Arthur gave her the blue mandala.

One of the most important descriptions in the novel is that of Mandala dance, which Arthur performed amongst the black berry bushes before Mrs. Poulter. The dance closely resembles "Nyasa," a complex method of "Tantra Sadhana," as a solitary meditative ritual by which a sadhaka prepares himself for proper "Puja." Arthur's Dance had four corners in which he wove the figures of Dulcie, Mrs. Poulter, Waldo and himself to form a geometric design. He danced in and out of the figures of Dulcie and Mrs. Poulter which suggests "Antarmatarika nyasa" and "Bahyamatarika nyasa" of the Buddhist tantra or Hindu "Shakta-tantra Upasana."

While performing his Mandala dance he was in a trance and was totally unaware of his bleeding hands, then he fell down. There was a tree which he recognized as a "Wheel-Tree" under which a Chinese woman stood looking angrily at him. The "Wheel-Tree" symbolizes "Chakras" or open lotuses mentioned in "Yoga" or "Tantra" philosophy. Tantric Buddhism believes in four "Chakras" whereas Hindus think there are six or eight "Chakras." It may be said that the "Wheel-Tree" and the dance near it symbolize "Chakra-puja" mentioned in the great book called *Kulavali Nirnaya* and the Chinese woman may be considered a symbolic reference to "Chinese Taoism" which is akin to "Tantra Sadhana."

Coming to the innermost circle of the symbolic design the colours of Arthur's Solid Mandalas reveal different symbols, Arthur has four solid mandalas; they are blue, yellow, white and the last (his own) is green and red knotted together. These colours become meaningful when we see them from tantric point of view.

According to the philosophy of Shakti-cult there are ten Mahavidyas who are the manifestations of the one all-powerful mother goddess "Shakti." She is also known as Durga or Chamunda. Among the ten Mahavidyas Kali and Tara are very important deities of the tantric-cult. Tara, it is believed, gives very quick response to prayer or tantra sadhana. Tara again has three manifestations of her own, namely Ugra-tara, Ekjata and Neelsaraswati. They are worshipped in Bengal, Tibet and China. The tantric method of "Tara Upasana" is, of course, with yantra and mantra. She sits on white lotus, holds blue lotus in hand and has a golden lock of hair.

If Arthur is considered the worshiper of Tara, his blue mandala, a symbol of universal love, represents Neelsaraswati and the blue mandala given to Dulcie as a token of his love makes enough sense. She accepted it and also thanked him for what he "told" her. Perhaps Arthur initiated her in the fold of Tantra-cult. The yellow (golden) mandala which symbolizes hope, stands for "Ekjata" devata who has one golden lock of hair symbolizing the rays of the sun and hope. At the time of mandala dance, the sun was shining brightly and Mrs. Poulter had let her hair loose. Waldo gave her the yellow mandala (because she was childless) as a hope of begetting children, but she was too afraid to use it.

The third (white) mandala reserved for Waldo (supposed to be the dwelling place of Ugra Tara) also suggests the sun or "Star." She is also the deity of the "Power of words" and prose-poetry, known as "Wakshakti" or "Gadya-Padya rupa." Since Waldo has a flair for language, Tara is the right deity for him to worship, hence Arthur offered him that mandala, but Waldo refused it. Only Dulcie had used her mandala and lived happily with her husband, children and grandchildren.

Arthur's own mandala, green and red, symbolizes double sex and union of Shiva and Shakti, as per the Tantric colours.

The last chapter is about Mrs. Poulter and the "Zeitgeist." This German word means the spirit of the time. From the point of view of "Tantra Shastra" this may be "Kala" the god of time. But since it is about Mrs. Poulter, the time spirit should be considered as "Kali" or "Mahakali" one of the three manifestations of mother goddess, and "Mother" is the symbol of love, forgiveness and protection.

After killing Waldo and wandering aimlessly like a mad man, Arthur comes to Mrs. Poulter's house and tells her that he had killed Waldo. But Mrs. Poulter, with very calm and firm attitude consoles him, caresses this old man's head with love and gives him courage. Mrs. Poulter protects him from the police inspector.

This protecting spirit is of Mahakali who kills enemies to save her devotees. Hence the sub-title "Zeitgeist" symbolizes "Kali." Mrs. Poulter's role ends the novel with hope for Arthur who has been taken to the lunatic asylum.

## NOTES

1. Patrick White, *The Solid Mandala* (New York: Viking, 1966), p. 9.
2. *The Random House Dictionary*, ed. Jess Stein et. al. (n.d.), p. 812.

# The Influence of Eliot's *Waste Land* on Patrick White's *Living and the Dead*

K. CHELLAPPAN and N.E. PAVITHRA

Patrick White belongs to the great tradition of novelists such as Dostoevsky, Tolstoy, Lawrence and Joyce in his epic vision of life and his concern with man's place in the universe, though he confines his milieu to Australia. His novels too have as the basic theme, mankind's eternal quest for, and a value in existence. His heroes seek "true permanence beneath the illusory flux, the true freedom which is valid even beyond physical death.[1] Dostoevsky presents a close parallel as there is the same close scrutiny and soul searching of characters in his novels. White shares with Tolstoy his criticism of the life of the bourgeois society and his attitude to physical love as something lewd and incapable of providing real happiness to mankind. In this aspect he differs from Lawrence, but he shares with him a sympathy with those people who are striving to "live," fighting against the "sterile" and the "dead." From Joyce, White has adapted the inner monologue and the "stream of consciousness."

But as much as these novelists, T.S. Eliot also seems to have been a major influence on the early works of White. White particularly shares Eliot's belief that modern man fears that the springs of spiritual nourishment are dead even while they live. Talking of influence, he wrote:

> Joyce and Lawrence, yes, at the time when I began to write. I certainly began to read Dostoevsky about the same time, and have read all his important novels, but it would not have occurred to me that I had been influenced by anybody so remote from myself, geographically understand his temperament fairly well. Most certainly I shouldn't have made use of

the stream of consciousness if it hadn't been for Joyce.[2]

Though no mention is made of Eliot, one can trace Eliot's *Waste Land* (1922) as the principal source of inspiration for White's second novel *The Living and the Dead.* (1941) It is his only novel which is set outside Australia. It registers his feelings towards England, which, after the war, appeared to him sterile. The London of *The Living and the Dead* is reminiscent of Eliot's "unreal city." As Burns says, the novel is "Eliot's *Waste Land* in extenso."[3] Bjorksten also associates Elyot, the principal character of *The Living and the Dead* with Eliot and *The Waste Land*, the sterile and dead. The genuine and artistic power of Eliot's poem must have influenced White and this paper proposes to make a study of the impact of Eliot's *Waste Land* and White's *The Living and the Dead.*

The very titles *Waste Land* and *Living and the Dead* are strictly similar as they embody the theme of life and death, suggesting man's struggle through a death-in-life existence. Eliot and White saw a complete breakdown of culture, religion and civilization in London. This modern city was an "unreal city of shattered institutions, strained nerves and bankrupt ideals, where life no longer seemed serious or coherent,"[4] and where people seemed already dead. *The Waste Land* is a picture of this modern world inhabited by those for whom life provides only a "heap of broken images"[5] and "fear in a handful of dust." (*WL*, 30) Similarly *The Living and the Dead* portrays the metallic contemporary existence where people are divided into two groups--the spiritually living and the living dead. There is emotional and spiritual starvation and the two works have their protagonists, Tiresias and Elyot, struggling to find meaning in an apparently meaningless universe. They are enveloped in an atmosphere of terrible dreariness and long for a purpose and vitality that would redeem their "dead" life. But, their will to believe is frustrated by their fear of life, and they dislike to be roused from their sterile existence. They refuse to leave their "dead" world and seek solace in death. Tiresias is merely an onlooker watching modern civilization which to him is wholly futile and dead. He makes no move on his part to help the "dead" live again. Elyot also stands audience to what is happening around him. He feels cut off from the family. He has no part in anything. He becomes an observer and not a participant, "It began to occupy him more and more, his not being part of anything. . . . He stood a long way off and watched."[6] Aware of his life as audience, when life gets too much to observe he escapes behind a study door. He "does not make use of opportunities to become alive, for him there is no rooted existence in the future or in his own mental make-up. His security is the past, a world of the dead."[7] He only reflects on the past, on everything absent from the present: "It was so easy to substitute the dead for the living, to build a cocoon of experience away from the noises in the street." (*LD*, 19) This unwillingness to live results in an inverted response to nature and love.

Nature and the external world are used to reflect the inner mind of Elyot, precisely because, he is unable, until the end, to relate to nature. He retreats further and further from life into his study. In the poem, the first line "April is the cruellest month" (*WL*, 1) shows that April the month of warmth and joy is anticipated with fear. Tiresias silently observes with dismay, the coming of April, as the people of *The Waste Land* are incapable of participating in the process of the renewal of the earth. April is linked with "memory and desire," (*WL*, 3) and, Winter, the symbol of spiritual decay, keeps them warm.

Love, in this sterile civilization, is destructive rather than creative. In the second section of the poem titled "A Game of Chess" Eliot indicates the failure of a sex-relationship in the modern world. The game of chess is played to hide the seduction of a young girl by a nobleman. Sex in *The Waste Land* in full of intrigue, falsehood and fraud, and true love cannot exist or blossom there, as depicted in the episode of the Hyacinth girl. White's views concur with Eliot's. Love ends in frustration in *The Living and the Dead* also. Catherine's love for her husband is short-lived and physical, children being born in due course. For both brother and sister sex is a ceremony fraught with sadness. Eden has a diastrous affair, becomes pregnant and has an abortion. The man was "bland, unseeing, obsessed with his own feelings" (*LD*, 147) and the sex was dry and lifeless, "a cheating of the flesh." (*LD*, 147) At the loss of her virginity her only thought was, "this then was sex, the rumpled bed, the sense of aching nausea, the dead weight." (*LD*, 147) Eliot shuddered whenever he thought of his affair with Hildegard in Germany, and his intimacy with Muriel, his Jewish mistress is only "the last flicker of boredom experienced by two people that habit kept united." (*LD*, 277) He is repelled by her sexual directedness, and he feels distaste for the softness of flesh in his next lover, Conny Tiarks. Interwoven with this loveless condition is his inability to lend a helping hand. As he returns from the station, he witnesses an accident. A drunken man is hit by a bus. He could see what was going to happen. He could see "the bus, ballooning down. . . . I must do this, his mind shouted. . . . The whole neighbourhood moved. Except his feet. He was anchored where he stood. He was the audience to a piece of distant pantomime." (*LD*, 13-14) Just as he could not make contact with the drunken man he is unable to make contact with Eden: "He closed himself to sentimental regret." (*LD*, 13) "He failed, deliberately. Because this was something he must not touch on." (*LD*, 12) This failure or betrayal in decisive situations as a consequence of lack of love is present in Tiresias too. There is a failure of action in his response to the Hyacinth girl's plight:

> I could not speak, and my eyes failed, I was neither
> Living nor dead. (*WL*, 39-40)

This failure to act shows that just as they stood audience to the incidents, so , too, they stand audience to life.

Sex was no part of either Eliot's or White's vision. They express distress at the sterile relationships and the drying up of the springs of spiritual emotion, and the steep decline of moral values. They believed that suffering is a necessary route to spiritual progress beneficial both to the individual who suffers and to those involved in the suffering. This thinking is due to an influence of their Christian values. It led them to demonstrate the necessity of suffering in human life. Eliot suggests through the story of Philomela that only through death and suffering can the transformation of sinful mortal life be achieved. White grapples with the same problem, and Joe's death is the solution. He is killed in Spain, and Eden decides to go there because "she was convinced of the rightness of this." (*LD*, 331) She goes out to confront life, and her decision throws light on the central meaning of Eliot's and White's thought: "The arch-enemies were the stultifying, the living dead. The living chose to oppose these, either in Eden's way, by the protest of self-destruction, or by what if not an intense form of living." (*LD*, 331) For them the first step towards a redemptive vision is forming an emotional relationship. This is absent in the wastelanders and Elyot. Just as the former get no inspiration from the "hooded" figure of Christ, Elyot does not understand Eden's participation and he retreats away. Elyot drifts into a state of limbo "bound nowhere in particular." (*LD*, 334) The journey he has undertaken seems to have no end. Like the journeys and quests of the characters in *The Waste Land* there is no real end in sight. "There was no end to this in the bus, trundling down its dark tunnel." (*LD*, 358) This was White's vision. He believed that the supreme enlightenment is to realize that one is part of the continuum leading towards but never reaching, save through vision, the centre of God. But Elyot grows into no state of satisfaction as there is too much consciousness, consciousness of too much, a similar plight in *The Waste Land.* They do not realize the inner way, leaving them with an ashen sort of existence, something endured rather than lived. This strong note of defeatism is apparent in both works, which express the unpleasant reality of life today, a world where people do not live but merely exist. However, the writers set the stage for a new beginning. Eliot leaves it to man to build a new order and make his own contribution to the revitalizing of broken tradition. There is hope for the individual who seeks his self-purification. The last words "Shantih, Shantih, Shantih" (*WL*, 433) signify some hope for peace, the peace that transcends fragmented life. White also attempts to present a positive ending. He tries to bring Elyot into the company of the living and remove him from his deathly isolation through the image of him waking up from sleep. He yawns and feels like "someone who had been asleep and had only, just woken." (*LD*, 358) In waking he does not leave the mystery of failure unresolved. As Ann McCulloch says, "failure is not resolved but it is demystified by being consciously explored. He surfaces from the fog and deadlines of retreat and thus what is implied is an awakening, from non-commitment, even if commitment is not achieved."[8]

*The Waste Land* and *The Living and the Dead* now come a full circle, but we do not get the impression of having reached an ending. At the end of the poem as in the beginning, the sterile world remains unchanged. In the last chapter of the novel we return to the situation of the beginning with Elyot alone in the house thinking of the past. The cyclic pattern is woven in *The Waste Land* with the use of fertility myths as decay and death are cyclical processes. In *The Living and the Dead* the circle is drawn by the three characters, Catherine, her daughter Eden, and her son Elyot, enclosed in a circle.

Each age creates its own literary language and Eliot employs Joyce's stream of consciousness technique. The entire poem is a series of disjointed thoughts brought to unity through a mythical mode. White also explores the same theme of the sterility in the existence of modern man using the stream of consciousness technique. He does not resort to myth, instead, the book forages endlessly through the minds of the characters through his or her own memories. It is full of reflections, emotional stresses, wistful flickering desires. Thinking about his sister, his mother and the people he has known, Elyot gives us a clear picture of each individual. This series of impressionistic glimpses that the reader gets from the novel is similar to the poem where each episode creates an impression for itself. The episodes and scenes are not logically connected or smoothly linked. There are abrupt transitions from one to another as Tiresias, the seer, reflects on the events of the past and present. Distance of time and space is destroyed and the movement acquires a spatial form. *The Living and the Dead* also opens on a sadder, wiser man ruminating on what has passed. The substance of the novel is what lies latent in the space between the two moments of Elyot's arrival at the station and his departure from it. He, like Tiresias, is the central consciousness, assimilating the characters together. He is aware of how those he has known have tried "to resist the shapelessness" which "he had not experienced himself, but sensed." (*LD*, 20) In the deserted house, quiet and full of dead feelings, thoughts of his sister and mother crowd his mind. Catherine, Eden and he were three people in the same house, each in a distinctive box, there was little intercourse between these." (*LD*, 248) Yet in spite of his detachment he realizes that "alone, he was yet not alone uniting as he did the themes of so many other lives." (*LD*, 333) He plays the same role as Tiresias who has no character or personality of his own, for he acquires identity not through individuality, but through acting as the unifying consciousness. Eliot himself says "just as the one-eyed merchant, seller of currants, melts into the phonecian sailor, and the latter is not wholly distinct from Ferdinand Prince of Naples, so all the women are one woman, and the two sexes meet in Tiresias. What Tiresias sees in fact, is the substance of the poem."[9] Thus, there is a unity imparted by the protagonists. There is no unity of self, but a unity achieved through the working of the conscious and unconscious psyche of different characters. In spite of the apparent chaos of episodes, thoughts and actions, a harmony is perceived in the narratives.

To say that all the characters meet in Tiresias is to suggest that archetypal identities emerge from large archetypes, in the way smaller Chinese boxes emerge from the larger. This archetypal image is adopted by White too. The metaphors of the Chinese boxes is used to present Elyot's mind: "One inside the other leading to an infinity of other boxes to an infinity of purpose." (*LD*, 333) The first boxes which suggest the image to Elyot's mind follow from his recognition of his own house which contains the material possessions and aspirations of those who have occupied it. There is thus a constant retreat into the past. Past and present are inextricably entangled. Past experiences have brought the characters to their present state of life, and while a few try to go beyond it, Elyot and his kind get drawn further into themselves. "We think of the key, each in his prison/Thinking of the key, each confirms a prison." (*WL*, 413-14) The contrast is constantly made between those who may live and learn to know themselves and to live with the knowledge of this world, and those who are dead and will never know anything. This juxtaposition serves to enhance the theme of life and death, in the poem also. In *The Waste Land* the sharp contrasts between past and present, fertility and barrenness, life and death serves to focus on the degeneration of values and the spiritual aridity in contemporary society. The rich description of the Renaissance life is set against the banal scene of the pub. Similarly the vulgar seduction of the typist by the "small house agent clerk" is contrasted with the glimpses of Elizabeth and Leicester sailing on Spencer's "sweet Thames." The romance conspicuous of the past is absent in modern relationships. Sex, which is sterile, breeding not life and fulfilment but disgust is illustrated through Philomela's rape by the barbarous king. The theme of sterility embodied in Belladona is strengthened by the portrayal of Lil who already has five children. They seem to embody and betray fertility. "The Fire Sermon" and "Death by Water" are again another contrast. Dying here suggests, rebirth, the possibility of resurrection. Through symbolism, water, rain and sea representing spiritual vitality is contrasted to rock, sand and stone standing for death and spiritual insensitivity.

Images are used by Eliot to depict the sordidness, and ugly

soulless nature of contemporary existence. The city of London in *The Waste Land* becomes an image of hell, like Dante's city in the Inferno, where the "damned" in hell perpetually move towards a constantly shifting ideal. Dante's words to Virgil,

> It never would have entered in my head
> There were so many men who death had slain
> (trans. Dorothy Sayers, 55-57)

is echoed by Eliot:

> A crowd flowed over London Bridge, so many,
> I had not thought death had undone so many. (*WL*, 62-63)

Civilization is dying of spiritual drought and nothing can grow from this sterile land

> What are the roots that clutch, what branches grow
> Out of this stony rubbish. (*WL*, 20)

The London in *The Living and the Dead* is also bereft of anything virtuous or joyful. Elyot "swims in the confused sea that was anybody's London." (*LD*, 22) Images of death haunt him. He himself is described in terms of a skull, a traditional emblem of death: "The sockets of his eyes were dark. Two empty saucers in the bone." (*LD*, 11) Eliot and White refer to dust, the Biblical allusion that to dust man shall return. Eliot speaks of "fear in a handful of dust" (*WL*, 30) while White likens Elyot's devotion to scholarship to a "devotion to dust." For Elyot, the emotion had gone out of his life, his life like his work was arranged in "numbered pages" (*LD*, 190) and he is a mere "rattler of bones." He is typical of the sterile man in the waste land, where the only noise heard is the "rattle of bones." (*WL*, 186)

A strong parallel thus runs between *The Waste Land* and *The Living and the Dead*. Eliot and White deal with the theme of sterility and spiritual starvation in the life of modern man. The titles of their works are incidentally symbolic of the atmosphere of dreariness, death and decay. White follows the structural pattern adopted by Eliot to express his vision. In *The Waste Land* the protagonist Tiresias speculates on life gliding off into memory.

Similarly, Elyot in *The Living and the Dead* ruminates on the past. It is through their reflections that the theme of barrenness is presented. The circular pattern is employed by the writers and the works are rich in the use of similar images and symbols. Though characters come and go and thoughts are at random there is a unity of feeling, an inclusive consciousness created, through the protagonists. According to Shaw, a comparative, influence is "not confined to individual details or images or borrowings or even sources--it is something pervasive, something organically involved in and presented through artistic works."[10] And we have seen that in White's novel there are not only echoes and images from Eliot's *The Waste Land* but the overall atmosphere and the very exploration of theme shows a clear and consistent affinity with Eliot's poem. Hence we tend to agree with Walsh that, "for all its skill and sureness in registering with fidelity, it *(The Living and the Dead)* shows clear evidence of the author's reading of Eliot, not in the way of reference and quotation but rather of reading as influence on his sensibility."[11]

## NOTES

1. Patricia Morley, *The Mystery of Unity* (London: McGill-Green's University Press, 1972), p. 1.
2. Ingmar Bjorksten, *Patrick White--A General Introduction* (Queensland: Univ. of Queensland Press, 1976), p. 3.
3. D.R. Burns, *The Directions of Australian Fiction 1920-74* (Melbourne: Casell Australia, 1975), p. 162.
4. Cox, ed., *T.S. Eliot: The Waste Land* (London: Macmillan, 1968), p. 101.
5. T.S. Eliot, *The Waste Land*, l. 22.
6. Patrick White, *The Living and the Dead* (London: Penguin, 1941), p. 106.
7. Ingmar Bjorksten, p. 33.
8. Ann McCulloch, "Patrick White's Novels and Nietzsche," *Australian Literature Studies,* Vol. 9, No. 2 (May 1980), p. 313.
9. F.R. Leavis, "The Waste Land" in *T.S. Eliot: A Collection of Critical Essays*, ed. Hugh Kenner (N.J.: Prentice Hall, 1962),

p. 91.

10. T.J. Shaw, "Literary Indebtedness and Comparative Literary Studies," ed. Stallknect and Frenz, *Comparative Literature--Method and Perspective* (U.S.A: Southern Illinois Univ. Press, 1961), p. 91.
11. William Walsh, *Patrick White's Fiction* (Australia: George Allen and Unwin, 1977), p. 7.

# Origins of Australian Poetry

JAGDISH RAI

Here rhyme was first framed without fashion
Song shaped without form.

So spoke Adam Lindsay Gordon about the origins of Australian poetry.[1] In fact, the birth of Australian poetry and the nourishing of its traditions is much more curious than this. It was the time when the romantic movement in Europe was at its prime and the poetic sensibility was being reoriented on the cult of beauty and enchantment. The Australian bush was far from supplying such founts of inspiration. In England it were the beauteous forms, the daffodils, the enchanting song of the highland lass, the Grecian urns and the cuckoo birds which supplied raptures and ecstasies to the poetic imagination. Australia, in the given circumstances could offer nothing more than the evergreen and the never-green eucalyptus, the scrub land, the vast arid sweeps of desert, the lizard, the drowsy snake, the awkward Kangaroo and the emu which could neither sing nor fly. And since the men who were supposed to write poetry in, about and for Australia had come from England, they could not be expected to feel inspired for poetic ventures. For the poetic emotion everything seemed to be perverse.

Not only that, even the men and women who were destined to be the premier inhabitants of Australia were people of a curious stamp. They were, most of them, convicts and the rest were police troopers supposed to administer the affairs of this British penal colony. Sometime later they were joined by settlers who were lured by the prospect of finding gold in Australia. Such was the geography and such were the beginnings of history in Australia, and both seemed to be uncongenial and unconducive to poetic genre. The latter seemed to be more so. (The explorers and the navigators who had touched the Australian shores earlier had already created a mental climate which consisted in a kind of prejudice). In fact the history of Australia had begun much earlier than the establishment of the British penal colony in 1788 in the sense that the exploratory writings about Australia had already conditioned and generated certain attitudes almost to the proximity of prejudices. The most contributive of these explorers were the famous Tasman (1642), William Dampier (1688), James Cook (1768-71), Major Ross (1788) and Charles Darwin (1832).[2] These were the men whose explorations coloured the European vision of the Terra Australis one way or the other. Tasman who discovered the present day Tasmania talked of the presence of ogre like beings in the region. William Dampier's account of the Australian flora and the natives is equally dampening. James Cook, however, gave a very happy impression of Australia. According to him it was a beautiful country and he compared it to "a gentleman's park."[3] Major Ross and Charles Darwin avowed their open dislike of the country and whatever it stood for. After the setting up of the colony, of those who had found the land disgusting Major Ross was the severest: "In the whole world there is not a worse country than what we have yet seen of this; all that is contiguous to us is so very barren and forbidding that it may with truth be said that--here nature is reversed."[4] Ross's judgment on Australia's aesthetic worth dropped like a seed in the literary climate of the penal colony simultaneously with its foundation stone and provided a theme for poetic endeavours for quite a few decades to come. The idea of the land of reversed nature went at once into the air and took several morphean shapes. Lang came forth with his idea of the land of primeval curse:

> If anything with the breath of life is visible at all, it is the timid grey lizard hiding itself in the crevices of rocks or the solitary black snake stretched at full length on the white sand or the busy ant rearing his slander pyramid of yellowish clay, . . . In such forbidding places the mind unavoidably partakes of the gloominess of nature; and the only idea that has forcible hold of it is, that such must assuredly be the region on which the ancient primeval curse to which the earth was subjected for the sin of man, has specially lighted.[5]

Australia thus was projected as a land hostile both to man and art. Major Ross the man of administration[6] and Lang, a poet, had set the literary tone in the new born colony and the parent country alike.

However, Captain Cook's impressions had not died out completely. An impersonal historical precedent had already fertilized them. The American colonial experience was still fresh. The penal colony was no more than a suburb of the new land and there was every chance of discovering a wonder land in the interior of Australia. There was evidence of rivers flowing inward to the heartland and could lead to great sea-like lakes as they exist in America. Thus at the time, and even much before that time of founding the penal settlement of New South Wales two simultaneous and dichotomous views of Australia had developed among people of creative dispositions. For some it was a terrifying land; dry wild and ugly where dumb birds slept by day and woke by night, where there was no change of seasons and thus no spring season to stir the aesthetic sense, where the black snake, the awkward Kangaroo and antique ants repelled the seeker of natural beauty. For others, it was a land of promise which was going to make up for the loss of America in every sense; power, riches and artistic wealth.[7] The convict emigrants and their caretakers brought both of these presentiments along with them. This gave rise to two kinds of poetic writing about Australia at two different places and by two kinds of people. In England there were people who were writing on Australia out of their mental vision. They had never seen Australia. In the Australian colony there were people who were trying to interpret the worth of the new land in terms of English standards. They had no affection for the land but being the standard bearers of the Empire they had to think well of it and speak well of it.

It is interesting to note that the people who were the first to write poetry in the penal colony were important men of the official class. Barron Field who was himself a poet and who has the credit of bringing out the first collection of Australian poetry was a judge of the Supreme Court in Sydney. Michael Massey Robinson who has the credit of having written first Odes on Australia was the confidential secretary of the then governor and later on was an important official in the police department. Henry Parkes was a politician and was for quite sometime the premier of New South Wales. Though recognized as poets in their day, they were rather writers of poetry in the Australian context. There was a touch of formality, pretension, propaganda and artificiality in what they wrote. Two archetypal ideas, Major Ross's idea of "the reversal of nature'' and Lang's idea of the ''land of primeval curse'' find expression in variant shades. Field's versification on Kangaroo is quite representative in this regard. Kangaroo, according to the poet, is symbolic of and embodies the awkward spirit of Australia and yet redeems it from shame:

> Kangaroo! Kangaroo!
> Thou spirit of Australia
> That redeems from utter failure
> From perfect desolation
> And warrants the creation
> Of this fifth part of the earth
> Which would seem an after birth
> Not conceived in the beginning
> (For God blessed his work at first,
> And saw that it was good),
> But merged at the first sinning
> When the ground was therefore curst
> And hence this barren wood.[8]

The ideas come from Ross and Lang. Versification comes from the poet. The tone is mongerel and dogerel. The verses reflect a sense of self ashamedness, a tendency to jeer at restrained by the tendency to withhold; an official of the crown stifling his personal mirth and jibe for the sake of decorum, softening the joke with after praise:

> For howsoever anomalous,
> Thou art not yet incongruous,
> Repugnant or preposterous
> Better proportioned animal,
> More graceful or ethereal
> Was never followed by the hound
> With fifty steps to thy one bound.

It is worthwhile to have a sample from Henry Parkes as well:

> The moonlight of a milder clime
> Is round me poured over scenes sublime
> But I would fly from all earth's light

And grandeur to behold tonight
My native land . . .[9]

Native land here refers to England. This versification reflects a common trend. Australia is viewed in contrast with England, is found wanting in beauteous forms and the resulting mood is that of self pity. With English blood and the English spirit, these people looked at Australia as outsiders but pretended at the same time to be its admirers.

Back in England a similar versification on Australia was going on. In the very year 1788, the year in which Major Ross had dropped the key metaphor of the land of reversed nature, one finds a different vision of Australia in a poem written by Erasmus Darwin, the grandfather of the famous Charles Darwin. The poem was written to celebrate the arrival in England of samples of Australian clay. The poem cherishes great hopes and visionary scenes of Australia:

There, ray'd from cities o'er the cultur'd land
Shall bright canals and solid roads expand
There the proud arch, colossus like, bestride
Yon glittering streams and bound the changing tide
Embellished villas crown the landscape scene
Forms wave with gold and Orchards blush between.

The vision makes an interesting contrast with the impressions and accounts of Australia given by Ross, Fielding, Lang and other men who had had practical experience of the landscape scene. Erasmus Darwin was followed by others to the same tune. Lisle Bowles turned out almost an epic on the glorious discovery of Australia and upon the romantic charms of the discovery talking of the imagined primeval glory of the umbrageous forests

. . . through whose boughs
Mossy and damp, for many a league, the morn
With languid beam scarce pierces, here and there
Touching some solitary trunk, the rest
Dark waving, in the noxious atmosphere.[10]

In contrast to this there were poets who had drawn their material from the travelogues of Australia. They portrayed very gloomy views of Australia for those who meant to migrate to the new land.

This poetic activity going on simultaneously at two places widely apart had a touch of paradox about it. Many of them had not seen the country they were praising or denouncing. Even those who had seen it and had come to inhabit it were doing so in a perfunctory way. It was simply the presentation of a point of view and points of view do not make poetry. It was motivated by the exterior consideration of official propaganda on one side and the display of self pity on the other. On one side there was illusion; on the other, the disillusion; both exaggerated and a little pertended.

And in the midst of this poetic noise was born genuine Australian poetry which smelled of Australian air and soil and breathed the Australian spirit as it was. This was done by poets who were born on the Australian soil and whose spirits had become acclimatized to its view from their very first breath. They looked for their motherland not on England but on Australia. Whatever it was, to them Australia was dear. The credit of being the first to sing of Australia in this vein goes to a young Australia-born student at Cambridge. William Wentworth by name, he presented a poem at a poetic contest in 1823. In this poem titled "Australasia" he not only proudly sang of Australia as his motherland but also presented the Australian scene along with its aborigines in a warm and affectionate light. This was like a call for the colonial poets to shed their sense of shame for being the colonials of a rejected world, and the call was taken up duly and in time. There were poets like Harpur, Gordon and Kendall who looked on Australia with affection and a kind of warmth. It was for them to create a repertoire of symbols drawn from Australian landscape and Australian life.

The birth of Australian poetry is unique and peculiar in a way in which no other such literary phenomenon seems to have been. Firstly because the Australian poetry has gone through genuine pains of birth while coming forth under circumstances and in a geography most uncongenial for such a naissance. Secondly and more importantly, because the birth of Australian poetry provides an occasion for fresh thinking on the nature of poetry and poetic motivation in the same way in which the early romantic poetry of England was doing almost at the same time the Australian poetry was being attempted. But at that time the genuine Australian poetry was too meagre, infantine and obscure to attract notice and to venture comparisons. According to the then leading poets poetry was born of the overflow of emotion recollected in tranquillity. This conception enunciates both the poetic process and the poetic material. Emotion aroused undergoing sublimation and transformation in the poet's imagination and pouring forth at a tranquil moment. And this concept can be very easily illustrated with the poetry of the exponents of this theory. Things of beauty in the physical, moral and spiritual world aroused in the poet the desired poetic emotion and set in the poetic process. In the charged atmosphere of the new romantic enthusiasm everything was taken for granted and these new conceptions worked very well.

But now that we can see things from a distance we can perhaps see them in a better perspective. Going by these definitions of the essence of poetry one wonders if the English Romantics, had they been in Australia at the time, would have been able to write poetry at all. The absence of the "beauteous forms" and the gloom of the bush would have dampened their emotive powers. And yet, though obscurely, a poetry of a very rich quality was written in Australia and on Australia at that very time. And there is the rub. It appears that perhaps there was something more elemental to the nature of poetry which remained unobserved and uncomprehended because in literature it is generally the specimen which precedes the definition and the new element had not yet become incarnated. If we set Harpur's poetry side by side with the contemporary English poetry we find that there is something qualitatively new and elemental in the former which is lacking to the latter. One has the passing fancy that perhaps Harpur had evolved a new kind of poetry in the same way in which Shakespeare had created a new kind of drama. In Harpur's poetry we do not find rapture and emotion collected or recollected. It was natural because Australia of those days could not offer occasions for these. And yet there is something more enduring and impressive than the emotion in his poems.

When we put it to the touchstone of contemporary poetic theories Harpur's poetry seems to announce "who bothers about beauteous forms and overflow of emotion?" His poetry definitely does not beg that poetic paraphernalia. And yet it has a touch of class and quality of its own. Of course its formal structure does reflect the influence of the contemporary acknowledged and representative English poets but these influences are superficial. The spirit is elementally and qualitatively different. For example, "A

Midsummer Noon'' opens like

Not a sound disturbs the air,
There is quiet everywhere
Over plains and over woods
What a mighty stillness broods.

This is how most of the contemporary English poets opened their poems and yet it is quite a different song:

All the birds and insects keep
Where the coolest shadows sleep;
Even the busy ants are found
Resting in their pebbled mound
Even the locust clingeth now
Silent to the barky bough
Over hills and over plains
Quiet, vast and slumberous reigns.[11]

This is poetry with the smell of Australia, with the throb of the bush and the burning and drowsy breath of the Australian sun reigning over its vastness. The antique ants, the pebbled mound, the locust, the barky bough, the dragon hornet and the beetle are the material purely Australian and far from beautiful; but what matter? The purpose is not to belaud or to belittle but to woo and capture the spirit which informs and breathes through this noon time Australia; and the cumulating impression which the poem leaves with us is that the sleeping shadows, the slumberous quiet and even the ever wakeful rill are one with this spirit of drowse which seems to distill from the sun, the air, the earth and the mentioned objects and finally submerges them. The poem is packed with evocative potential.

In a Wordsworthian poem emotional subjectivism dominates. In a moment you know which way the poet wears his heart

No mate, no comrade Lucy knew
She dwelt on a wide moor
The sweetest thing that ever grew
Beside a human door.[12]

Or

> No Nightingale did ever chant
> So sweetly to reposing bands
> Of travellers in some shady haunt
> Among Arabian sands;
> A voice so thrilling ne'er was heard
> In springtime from the cuckoo bird.[13]

The direction of the sentimental thrust needs no comments, Harpur's is the poetry of emotional seclusion. Though he did not pronounce upon critical theories of poetry, he seems to have his own view of it, a view different from the current opinions. (And this view is reflected in almost all his good poetry, be it a narrative or otherwise.) His poetry issues not from emotion but from a warm affection which does not suffer from prejudices positive or negative and which keeps a reasonable distance both from emotional indifference and involvement. It is more of an identification with the object of his cotemplation, a sense of oneness which does not depend upon fervour and emotion. A woman may be ugly and shabby in looks and accent but yet to the child born of her flesh and blood she is the object of affection and warmth. It is this affectional bond and sense of identification with Australia and everything Australian which runs like the central trait in Harpur's poetry, be it a narrative like the "Creek of Four Graves" or "A Storm on the Mountains" or "The Mid Summer Noon in the Australian Forest." The land of "primeval curse," of "reversed nature" and "universal gloom" produced in him a sense of wonder bordering on affection.

Though there were some others like Gordon and Kendall who displayed occasional moods of affection for Australia and garnered a very useful treasure of Australian symbols for the coming generations of Australian poets it is Harpur who seems to have set the tone of the Australian poetic tradition. It is from this tone that veritable Australian poetry has resulted and this trait continues to be central to genuine Australian poetry even today. It is this affectional aspect of poetry which has been a sustaining influence in Australian poets. One feels tempted to skip over to a modern poet like Judith Wright to illustrate Harpur's seminal contribution to the Australian poetry. One can have, for example, her very short poem on the kite. A kite as a subject of poetry sounds rather awkward. But it is an Australian kite and look, how the affectional bond turns it into a symbol of grim vigour and struggle of Australia, beauty born of hunger and force:

> Carved out of strength, the furious kite
> shoulders off the winds hate
> The black mark that bars his white
> is the pride and hunger of Cain
> Perfect, precise, the angry calm
> of his closed body, that snow storm
> of his still eye that threatens harm
> Hunger and force his beauty made
> and turned a bird to a knife blade.[14]

One wonders if it is the evolution of the kite or the evolution of the Australian nation from its colonial origins itself which the poetess is singing about. And do not the tone and the touch of affection give one the passing fancy that it is perhaps a poem from Harpur?

## NOTES

1. Adam Lindsay Gordon, Australian poet (1833-70), bush balladist and landscapist. The quoted lines occur in his poem "A Dedication." He lived in Australia from 1853 to 1870.
2. Tasman, a great Dutch navigator and explorer, touched the western coast of Australia in 1642.

   William Dampier, a great English seaman, explorer and author, spent three months on Australian coast in 1688, is profoundly respected for his travel literature and the accuracy of observation.

   James Cook, a great English navigator and cartographer, surveyed 200 mile eastern coast of Australia in 1777.

   Charles Darwin, renowned naturalist and exponent of the Principle of Organic Evolution, sailed to Australia in 1831.
3. James Cook had seen only the eastern coast of Australia. The eastern uplands have their share of natural charm. Moreover he was on an official mission of exploration and was bound to speak well.

4. Major Ross, *Historical Records of New South Wales* (Sydney, 1788), I, ii, p.172.
5. John Dunmore Lang, *A Historical and Statistical Account of New South Wales* (Sydney, 1834), I, p. 354.
6. Major Ross was at the time the lieutenant governor of New South Wales.
7. Thomas Campbell, "Lines on the Departure of Emigrants for New South Wales" (Sydney, 1828). The following lines from Campbell's poem embody the imagined dreams of promise which the new settlement held out to the more optimistic of the Englishmen:

   Untracked in deserts lies the marble mine
   Undug the ore that 'midst thy roofs shall shine
   Unborn the hands but worn they are to be
   For Australasia, that shall give to thee
   Proud temple domes. . . .

   These lines have been addressed to England.
8. Barron Field, *First Fruits of Australian Poetry*, "Kangaroo" (Sydney, 1819).
9. The lines occur in Parke's first book of verse published in Sydney in 1842.
10. William Lisle Bowles, *Spirit of Discovery* (England, 1804).
11. Charles Harpur, "A Midsummer Noon in the Australian Forest."
12. William Wordsworth, "Lucy Gray."
13. William Wordsworth, "Solitary Reaper." "The sweetest thing" and "voice so thrilling" deserve notice.
14. Judith Wright, "Black-Shouldered Kite."

# McAuley, Eliot and English Poetic Tradition

S.K. TIKOO

James McAuley is considered to be one of the important modern poets of Australia and placed alongside A.D. Hope, Judith Wright, Mary Gilmore, Douglas Stewart and others. My purpose in this essay is to suggest that despite the fact that he is a modern Australian poet he can be placed in the English poetic tradition alongside T.S. Eliot, a most important exponent of that tradition which runs from Chaucer to the metaphysicals to the beginnings of the 1920s when the vogue for metaphysical poetry began anew and critical efforts were made to reinvigorate studies in that poetry. To be precise, McAuley has some things in common with Eliot--his classicism, Catholicism, an identical attitude towards the supernatural, and an active interest in politics (though they had different political ideologies).

Although it is difficult to examine the entire *ouvre* of McAuley I propose to analyze two poems of his to enlist his attitude to life and death and love. He seems to be preoccupied in some of his poems specifically with the theme of death. At the outset of this analysis, it is possible to notice that he writes in the meditative mode of the English metaphysical poets in whose revival and popularity in this century Eliot played a very significant role. Some of McAuley's poems illustrate the metaphysical concern with the melancholy and the dreary predominating over the bright and the cheerful aspects of life. This can be seen in his recurring concern with the themes of love and death.

As the poet states in the very first stanza of the poem "A Leaf of Sage," it is a tale from Boccaccio's *Decameron*. His rendering of this tale reveals his interest to revive traditional verse forms. However, the tale is poignant because of its theme of unfulfilled love, pathos and grief, and adequately brings out the poet's predilection for the romantic and the dreary. It is a tale of a charming, budding love-relationship between Pasquino and Simona:

> Pasquino lingered while Simona span
> And as he watched, her spindle seemed to draw
> The fibre of his feelings till they ran
> Twisting to coloured threads, which Love began
> To weave into the pattern he foresaw.[1]

The growth and flowering of their love subtly sentimentalized by the entrancing image of the colourful threads woven on the spindle is further brought home to the reader by a reference to the advance of day from its dewy morning to the golden noonday. But the romantic horizon of their courtship is soon overcast with clouds of gloom. They are reminded of an ancient saying which if followed up in deed could immortalize their love. The saying is, "Eat sage in May if you would live for aye." The lover is only too glad to satisfy his beloved's desire to rub the sage leaf on his teeth which will impart aromatic flavour to his breath and make their kiss ambrosial. As soon as the happy command is carried out by Pasquino he is transformed into "a swollen corpse." The golden noonday is blighted by "the thumb of Darkness" which acts like the cruel Fate of classical antiquity. The pathos in the event is intensified beyond measure when the beloved is accused of having poisoned and murdered her lover. Unconvinced by the accusation levelled against her the judge hears first-hand from Simona as to what had transpired at the scene of the event. To prove her innocence she demonstrates exactly how Pasquino had rubbed the sage leaf on his teeth and having done likewise succumbs to death within a few moments. The sage leaf took a toll of two human lives.

This is a truly delightful poetic narrative in the traditional romantic-tragic mode even though the tale is essentially derived from *Decameron*. McAuley's rendering is powerful because of the simplicity and lucidity and pathos with which the tragic situation is unfolded. The lovers by an ironically ignorant act terminate their own lives and do not so much as see the flowering of their love into maturity and ripeness. A good deal of suspense is aroused because the tragedy seems to have been wrought by the working of some inhuman, evil agency. Upon the magisterial enquiry conducted into the incident it is found out that the aromatic sage leaf had been poisoned by a toad which was discovered to be squatting within the hollow of the sage tree when it was cut down. The toad thus virtually plays the role of Satan or the Darkness. The blighting of good by evil not only reintroduces the biblical theme of the Adamic temptation and fall, but also underlines McAuley's, as much as Boccaccio's, world-view embedded in the narrative. The poet seems to believe that human love or goodness cannot exist unless sanctioned by the powers above. As Jennifer Strauss, an Australian critic, has aptly noted, McAuley was able to see the world in a Christian light "as a world to which love was available as an act of grace."[2] It also points to his religious belief that this worldly love is poisoned or marred by death, and that the only true and lasting love possible is divine love and faith in Christ. In this sense McAuley's outlook on life is reminiscent of the views and belief of poets such as Eliot who displays a deeply religious consciousness beneath the secular facade of their poetry. However, this spiritual awareness informs McAuley's poetry written after his conversion to Catholicism in 1952. His "Celebration of Divine Love" is a product of his post-conversion sensibility. It is as one might say "The Ash Wednesday" of McAuley. We may also turn now to a detailed analysis of his other poem, "The Cloak," which is admirable for illustrating his conformity to English poetic tradition and for focusing on his poetical power at a late stage of his life when he had become matured and his attitude to life and death underwent a definite change following his conversion.

The death theme is predominant in the poem. But Death is viewed not as a frightful persecutor or avenger or as an agent of cruel Fate, but in a comical vein as a powerful, mysterious, tricky Magician. It has no magic wand and no volunteers to carry out his behests but acts solely on his own. The only instrument it carried with it is a crimson-lined cloak. Truly like a magician it spreads out the cloak and throws it on the watching audience around it. At each performance a member of the "crowd" disappears. It is an interesting but not a frightening view of the mysterious ravager of life. Death shocks and dazes the near and dear ones of the afflicted, but that is not how McAuley portrays this shocker. He finds it as an enervating force for it fills the onlookers with "a decent numbness" or unshapen or uncontrollable ("raw") grief. There is also a slight ambiguity about the line "No volunteers?" which might mean either that Death comes and performs like a Magician without professional assistants or that no one volunteers to surrender to Death until it seizes one. Obviously, indifference to Death is shown because life, despite its miseries or unpleasantnesses, is dear to everyone. Even if one has passed time uneventfully or has not lived life in a true sense life is precious. This is the usual human attitude to life and death. Besides, death is not only least welcome but also no one can meet its challenge. Perhaps in one situation death may be welcome. This is, when it removes from the scene one who has been grievously wronged by us and whose sight is a perpetual reminder to us of our shame and guilt. But to wish someone death for that reason is a sort of "obscene relief" which only the mean minds may seek or welcome. On the contrary, only a heroic welcome will mitigate Death's power to frighten human beings.

Even though Death is cast in a lighter vein as a Magician which has a mysterious power to cause living beings to vanish away, yet the awe-inspiring aspect of this figure is delineated in no less frightful terms. The crimson-lining of the cloak is suggestive of the danger, pain, etc. and invokes feelings which haunt the mind with a sense of fear for the victims. Just as the cloak symbolizes death so the crimson colour symbolizes danger. Traditionally, red colour has been assigned varied significance. For the religious minded it signifies spiritual renunciation. The revolutionaries make it their chief symbol. A poet, such as W.B. Yeats, uses it to symbolize passion for his beloved, whether personal or his country. With McAuley it seems to suggest the mystery of the other world into which the claok will transport the victims. However, no further comment on its significance may be appropriate because "death does not comment or explain." The cloak then seems to be a symbol for death that carries the victims into what may possibly be even a better world than the one he is taken out of.

That world has order, symmetry and proportion which, by implication, the poet finds absent from his world. This is a poetic vision of a world made according to classical principles. A glimpse of that world is provided in a dream vision of it wherein he sees "the jade mountain veined with crystal streams." But is, in fact, a world as one sees in reality. The mountain looks like a magnificent body and the streams of crystal clear water flowing down its slopes appear like its veins. The natural objects--mountain and streams--are humanized to make them look more real. This is certainly anthropomorphism used in the way Robert Frost uses in his poems or Aesop in *Fables*. The dream world becomes real enough and resembles the actual world. Perhaps the implication is that the poet admits the possibility of realization of the dream world through the very world in which he lives. The harmony, lyricism and the poetic sentiment expressed in the poem refine the essential harshness of the sombre subject matter of death.

Instead of experiencing the fright caused by death the reader is bemused at the comical contemplation of its destructive or life-negating performance. However, mention is made of the experience of despondency that comes about and the sense of the void created by the vanishing away of an intimate friend or relative into the other world from which no dead return. Thus the reality of death is not travestied but honestly acknowledged. Death is recognized as a necessary corollary to life. Instead of repelling, the thought of death acquires a charming Keatsian ring of "easeful death" with which one may fall in love. There is a distinct change of mood at the end of the poem. The beginning was made with presenting a comical picture of death as a Magician, but the end is marked by a serious acceptance of the kind of redemptive role that it performs. Some element of reluctance is also noticeable in the initial view of death because of the poet's awareness that he is only fifty years old and has scarcely lived in the true sense of living life. Those fifty years had simply "gone away" without giving him any sense of satisfaction. During that short span he had also witnessed many intimate and known ones snatched away by Death and carried into its mysterious territory. The remaining crowd including the poet is left astonished, feeling the void and experiencing grief and a numbness of sense. The magical performance leaves the interested audience dazed and incapable of reckoning with the tricks it plays each time a member is transported into that mysterious world.

The treatment of a hackneyed but eternally puzzling subject matter of the omnipotence of death in the terms of a magician performing subtle feats not only lightens the desultory aspect of the theme but also renders it thought-provoking. The sixteenth century English essayist, Francis Bacon gives an exhaustive but witty exposition of the ways in which Death overtakes human beings and perceives it as a mysterious, awesome power or fate which human beings must suffer according to their various deserts. McAuley sees Death not merely as the final arbiter of the fate of individuals, but also as an inexplicable agency which causes both delight and puzzlement to the onlookers. It produces an "astonished void" in their minds. It is comic for the feeling of grief is overcome by a captivating harmony induced by the poetic vision of "the jade mountain veined with crystal streams." The darkness associated in the mind with the darkness of the underworld of the dead, powerfully envisioned by Dante's Limbo, is overcome by the soothing quality of this vision.

It may, however, be noted that McAuley's vision is only faintly contemplated but not visualized. The contemplation makes it more poetical than real and, therefore, less religious than the vision provided by Dante or Yeats or Eliot. However, Eliot makes it more incisive and sharp by clothing his vision of death and hell in contemporary terms:

> A crowd flowed over the London bridge, so many,
> I had not thought death had undone so many.[3]

Eliot presents death as a massive killer. Now the point is that McAuley's handling of death is suave and comic compared with the serious and even religious treatment of it by Eliot.

In "The Cloak" there is a unique commingling of different elements or the main strands of the English poetic tradition--the medieval (the Magician figure), the metaphysical (the cloak and Darkness), the seventeenth century ironical-satirical (exposure of scandalous conduct of evildoers who seek "obscene relief"), pre-Romantic (the elegiac tone reminiscent of Gray), the Romantic, Keatsian ("decent numbness of sense" recalling "Ode to a Nightingale"), the Augustan (implied preference for classical virtues specifically named, symmetry, proportion, etc.). These various elements certainly evoke a strange complexity of feeling which is finally resolved on a note of tacit approval of the role played by the eternally destructive performer. Understandably, McAuley's desire to preserve the traditional standards and values, already underlined by an Australian writer-critic Vivian Smith,[4] is manifest in "The Cloak." His fascination for continuation of the European tradition is suggested by his later opposition to neo-nationalism of the Jindyworobaks which contributed to his becoming controversial and somewhat less popular in the latter part of his life. His latent desire to preserve and promote the age-old tradition is reflected in his imparting to his poetry an intellectual and an argumentative quality which is a predominating characteristic of English metaphysical poetry.

It has aptly been observed that in McAuley's poetry there is the mingling of intellect and vision which "predominates over concrete experience, the idea over the observation."[5] "The Cloak," I think, is one of his poems in which "the conflict between feeling and emotion, intellect and will, issuing occasionally in sentimentality, occasionally in cynicism,"[6] does not become manifest. In fact, both will and cynicism are kept out of the poem. Besides, the poem depicts not a conflict but a steady change in the poet's mind from a state of puzzlement at the subtle tricks performed by the proverbial Magician to the state of ultimate acceptance and affirmation of its role. Instead of experiencing any conflict or tension, the poet's as well as the reader's mind must experience a serene calm precisely similar to that experienced at the end of a successful argument or from the revelation of a new awareness of tranquillity after meditation. At least, for once, there are no such pressures behind the poem as the ones noticed by McAuley's contemporary poet-critic Judith Wright who observed; "Sometimes the pressures behind his poems seemed too rigidly held under control: sometimes they seemed falsified by intellectual elaboration and too recondite allusion."[7]

It is possible to argue that "The Cloak" does not stand as a unique and representative instance of the type of poetry that McAuley wrote. But it is important to know the reason for a detailed discussion undertaken here. The poem seems to be significant in the writings of McAuley because it bears testimony to the poet's intellectual development since his earlier treatment of the themes of life, death and love in "A Leaf of Sage." There is a striking transformation of his early perception of the world and his attitude to these themes. In "The Cloak" the supernatural view takes over and reflects his new perception. Besides, this poem throws further light on McAuley's poetic tendencies and preoccupations. It also develops a subtle connection with one of his most popular poems, "Captain Quiros," in that both the poems reflects the poet's affirmation of his belief that "this-worldly fulfilment is impossible."[8] The latter poem shows the poet's readiness to welcome death which may effect a transition of the unhappy multitude into the other hopefully happy world. Both the poems discursively present the idea of the other world. But it is precisely in "The

Cloak" that McAuley's concern with the supernatural and the transcendental becomes poetically effective. The lines achieve a lyrical quality of the kind that McAuley achieved in his early lyrics.

The lyricism in much of his poetry--in "At Rugby Lagoon," "In Northern Tasmania," "Black Swans" which are considered among his finest lyrics--enhances the quality of resignation and the valedictory mood which ultimately grips the reader of "The Cloak." The mood of an early lyric evoked by the lines--

> At dusk I look out through old elms
> where mud-pools at the gatepost shine,
> A way of life is in decline,
>
> And only those who lived it know
> What it is time overwhelms,
> Which they must gradually let go[9]--

is recaptured but it is overcome by a mood of quiet contemplation and acceptance that one day this life would also pass away. The human beings cannot but surrender to death and disappear, "Leaving in us an astonished void, a fear/ A decent numbness, or raw grief." The rest of the spectators ( "The house is packed") witness the action of Death on the stage of life (echoing Shakespeare's poetic line, "The world's but a stage") and reconcile themselves to it. The Catholic in McAuley finally perceives the divine design behind the action of the Magician-actor for the former firmly endorses the "act" ("he doesn''t need to change the act") at the end of the poem.

McAuley, thus, employs sensuous imagery--the Magician, crimson-lined cloak, the jade mountain, caped darkness, transparent streams, etc.--to present a theme which is essentially sombre and melancholic. To one who deals with death the past itself appears glorious and becomes a theme in itself. In fact, the poet displays his interest in reminiscing the glory and the greatness of the past. It is particularly true of his lyrical sequences and sets collected under the title *A Vision of Ceremony* which contains one poem, "Black Swan," that was written purposely "to reawaken his readers to the life of the spirit and the sense of recovered spiritual gains."[10] In order to deal with the past of religion and orthodoxy he activates "the simplest traditional lyrical modes"[11] which makes some of his poems didactic in intention and also touching in appeal. As has been pointed out by one critic, he uses stylistic devices to modulate imagistic contrasts such as the contrast between images of light and darkness.

Clearly, as in "To the Holy Spirit," in "The Cloak" too, McAuley shows his inclination to write in the spirit of the metaphysical poets and so clothes abstract, supernatural concepts with concrete natural concepts. As Vivian Smith has rightly observed, in the former poem McAuley "invokes the Holy Spirit in the figure of a bird of paradise."[12] Similarly, in the latter poem he invokes Death in the comical figure of the Magician which will transact business subtly and dubiously between this world and the other, invisible world. Likewise, just as another poem of his, "St. John's Park," is known "for its emotional tone, colour and balancing and interrelation of a succession of images,"[13] so is "The Cloak" found admirable for its complex emotional tone, its complexity finally resolved by evocation of feelings of orthodox awe and resignation. It exhibits a transition from the dreary bleakness of "caped darkness" to the brightness and transparency of "crystal streams."

It may be appropriate to say that in this meditative lyric "The Cloak" McAuley surely furnishes evidence which suggests that he is also in line with his contemporary Australian poets, viz. Webb, Hope, Judith Wright and Douglas Stewart all of whom had been trying to bring about a synthesis of European culture and Australian reality. They carry deep within their sensibility the influence of the European, particularly English, poetic tradition. They also pursue identical spiritual paths in their meditations on man's true destiny. The vision of life presented in the poem has a traditionally familiar ring which we get in the poetry of Donne or other metaphysicals. In one poem of McAuley we are particularly reminded of the geometrical figure of a pair of compasses, which Donne introduces in "A Valediction Forbidding Mourning" to illustrate the permanent union of true lovers despite their physical separation. This happens through McAuley's use of the geometrical figure of the "pentagon" to describe indirectly the world of the spirit in contradistinction with "the pentagon of pleasure" built by the senses:

Love so is
Despair, being spirit too.
Hair and eyes in love can do

Lips can kiss;

Five senses build
A pentagon of pleasure:
But mind, exceeding common measure,
Is unfulfilled.[14]

It may be seen here that the theme of love unambiguously acquires a metaphysical dimension as mere sensuous pleasures fail to satisfy the mind's deep craving for love. Here, McAuley moves a step ahead of Eliot in creating this sensuous image in a truly metaphysical spirit. And yet the essential difference between Donne and McAuley is evident. Donne uses the geometrical figure to underline the essential spirituality of true love, but McAuley reverses this use made by Donne and instead uses it to suggest the inadequacy of the magnificent physical reality built by the sense which is no doubt transitory and subject to change.

In conclusion a word must also be said about one more element common between Eliot and McAuley briefly hinted earlier. That is, their insistence on or interest in promoting classical virtues, viz. refinement, symmetry, proportion, etc. stated in "The Cloak." Eliot's declaration that he is a classicist in literature, Anglo-Catholic in religion and royalist in politics is fittingly matched by McAuley's emphasis on classicism and his adaptation of the classical epic to Christian insistence on recognition of man's sinfulness as a fundamental fact of life. The classical approach to Christianity recognizes the need to shun sin (because it violates the moral order of the universe) and save the sinner. Both Eliot and McAuley go to classical antiquity: the former for building the plot-outlines of his plays or for developing ancient myths as controlling devices in the poetic presentation of modern reality in *The Waste Land*, the latter adapts the classical material of the roles of Philoctetes, Herakles and Prometheus in dealing with the heroic themes in his attempts at heroic poetry. As Jennifer Strauss has remarked in her admirable study of the poetry of McAuley: "In 'Hero and the Hydra' McAuley examines classical myth, not so much to see if it can yield a model of redemption for a sickness of modernity as to express the agony of a civilization which seemed to have lost its principle of coherence, unable to bring together the twin themes of order and justice in the soul."[15]

Thus both Eliot and McAuley conceive their poetic ideals and visions in terms of their Christian perception of the modern world as sick, diseased, corrupt, and without a sense of direction or coherence. But while Eliot sees the possibility of its redemption directly through affirmation of faith in moral values, McAuley, who had earlier expressed firm conviction in the heroic struggle of man, finally affirms the moral order. The passionate devotion of both Eliot and McAuley to classical learning can be adequately defended since both saw the present day world as being in a chaotic state--which was borne out by their realization of the havoc wrought by the World Wars and the involvement of both Australia and England in the two Wars--and hence their need for reclamation and order.

Eliot and McAuley can also be recognized as strong advocates of the need for upholding European tradition. While Eliot's Eurocentrism is well known, McAuley's inclination to develop Australian literature in the European tradition is partly corroborrated by his later repudiation of the Jindyworobak nationalism of which he was a supporter at an earlier time. McAuley's intellectual development from that time onwards has already been taken note of: "By 1945, however, he was writing dismissively of their 'sovereign art-provoking lotion' in Jindyworobaksheesh."[16] Clearly, he is turning towards a poetry which is not merely nationalistic but also universally valid. It is due to this changed outlook that the poet vehemently attacks his contemporary Bernard O'Dowd and others in whose poetry he did not find anything worthwhile to help create an appropriate mental climate conducive to poetic activity.

Along with his poetic activity there is also the political activity in which McAuley actively participated and in which, though his ideology is different, he again comes close to Eliot. McAuley recognizes the right of every individual to participate in politics but he would advise them to shun politics and instead turn to their private gardens and cultivate roses. His preference for the rose and garden symbols implies his desire for creativity in which one could experience the mingling of the natural and the supernatural. One may recall Eliot's fascination too for the rose and garden symbols in his poetry. If one goes further back, then the employment of rose symbol can also be seen in the poetry of W.B. Yeats and other poets. The point is that the employment of the rose and garden symbols is also a part of the English poetic tradition, and that

McAuley's poetic creativity is by and large firmly grounded in the English poetic tradition despite his initial flirting with (Australian) Jindyworobaksheeism.

## NOTES

1. Cf. *The Penguin Book of Australian Verse*, ed. Harry Haseltine (Penguin, Rep. 1982), p. 297. All subsequent quotations from McAuley's poems are taken from this.
2. See Jennifer Strauss, "From Heroism to *Pietas*," in *Meanjin* (Melbourne University), Vol. 48, No. 3, Spring 1989, p. 605.
3. T.S. Eliot, "The Waste Land," *Collected Poems 1909-62* (London: Faber and Faber, 1963), p. 65, lines 62-63.
4. Vivian Smith, "Poetry," *The Oxford History of Australian Literature*, ed. Leonie Kramner (Oxford Univ. Press, 1981), p. 383.
5. *Ibid.*
6. *Ibid.*
7. *Ibid.*, p. 384
8. *Ibid.*, p. 389
9. *Ibid.*
10. *Ibid.*
11. *Ibid.*
12. *Ibid.*
13. *Ibid.*
14. Cf. *Collected Poems (of James McAuley) 1936-70*, No. 3 (Sydney: Angus and Robertson, 1970).
15. See *Meanjin*, Vol. 48, No. 3, 1989, p. 603.
16. *Ibid.*, p. 599.

# Mirroring the Land: The Nature Poetry in Australian Literature

SOMA BANERJEE

The country grows
Into the image of the people
And the people grow
Into the likeness of the country
Till to the soul's geographer
Each becomes the symbol of the other.

Max Dann

Spengler had once commented that the continents shape everything within their shores to a special, almost demiurgic blueprint. It is no wonder that verses emerging from Australia have the spiky brilliance of the banksia, the etherealness of the ghost-gums under which patter Earth's weirdest creatures, and the sun-hazed vastness of the outback. The poets crave that they be given "A harsh land to wring music from." They want words that are "cutting harsh/as wattle-birds notes in dusty gums/crying at noon" and embue strength and austerity from the soil that "swings, like heart and blood/from heat to mist."[1] The images are best received as an arena of powerful, shifting impressions, through which we are constantly moving into deeper perceptions of this mysterious continent and its poets--who use the English language in a highly personal, often idiosyncratic way. The condensed brilliancy of illustration is stunning--the unusual setting and phrase open all inlets of side-view and perspective, excite the imagination and cling to memory.

Bernard O'Dowd, that fiercely independent Australian, visualized his native land as the "Last sea-thing dredged by sailor Time from Space" and questions: "Are you a drift Sargasso where the West/In halcyon calm rebuilds her fatal nest?" Through the showy learning and tangled metaphors of this sonnet emerges the fervour of a whole nation of literati struggling to carve out a path away from the literary oppression of overseas authority. Those critics held that language could never trace the intricate nuances of experience, and efforts in that direction only freeze and distort the vital deliquescence of experience into abstract shapes. Such pronouncements were ridiculous in context of this dream-soaked, vision-drenched land, and its bewitched poets, who had been shorn free of the tangled growth of erudition. An unique pattern of style is noticeable in most of the Australian creative artists. The spirit of their extraordinary continent are transmuted into the warp and woof of imagery and aesthetic treatment, and the poetic imagination is exercised with exhilarating freshness. Gilbert Slessor in "South Country" brings home an awe-inspiring, very Australian vastness:

> And over the flat earth of empty farms
> The monstrous continent of air floats back
> Coloured with rotting sunlight and the black
> Bruised flesh of thunderstorms.
>   Air arched, enormous, pounding the bony ridges
>   Ditches and hutches, with a drench of light
>   So huge, from such infinitude of height
>   You walk on the sky's beach.[2]

Images are knit up into a superb harmony of impressions and cast a plenary spell. The external world corresponds to the inner reality and the rhythm of the visual landscape reverberates within the brain. "I had no human word" admits Ronald Robinson, except "The speech that silence shapes but keeps a ruin and the writhe of thin/ ghost-gums against their rain-blue deeps/ of night and range I drank in." He saw the nature of mountains change-- "deepen and free from mood to mood/ . . . and found where dark heliotrope/ shadows pied a ranges power/mauve purple at the foothills slope/ the parakelia, the desert flower."[3]

Clumsy, fumbling attempts to wrest out the land's secrets, or to hunt analogies in a British context is futile. English language is but a fragile, tenuous link here, through which the poet conveys the magic and the exotic impressions to the outside world. William Walsh stresses that Australian writers, like the rest of their commonwealth counterparts, believe that immediate experience and its expression in language are not two wholly different things. He says: "Language in Britain may be a kind of treachery; in the Commonwealth it is taken to be a sort of loyalty."

The "lost world feeling" that the Britons so scoff at, has its own special charm. It is present in the minor English speaking cultures, where expressions obsolete elsewhere survive. Attitudes evolve their own directions, often tangent to the original. Language here is not an invalid surrogate for experience, but a new, living entity, all the stronger for its hybridization. A real sense of a more uninhibited life springs from the English literature coming from countries far removed from England. It has a spontaneity, a raw energy, emotional rather than intellectual, and this underlies the work in most Commonwealth countries. It is revealed in the creative insurance and vivid imagination of a Patrick White, the cerebral athletics of A.D. Hope, in the tantalizing fabric of R.K. Narayan's Malgudi Tales, as in the cataclysmic, bleak power of Morely Callaghan's Canadianness. The peasant sagacity and muscularity of V.S. Naipaul's prose has it, and so is it present in the emotional, very Bengali turbulence of Nirad Chaudhuri.

Eliot saw a living bond between an artist and the whole atmosphere of ideas that make up his tradition. The poetic mind is the catalyst putting the concepts of its milieu into words; the poem develops like an egg, "the dark embryo" of which is created by tradition shaping the poetic mind. A serious writer is ever involved in the process of accumulating the spiritual experience of his race, and draw the exact curve of the specific sensibility of his time upon the graph chart of aesthetics. With the suffocating pressure of British literary criticism removed from him, he is at once the defender and analyst of his society. He feels that he is contributing not to the literature of some nebulous, vaguely existing Commonwealth, but to his very own Australia, India, Canada, Africa or the West Indies. The idea of melting down all individual identity in the gigantic churning-bowl of the Commonwealth is revolting. New Zealanders are fiercely protective of their identity of not being Australians. West Indians do not care to be dubbed as British, Jamaicans or Antiguans. Each race is distinct, ironically inverting Forster's liberal apophethegm into "Only disconnect."

Australia and India, now far apart and once geologically united in the continent of Asia, have more in common than is usually imagined. Both are countries of fantastic contrasts; with deserts, tropical rain forests and snow-capped ranges co-existing. Primeval, brooding lands--the last of the world's lost species roam here, and the medley of exotic flora and fauna is mind-boggling. Both are so unusual, that nowhere else on the globe can one find a close analogy. India is immensely ancient, culturally, when compared to Australia, where people have a light burden of time, so that it is still personal--to be measured in terms of great-grandfathers, not past civilizations. David Campbell relates of a stockman, under "collibahs" that "were twisted steel." In the mirage-laden, distorting air, he hallucinates that it is the future generation--the stockman's grandson before him. Yet the tradition of writing a highly personalized English put the two at par. It is the Australian's native tongue, however; and a second, adapted language for Indians, as for Africans. An autonomous form with its own idiom and usage to fit the requirements of the Indian temperament, the very fact that English is learnt and not simply assimilated adds a peculiar flavour to it. Poetry, the most sensitive of literary forms, uses it with force and delicacy, and taps the resources of an alien language to express things Indian. Nissim Ezekiel's, "You have the tone of vice for true or false/A sense of seasons, place and element/Your sunniness is not obscured/By people, gods or ghosts within the blood/You quietly burn and find the fire god," and Moraes's "I shall be he whom you will never find/Except in me; I am the last pretence/Dark angel of the world; who moves behind/Dayfall, and whispers truth to innocence/Hurting it to tears," are examples of heights attained. Despite the "woolly terminology of Indian philosophic tradition often influencing poets, Indian poetry has gained a prominent status in world literature. Buddhadev Bose's argument that "Indo-Anglian poetry is a blind alley, lined with curio-shops, leading nowhere" rings hollow.[5]

In this essay, I intend to explore those special characteristics of Nature poetry--Australian and Indian--that reveal the uniqueness of the land that inspired them. Christopher Brennan, the first Australian poet to prove himself aesthetically adult, chants of "Fire in the heavens, and fire along the hills/and fire made solid in the flinty stone," while "Behind the veil of burning silence bound/ vast life's innumerous busy littleness/is hushed in vague-conjectured blur of sound" that dulls the brain, until "some dazzling puncture let the stridence throng/in the cicadas torture-point of song." But this typifies the poet's urge to write as a world-citizen. These lines could be describing an arid, burning valley in India, Mexico, Africa or the Middle East. Very similar is R. Parthasarathy in "This is the country the sun rules/Here stones have eyes; rivers hands." The poet's fastidious sensibility, reflected in polished lines, records a general landscape. In neither of the two extracts quoted are the special scent of Australia or India palpable. What I am emphasizing as the very personal nature poetry of a country, are poems that could be written nowhere else in the world--the substance round which poetic fervour builds up must be unique to the native soil. The landscape and the life of the land is translated, metamorphosed into poetry, as evident here in Ronald Robinson's ecstasy over black swans:

> If the land I crossed was dumb
> ravaged, stark with fires scars
> sudden, in green flames of scrub
> rose the blood-proud warpaths
> Savage was the place where night
> cried in winds about my ears where the honey-eater still
> sang clinging to the grass-tree spears.[7]

So potently is Australia evoked that the lines burn and throb with the colour and sounds of the Bush, and we can never dream of reading it as a general nature poem, or confuse it with the Irishness of Yeats "Wild swans at Coole." As distinctive, and laden with its own hushed dark beauty and burden of nostalgia are the poet Jibanananda's evocations in "Beauteous Bengal." He declares: "I have seen the face of Bengal/I no longer go seeking the world's beauty." His landscapes, flora and fauna are so unquiet, so deeply enmeshed in that land's fabric, that they are totally inextricable, and even transplanted with the subcontinent, would give an awkward impression. Yet Australia, like India, is a land that guards its mysteries.

> The truth is too close to the sorrow; the song you would sing
> It cannot go into the fever; you cannot go into the spring.

The reader's senses might be appeased--the scent, the light, the weird sounds, the unbelievable colours might be conveyed, yet

Nature does not allow the final curtain to be drawn from her ancient visage. The ultimate secret eludes us in our mental sojourn through this haunted, untamed land. The "naked and aboriginal feel/of Nobody's Land" for which the poet's dreaming flesh had ached over long years, is immensely old. This "nation of trees, drab green and desolate grey" is falsely called a young country:

> She is the last of lands, the emptiest
> A woman beyond her change of life, a breast
> Still tender, but within the womb is dry.[8]

A.D. Hope's controversial poem "Australia" reflects the white colonials's ambivalence towards the place of their inherited exile, evident in "The river of immense stupidity/Floods her monotonous tribe from Cairns to Perth." Urban Australia is shunned. "Her five cities, like five teeming sores" are the hotbeds of "chatter of cultured apes/which is called civilization over there." This situation has analogues in Canada or the West Indies. Poets turn for succour to the great open spaces "such savage and scarlet as no green hills dare Springs in that waste."

Love for the soil rings in James McAuley's brilliant Terra Australia. "It is your land of similes, the wattle/scatters its poller on the doubting heart." There is loneliness, but also an Edenic calm--

> The flowers are wide awake, the air gives ease
> There you come home; the magpies call you Jack
> And whistle like larrikins at you from the trees
> There too the angophora preaches on the hillsides
> With gestures of Moses; and the white cockatoo
> Perched on his limbs, screams with demonic pain
> And who shall say on what errand the insolent emu
> Walks between morning and night on the edge of the plain.[9]

More of the unique fauna appear in his Celebration of Love, and we have a distinct feeling that the creatures hidden under deck on the Noah's Ark have been released on this coninent. Parrots scatter, "shy wallabies/ peer out like secret selves among the rocks/A clod of earth moves and becomes a rabbit . . . these sober citizens of sweet content/Koalas, feel the tug of events/And look down from their sleepy galleries/In grave astonishment,"[10]

There is a poignant juxtaposition of the radiance and darkness of the same land, where "The dispassionate and shaven gum tree" calls the "kookaburras home" with open arms, and the "leaves make shadow dance and sunlight." The element of infused imaginative tragedy in McAuley's works is glimpsed in "the faint sterility that disheartens and derides where "Blue-green gums have a wild precision, a strict disorder/And the brown sheep poke at my dreams along the hillside."

An eerie sense of emptiness pervades Australia, specially the "red-centre"--the Back of Beyond the Bush. Its "hard archaic magic" infuses a peculiar nostalgia into the Australian soul, and wonder in the aliens. In "This wary gaunt oracular bush," "hot rock-knuckles amid this breathless bracken/Jut to the light that glints unwillingly/From every slack leaf, every crook and jag/of silvery deadwood."[11]

Here, heat is felt in the guts and light in one's bones, and the bush-ballads originated in this land "where drought visits and fire her daughter." The Bush is bounded by the huge eroded Macdonell Range, twisted in fantastic lunar shapes, the shimmering salt-coated lakes and the grotesque Olgas. It is an angular presence, elbow, lean as famine/Dry rasping, hot with prickles" where "glare not colour hangs/like gauge." We recall Alun Lewis' heat-shimmering "Mahratta Ghats," where "Dark peasants drag the sun upon their back" a land upon which Shiva has split his seed. "The valleys crack and burn" while viciously the exhausted plains/Sink their black teeth into the horny veins/straggling the hill's red thighs," and the "small gods" are pitiless.

K.N. Daruwalla's "Haranag" has a description akin to the Bush, its spinifex, its inflammability, its dry vegetation: "The bamboo-jungle grew around our house/an arthiritic forest/of tangled bone/spiked with leaf/You couldn't cut it/the stems had hardened so/The chopped limbs could not be moved/They were interlaced like bone shards/in a multiple fracture/You couldn't burn it was too green/ and if you burnt it in June/half the town would go cindering with it/and so the jungle stayed/and in its shadow/the porcupine and the bamboo-viper."[12]

A land of opposites, parts of Northern Australia have tropical climate, with the most exotic flora and fauna. The bower-bird teems here, as do wild pigs, kangaroos and crocodiles. Judith

Wright details the rain-forest, where, in the "bewildering midsummer of darkness/lit with ancient fern/laced with poison and thorn" the path winds under "hanging clouds of leaves and voiceless birds." Here "The priest stinging tree waits with his whips and fevers/under the hooded flowers that fall from the tree like blood." West Indian Edward Braithwaite's forests have the same sinister appeal. The wall like forest at Yeji in "tangled squat mahogany out/riders, and then the dense, the dark green tops, bright/shining standing trunks/wawa, dahoma, esa and/odum the doom/of the thick stretching green leaves gathered darkness.

Low ranges, shallow gullies filled with huge boulders, clumps of spinifex, acacia and short grass, and not sand, comprise the deserts of Western Australia. Showers bring out riots of wild flowers and screeching flocks of cockatoos. This is mirrored in the blooming of "parakelia, the desert flower" and "beyond all words I knew the rush of ash/grey wings that gloomed, with one response/storm grey to swerve with crimson flash."

The continent of Australia spreads out from a world of coral reefs and rain forests to territories of harsh cold. Tasmanian Christopher Koch's poems convey sense of silence and antiquity, of anguish winds and empty beaches. "Nothing moved but a heat dance" on Shelly Beach, where Aborigines had once camped. "In this forgotten ring of land/ Sentinelled with grey gums corpses/The dry grass was careless of its own soft death/And the banks at the water's edge watched him sullenly/ They were ill with an illness that was very old." Nature here is neither anthromorphic nor sympathetic, nor is it malevolently Learesque. It is the sublime inhumanity that is articulated in the dirge from Cymbeline.

Vivian Smith recalls Koch in mannerisms, and both delight in the glacial Tasmanian landscape, In "Sea Lion," "The wind cries out from the thorny dunes/from the tangled banksias sharp as wire." In "Bedlam Hill," the landscape is "empty as a blindman's stare," and the hills strewn with "fractured rock where the berry suckles the given stone." No "life moves beneath the stone" in these cold hills with "madness in their monotone." The very muteness is significant, for it induces a fullness to presence in our own bodies--a plenum of self-consciousness that can dispose of bridge-buiding between our experience and consciousness. He is lyrical in describing Portuguese Laurel, flowering "a harp of loosened fire/strung to praise the world." It gathers distance in itself, and is "spray and foam and floating snow/burning buds of stars, the Milky Way and trailing light/of long light years." We sense being blown outside the loop of time in this austere landscapes that is "torn and built from air," and where "shell stir in the pull of water, lift/fragile and holy faces to the sky."[13]

As evocative, but on a different emotional strain is Lawrence Bantleman's "Kanchajunga," where the sun is lewd and "a wind without a lung." Folksongs fill the foothills, and "As I root/I hear not armies overhead/I hear the flute. I hear/The summoning of India/To face the truth/There is some black rock. There some white/Some scraps with blade-thin edges/Shave the night.

Queensland, its blaze and rain, are captured in John Blight's "Thunderbolt" where "top-heavy clouds of noon/Crashing in five o'clock storms like guns" intimates how "Time soaked one so with wet" and "down the lightning bean stalk, hurtling down/Thundered the giant footsteps of rain." (Mary River Camp) In Soyinka's African analogue to this, "roaring vats of an unstopped heaven" drum on the Earth, that lies in "fevered distillations," for "Ogun is still on such/combatant angles, poised on a fresh descent/fiery axe heads fly about his feet."[14]

Australian and Indian literature, as indeed all Commonwealth literature, excel most when the distinctive flavour of the native soil comes through forcefully. As Walsh pointed out, "The future requires that the consciousness of the race be articulated in, and refined by, arts generated on its own soil, above all by the supremely expressive art of language since nothing has more human reality than the savour of home."[15] And the poets might echo James McAuley:

> And I am fitted to that land, as the soul is to the body
> I know its contractions, waste and sprawling indolence
> They are in me and its triumphs are my own
> Hard won in the thin and bitter years without pretence.

## NOTES

1. Ian Mudie, "This Land," *The Penguin Book of Australian Verse*.

2. Kenneth Slessor, "South Country," *Ibid.*
3. Ronald Robinson, "I had no human speech," *Ibid.*, p. 188.
4. William Walsh, *Readings in Commonwealth Literature*, Introduction, p. xi
5. P. Lal, ed., *Modern Indian Poetry in English.*
6. Christopher Brennan, "Fire in the Heavens," *The Penguin Book of Australian Verse*, p. 27.
7. R. Robinson, "Tumult of the Swans," *Ibid.*, p.187.
8. A.D. Hope, "Australia," *Ibid.*, p. 120.
9. James McAuley, "Terra Australia," p. 228.
10. James McAuley, "Celebration of Love," p. 230.
11. John Thompson, "The Traveller," p. 128.
12. K.N. Daruwallah, "Haranag," *An Anthology of Indo-English Poetry*, ed. Gauri Deshpande, p. 68.
13. Francis Webb, "For my Grandfather," *The Penguin Book of Australian Verse*, p. 274.
14. Wole Soyinka, "Idanre and Other Poems," p. 61.
15. William Walsh, p. xiii.

# A.D. Hope's Ulysses and Kate Llewellyn's Penelope: Two Modern Voices from the Past

MALATI MATHUR

The frequent use of myths is a prominent characteristic of A.D. Hope's poetry. The familiarity of the oft-repeated tales, is however, offset by Hope's shift of focus. It is like looking at the photograph of a long-familiar, almost drab, scene in which, though the details are all the same, freshness is provided through the capturing of the scene from a different angle of vision. It is in his imaginative and innovative use of myths that Hope's brilliance most clearly reveals itself and myths provide the most satisfactory answer, both philosophically and artistically, to the problems he encounters as a man and a poet.

Myth has been defined as "a story or complex of story elements taken as expressing, and therefore as implicitly symbolizing, certain deep-lying aspects of human and transhuman existence."[1] For Hope, myth

> serves as a pattern of meaning for himself and his fellow men . . . some of his best poems are those in which he has utilized the mythic core to the best advantage, revitalizing old stories to bring their significance up to date.[2]

However, myths are not there merely for their own sake. They do not serve as props brought into use for holding up shabbily constructed concepts or incompletely formed ideas. They serve, rather, as vehicles to express certain deeply thought out and strongly felt convictions. The most remarkable and distinctive feature of Hope's use of myths is the way in which he cleverly adapts them to speak directly to the modern man and woman, thus helping them to achieve an identity with an understanding, of the age-old characters. And always, there is the unexpected conclusion, a certain twist in the tale which helps to bring home the point the poet is trying to make, in a thoroughly dramatic fashion. As Vivian Smith has remarked:

> He is . . . one of the most allusive of Australian poets, with a large body of knowledge at his disposal. But he does not merely aim to recreate historically or atmospherically the history of the legends of the past, created on a single striking figure or group. The myths provide him with convenient familiar fictions. To use a myth situation and characters, however much they are reinterpreted or reversed, provides the poet with a ready-made foundation; the poem does not have to start below ground level to establish its basic reference and the poet can rely on the reader to supply a set of attitudes. Whether he develops or reverses them, he has not had to create them within the poem.[3]

In "The End of a Journey,"[4] Hope describes the feelings of Ulysses on his return to his island kingdom after all the excitement and danger-filled days of adventure and voyages. Interestingly enough, not once does Hope refer to Ulysses by name. His identity is established only through references to Circe, Priam and his burning town, the song of the sirens and so on.

The Ulysses we are introduced to here is not the noble hero of Dante, Homer or Tennyson. He is a twentieth century wanderer returned home: a rheumy, disillusioned old man, "a figure, seemingly incapable of mental or physical action, whose only certainty is that 'the Gods at last had left him.'"[5] The reader "is expected to contrast the Homeric story of high-souled adventure and dauntless determination with the prosaic sterility and loneliness presented."[6]

The very first stanza sets the tone. Finally back with Penelope, the night of reunion is not an ecstatic, deliriously joyful celebration of conjugal ties; it is "an old man sleeping with his housekeeper." "The embrace is a 'rape (-) by a stranger' . . . Penelope's traditional values of 'faith and valour' are undermined as she finds 'herself, faith wasted, valour lost.'"[7] Thus, the reunion, with all its attendant values of the sustenance of home and hearth and for which Ulysses had ignored the seductive song of the sirens, is transformed into a cold and meaningless act of barren sex:

> And he, for all the bloody passion it cost
> To have heard the sirens and yet have fled,
> Thought the night tedious, coughed and shook his head.

The slaughter of the suitors and indiscreet maidens is focussed on with grim clarity. For Hope, there is no justification for the senseless carnage; it is not the cleansing of the state as suggested by Homer--it is a wanton and capricious destruction of human life:

> A farm cart by the doorway dripped and stank,
> Piled with the victims of his mighty bow.
> Each with her broken neck, each with a blank,
> Small strangled face, the dead girls in a row
> Swing as the cold airs moved them to and fro.

The picture presented here--that of a farm cart 'piled' high with bodies--is shocking in its implicit reduction of human beings to the state of piled up garbage.

The long wished for object of our hero's wandering--the island kingdom of Ithaca--is, for the modern Ulysses, merely a "petty kingdom." Where Tennyson's hero, looking out across "the dark broad seas," muses that "some work of noble note, may yet be done,"[8] there is no such suggestion in Hope's presentation of this Ulysses of the present day for whom "the expectations of the fruitful conclusion to a quest are subverted."[9]

> Grimly he watched his enemy the sea
> Rage round the petty kingdom he called home;
> But now no trident threatened from the spray.
> He prayed but knew Athene would not come.
> The gods at last had left him, and the day
> Darkened about him.

There is no feeling here to correspond with Tennyson's sentiments that "old age hath yet his honour and his toil."[10] Hope's nameless revenant is, like his Byron, alone, "a castaway" on the "cruel shore" of his disillusionment:

In age and disenchantment to prolong
Stale years and chew the end of ancient wrong,
A castaway upon so cruel a shore.

Hope's Ulysses takes his place among the other twentieth century anti-heroes. "As a type of contemporary anonymous man, he is a fitting hero, perhaps, for the anxious age: this modern Ulysses, suffering an atrophy of will, is cut off from the sustaining rituals of love and family."[11]

Hope's poem is, in a sense, an echo of the Australian experience--"castaway" from the shores of England into a hostile, alien environment. The plight of Ulysses also duplicates the plight of creative writers like Hope. With no established literary tradition to draw upon, struggling to form an identity of their own as distinct from that of the British, writers in Australia felt the anguish of an acute feeling of having been cut off from their roots. "Having no focus and no central point of cultural reference, Australian writers have, of necessity, been more isolated."[12]

In "The End of a Journey," Hope refashions Homer's rendering, infusing the story with the mood of contemporary fiction which speaks directly to our age. Hope delineates the pathos and anti-climactic note of the homecoming, presenting a picture of life that has lost its magic--made all the more poignant because of the vivid memories of that magic which Ulysses revolves "in his skull." There is "an assertion of life in the acknowledgement that just as day is followed by darkness, years of excitement are eventually counterbalanced by dullness."[13] The feeling of flatness and disillusionment after the anticipation and excitement of the homecoming is intensely portrayed.

But what of Penelope--the type of the faithful wife, left behind for years together while her husband-King roams the farthest corners of the globe, never knowing when he would return or even whether he would return at all?

All our epics abound with descriptions of adventurous gallants and the saga of their journeys; not one makes an attempt to plumb the depths of the emotions of the women left behind. Kate Llewellyn, presenting the other point of view in "Penelope,"[14] describes the feelings of Ulysses's wife during all the years of his absence and then on his return.

The poem is a witty reply to Hope's "The End of a Journey."

With its dominant note of feminism, the poem reflects the mood of Australia in the 80s. There is a change of perspective, a look at the same situation as viewed by another, no less important participant, hitherto largely ignored.

The poem begins by addressing traditional wives with their traditional occupations--"knitters weavers or embroiderers"--inhabiting a world which complacently expects them to fill their hours with counting stitches while their wandering husbands seek to quench their lust for adventure and women. And then all those countless hours of Penelope's toil are laboriously undone each night:

> You who have been knitters
> weavers or embroiderers
> know what it meant
> nightly to undo the work of every day

Kate Lewellyn, like A.D. Hope, makes adept use of the myth. She takes up the threads of the story as we know it and expertly twists them around to present a different picture. Penelope here seeks to demolish the myth within the myth:

> after twenty years of that
> at my wits' ends they say
> I determined to give myself
> to anyone who could bend his bow
> facts yes facts
> the truth as always
> lies somewhere between

The "fact" that "they" present is markedly different from that what she has felt. She

> was weary of that cold cold bed
> it's not forever a woman
> who's known marriage and the birth of children
> can always act the nun

The repetition of "cold" serves to emphasize her loveless state of existence. She is no timid virgin unaware of the passion and intensity of physical love. She is a married woman who has borne children, one who has experienced to the full and responded to the demands of desire. Why, then, has she continued to exist in this barren, passionless state? Because that is the way of the world--that men can philander and women must wait to welcome them when they return to the security of home and hearth, sated by their wanderings:

> hoist to men's belief
> that they can adventure and take lovers
> and that woman wait

It is a world in which men have all the rights and the women all the duties.

But the modern Penelope wishes to set the record straight. It is not as though she did not want the warmth and caring of a lover. She is "at the point of giving in" when Fate brings her husband back:

> it was purely chance
> fortuitous
> and allowed me among all women
> to be exampled of the faithful

So it is not as though Penelope has remained faithful out of choice or an overwhelming lover for her absent husband. She has remained so because of her adherence to and reluctance to cross the strict standards (albeit double) set by society. Even the norms of society would not have stopped her for very long if chance had not brought her husband back at just the right time. This is the point Kate Llewellyn very clearly and unequivocally makes.

The next line is completely modern both in tone and choice of phrase--"I was hot to trot" and compels the reader to rearrange the picture of Penelope, to make alterations in the image handed down by tradition.

Penelope and Ulysses, now virtual strangers (A.D. Hope's "The End of a Journey" makes this point), are united in an alien and unfriendly Ithaca. In the original version of the myth, "wise" Penelope's initial response to Odysseus is tentative and sceptical: Odysseus accuses her of "having a heart that cannot be softened. No other woman in the world would harden her heart to stand thus aloof from her husband." But, having tested him, she softens--"so welcome to her was the sight of her lord, (that) her white arms she would never quite let go from his neck."[15]

Implicit in the above lines is the belief that it is the duty of all "good" wives to welcome their errant husbands whole-heartedly with not a thought for their vagrant spouse's (mis)adventures in other lands and other beds. Twenty years of absence, apparently, should count for nothing. All that should matter (if the wife is good and loving) is that the husband is back home again.

This outrageous sentiment is enough to incite all self-respecting women to rise up in arms and that is precisely what Llewellyn seems to be doing.

Robert Lowell, in his poem "Ulysses and Circe"[16] offers a slight deviation in the depiction of Penelope's feelings at the return of Ulysses:

> She sees no feat
> in his flight or his flight back.

She knows he is not as "invincible as he once was." Lowell's treatment is a step towards the feminism of today while Kate Llewellyn's poem rearranges the entire scenario, presenting a picture that seems topsy-turvy and entirely at variance with the familiar legend.

However, in spite of the fact that Penelope wanted to rebel, an awareness of the conventions of an orthodox society forces her to suppress her desires. Lacking the courage to fling all constraints aside, she waits, while the dull edge of her desperation is slowly but relentlessly whetted and she gears herself up to kick society full in its complacent face. And then her husband returns. There is no feeling of joy or a sense of faith rewarded, there is only regret:

> their expectations had a role
> and kept me an unstable undoer of my work
> it left me an older woman
> it murdered my only friends.

Her faith has been "wasted" as A.D. Hope puts it; there is the pang of a loss keenly felt. What has been the fallout of her famed faithfulness? It has left her unstable--weaving and unravelling the results of her toil; it has left her older--living through years of barren loneliness; and it has left her friendless--how poignant is the line "their feet fluttered in the wind"! The slaughter of innocents is echoed in Hope's lines:

> the dead girls in a row
> swung as the cold airs moved them to and fro

There is precedent in Homer for Penelope's aging. Tennyson's Penelope is "aged":

> By this still hearth, among these barren crags,
> Match'd with an aged wife. . . .[17]

Hope transforms her fabled patience into passivity, a lack of will, in the process stripping her of dignity and spirit. Kate Llewellyn's Penelope is "an older woman" but one with a mind of her own. She is capable of self-analysis and understanding.

And what of the adventurous husband? Does he exhibit any signs of sensitivity of her mental state or an appreciation of what she has lived through? Oh no! With the complacency typical of selfish males, he takes it for granted that she should have waited faithfully for him and welcomed him back in spite of his having strayed so far and repeatedly from the conjugal bed. He does not realize that he has probably come home just in the nick of time and that had he delayed any longer, his wife might have given in to her needs and taken a lover: "he only just came home in time." The Penelope of today is no longer willing to play the role of the long waiting wife who is expected to find fulfilment only in the arms of her lawfully wedded spouse, no matter how much of a Casanova he is. She may be fettered by the expectations of an orthodox society with its separate codes of morality for men and women, but not for long; there is a clamour these days that men should recognize the woman's needs and aspirations too--she is as much a warm-blooded creature as any male and desire and passion course just as intensely through her veins, as in theirs.

The long suppressed desires which have made Penelope unstable are not even remotely sensed by her husband. Happy to be home again, he

smugly drinks his wine
and understands nothing

Picture if you will, a satisfied Ulysses continuing with the routine of existence, fulfilling all physical and sensual needs, so encapsulated in the cocoon of self that he cannot--or will not--feel the tendrils of Penelope's anguish brush delicately against him. And Penelope watches with an imperturbable face--knowing and feeling all--but revealing nothing. Who of the two is invested with dignity here? For whom but Penelope is there an instinctive welling up of sympathy enveloped in respect?

The two poems--A.D. Hope's "The End of a Journey" and Kate Llewellyn's "Penelope," taken together, appear as two sides of the same coin. Conspicuous in both is the strong feeling of regret. There is no sense of faith having been rewarded or the satisfaction and security of a long-awaited homecoming. Both the man and the woman experience feelings that the modern husband and wife can identify with. The rootless drifting and the return home, only to find that memories of home had been gold-washed than the reality; the long and patient wait; the thrusting aside of all temptations, only to discover that what one has waited for so eagerly brings not the sweetness of requital but the bitterness of ashes--these are common and relevant features of today's world in which the fast pace of living permits nothing to be held in abeyance. In this sense, both poems have skilfully adapted the familiar myth to fit and appeal to the modern mind and have transcreated the ancient story into one of today.

## NOTES

1. Alex Preminger, ed., *Princeton Encyclopedia of Poetry and Poetics* (Princeton: Princeton University Press, 1965), p. 538.
2. Suzanne Graham, "Myth and the Poetry of A.D. Hope," *Australian Literary Studies* (ALS), VII, 2 (Oct. 75), pp. 130-40.
3. Vivian Smith, *The Oxford History of Australian Literature*, Leonie Kramer, ed. (Melbourne: OUP, 1981), pp. 380-81.
4. A.D. Hope, *Collected Poems 1930-1965* (Sydney: Angus and

Robertson, 1968), pp. 1-2.

5. James Wieland, "A.D. Hope's Latter-Day Ulysses: 'The End of a Journey' and the Literary Background," *ALS*, X, 4, (Oct. 82), p. 474.
6. Suzanne Graham, pp. 130-40.
7. James Wieland, p. 472.
8. Alfred Tennyson, "Ulysses," *Fifteen Poets* (ELBS and Oxford at the Clarendon Press), p. 410.
9. James Wieland, p. 474.
10. Alfred Tennyson, p. 410.
11. James Wieland, p. 477.
12. Fay Zwicky, "A Question of Identity: Problems in Contemporary Australian Poetry," *Indian Association for Commonwealth Literature and Language Studies Newsletter*, 10 (July 1982), pp. 6-7.
13. Suzanne Graham, pp. 130-40.
14. Kate Llewellyan, "Penelope," *The Phoenix Review*, Special Issue on Hope's 80th Birthday (Winter 1987), pp. 47-48.
15. S.H. Butcher and A. Lang, trans., *The Odyssey of Homer* (1921; London: Macmillan, 1932) pp. 81-257.
16. Robert Lowell, "Ulysses and Circe," *Day by Day* (New York: Farrar, Straus and Giroux, 1977), pp. 3-10.
17. Tennyson, p. 408.

# Time and Change in Judith Wright

RADHARANI CHAKRAVARTY

Poets have always been preoccupied with the problem of time and change, but Judith Wright's positioning in Australia gives this theme a special resonance in her poetry. Perhaps her complex, and distinctly unconventional, conception of time and change has something to do with the geographical location of Australia in the southern hemisphere, with the resultant reversal of seasonal patterns prevalent in the northern half of the globe. As the descendant of white settlers in the Hunter Valley, Judith Wright inherits a hybrid mixture of northern and southern versions of time. Aware of the European seasonal calendar and of the "clock time" invented by civilization, she is also living and writing within the framework of the Australian seasonal cycle, surrounded by the timeless landscape of a vast, wild land which defies the limits of clockbound time. The tension between these different time-schemes lends tremendous intensity to her verse, which constantly suggests that interpretation of time and change is a matter of perspective. This tension also brings out her lifelong dissatisfaction with the existing state of affairs in Australia, and her conviction that constructive change is not only possible, but desperately needed.

Two kinds of time are juxtaposed, for example, in "Typists in the Phoenix Building." Inside the claustrophobic atmosphere of the insurance office, machines record the artificial, man-made divisions of clock time:

> Comptometers and calculators
> compute the frequency of fires,
> adduce the risk, add up the years.[1]

Outside the building, natural, seasonal time prevails:

Where will the inundation reach
whose cycle we can but await?
The city burns in summer's heat,
grass withers and the season's late . . .(*Ibid.*)

In recognizing the simultaneous prevalence of mechanical and seasonal measures of time, Judith Wright asserts the relativity of all human formulations. This relativity, with the accompanying awareness of multiple perspectives, is precisely what the Australian location would emphasize.

In different phases of Judith Wright's career, the theme of time and change acquires varying overtones. Its application is sometimes personal, sometimes political, and occasionally, spiritual or metaphysical. The idea of change, in her later works, is associated with the process of poetic creativity as well, stressing the need for constant innovation, in order to ensure continued significance. In all her poems, however, the longing for change is inspired by the general sense that an imperfect past impinges on an even more unsatisfactory present, creating the urgent need for a more promising future.

Judith Wright's cogently expressed dissatisfaction with the present arises from causes which are partly biographical. Although she is a fifth generation Australian, the fact that she is a white immigrant prevents her from developing a sense of belonging. "The trouble with our relationship to Australia is that we still don't live here. I was brought up in it, you might say, and have succeeded in absorbing it to some extent, but there's a tremendous amount still outside."[2] Her poetry, she claims, expresses "the state of mind that imposes itself upon rather than lives through, landscape and event."[3] In "Bullocky," for example, the native past is evoked, but the poet's tone is that of observer, rather than participant:

Grass is across the waggon tracks,
and plough strikes bone beneath the grass,
and vineyards cover all the slopes
where the dead teams were used to pass. (Heseltine, 280)

This inability to write as an "insider" creates the nagging sense of inadequacy which is often the starting point of Judith Wright's tireless quest for change.

As the Australian poet Rodney Hall points out, Wright's sense of maladjustment is aggravated by her near-deafness, which accounts for the predominance of alienated, solitary figures in her poetry.[4] The bullocky is alone, like the unborn child in "Woman to Man," and the typists encapsulated in the Phoenix Building.

The memory of two World Wars, described by Judith Wright in a filmed interview with James Murdoch, creates a lifelong hatred of brutality and explanation.[5] This surfaces in the call for social change in her poems, which insistently voice her humanitarian concerns. In the interview, Judith Wright says that the preoccupation of her early poems is "to express my sense that the emotions . . . have been perverted" by destructiveness.[6] She asserts that this complete disregard for other living beings is related to the way the whites use the land, as something to make money out of. Her poems, by contrast, attempt to reassert the values of love, compassion, and the desire to be part of nature instead of its ruler. In her first prose work, *The Generations of Men* (1959), she rewrites history on the basis of her grandfather's diaries, to prove that occupation of Australia was the beginning of violence and materialism.

Judith Wright's attitude to the colonization of Australia is in some ways comparable to that of her contemporary, A.D. Hope. In the poem called "Australia," for example, Hope describes the continent as

> a vast parasite robber-state
> Where second-hand Europeans pollulate
> Timidly on the edge of alien shores. (Heseltine, 190)

All the same, Hope's "savage" continent has

> Some spirit which escapes
> The learned doubt, the chatter of cultured apes
> Which is called civilization over there. (*Ibid.*)

Judith Wright's poems echo this sense of the land as the repository of values, which has been ravaged by the European invaders. Her sense of the past as history is consequently riddled with guilt. In "Australia 1970," for example, she says,

Die wild country, like the eaglehawk . . .
For we are conquerors and self-poisoners
More than scorpion or snake
and dying of the venoms that we make
Even while you die of us.[7]

Wright's poetry may be regarded as a facet of her lifelong involvement in humanitarian causes, ranging from organizations like the Wildlife Preservation Society to the Aboriginal Treaty Committee, which she joined in 1979. In "Two Dreamtimes," a poem about the wrong done to the aborigines, Kath Walker, the native poet, is addressed as "my shadow sister."

Angry protest against oppression is also voiced in "the Beanstalk, Meditated Later," in which the story of Jack and the Beanstalk is extended into Jack's old age. Jack now has the hindsight to recognize that exploitation, symbolized by the "giants," continues unabated, in spite of his single heroic act of destroying the beanstalk:

Giants have trampled earth and asked no pardon
Well, nor did I . . .
Now I've grown old.
but still the giants trample the sky. (Heseltine, 289)

Instead of accepting this repetitive pattern as inevitable, Jack makes a bid for apocalyptic change, which necessitates destruction before fresh construction can begin:

I'll post a proclamation--advertise--
find that farmer, buy his whole year's crop,
burn the lot, and see the, last seed dies . . . (*Ibid.*)

The protest against "dispossession, murder and injustice"[8] continues in *Cry for the Dead*, the prose sequel to *The Generations of Men*. At one stage in her career, Wright even stopped writing, as a gesture of anger against the callousness of Australian officialdom.

## II

Judith Wright's demand for a better future is best understood in relation to her special conception of time. "I am not driven by clocks," she insists,[9] and this is apparent from her refusal to divide time into the traditional compartments of past, present and future. Instead, time in her poems constitutes a fusion of these man-made categories, reminiscent of Bergson's concept of "pure duration." Bergson's *duree* is "the form which our conscious states assume when our ego lets itself *live*, when it refrains from separating its present state from its former states."[10] According to Bergson, true change can only be explained by true duration; it involves a dynamic interpenetration of past and present, not a mathematical succession of static states. Seen within the framework of this theory, Judith Wright's own ideas about time and change become easier to understand.

Her treatment of the theme of time also seems to owe a great deal to T.S. Eliot's *Four Quartets.* Like Eliot, Judith Wright recognizes that

> Time present and time past
> Are both perhaps present in time future
> And time future continued in time past.[11]

Her version of eternity has much in common with Eliot's

> Point of intersection of the timeless
> With time.[12]

In Judith Wright's poems, the sense of the past constantly saturates her awareness of the present. In some poems, this past is personal. "Request to a Year," for example, is about the poet's own great-grandmother. In "Australia 1970," the past is the ancient history of the continent:

> Die like the soldier-ant
> mindless and faithful to your million years. (Hall, 207)

Elsewhere, as in "Eve to Her Daughters," the past is projected through myth:

> Faults of character have their own logic
> and it always works out.

I observed this with Abel and Cain.
Perhaps the whole elaborate fable
right from the beginning
is meant to demonstrate this . . ."[13]

Often, Judith Wright's sense of the past has distinctly Australian overtones. In "South of my Day's Circle," written after the shift to Brisbane, New England becomes the land of memory of which personal recollection mingles with local history. The

high lean country
full of stories that still go walking in my sleep. (Heseltine, 281)

is dotted with local landmarks, such as "Thunderbolt at the top of Hungry Hill," or the Hillgrove, once a prosperous gold-mining district.

Wright's awareness of the past, however, never remains at the level of mere nostalgia. The past co-exists with the present, which contain within it the seeds of the future. The bullocky, for example, traverses vineyards which cover the bones of the dead; but the same bones foster the fruit of the future:

O vine, grow close upon that bone
and hold it with your rooted hand.
The prophet Moses feeds the grape,
and fruitful is the Promised Land. (Heseltine, 280)

Here, Wright's positive vision of the future is articulated through the myth of Moses.

While the vision in this poem is hopeful, it is elsewhere frequently tempered by an awareness of death. In "The Company of Lovers," for example, love gains intensity from a recognition of the inevitability of death:

Grope in the night to find me and embrace,
for the dark preludes of the drums begin,
and round us, round the company of lovers,
Death draws his cordons in. (Heseltine, 279)

In "The Harp and the King," death is associated with impotence, and the inability to create a future:

> Night and the terror of the soul come on,
> and out of me both water and seed have gone.
> What other generations shall I see?
> But make me trust my failure and my fall. (*Ibid.*, 285)

As "Habitat" demonstrates, death is the final answer to human vanity:

> Mirrors he waiting in tombs,
> Etruscan ladies
> tried to take them along;
> but glibly and faithlessly
> they answer the tomb-robber. (Hall, 203)

Judith Wright's vision of the future, as a combination of hope and fear, is clearly too complex to be dismissed as shallow optimism.

The future implicit in the present is frequently viewed from a strongly feminine point of view. The unborn child in "Woman to Man" is the seed of the future embedded in the present:

> The eyeless labourer in the night,
> the selfless, shapeless seed I hold.
> builds for its resurrection day. (Heseltine, 282)

Judith Wright insists that women are "more in touch, as it were, with life in the raw . . . women have to rely and should rely a good deal, on their emotional reaction to life; and I feel that one has, one's really walking a knife-edge there."[14] This emotional response is evident in poems such as "Stillborn," in which hope is replaced by despair:

> Such women weep for love
> of one who drew no breath
> and in the night they lie
> giving the breast to death.(Hampton, 71)

Wright's vision of time as a dynamic fusion of past, present and future, allows for tremendous compression in the use of poetic language. In "South of my Day's Circle," for example, words are used in a highly elliptical way. "My day's Circle" is glossed by Judith Wright as the daily round of routine activities.[15] Without understanding this terse, compressed phrase, it would be impossible to interpret the significance of New England in the poem, as located beyond the scope of everyday activity. In "Habitat," the single image of the mirrors encapsulates within itself the past and present, as well as the future:

> What will the last face
> look like?
> Mirrors know
> It will contain all faces, all
> human history
> (which mirrors remember). (Hall, 204)

Compression, ellipsis and extreme economy of language can occasionally create obscurity but they also add immeasurably to the intensity of poetic effect.

Beyond the time-bound world which forms the main arena for the conflicts that animate her poetry, Judith Wright sometimes suggests the dimly-sensed vastness of eternity. In "The Cycads," the image of timelessness is, typically, an impressive feature of the Australian landscape:

> Only the antique cycads sullenly
> keep the old bargain life has long since broken;
> and, cursed by age, through each chill century
> they watch the shrunken moon, but never die,
> for time forgets the promise he once made,
> and change forgets that they are left alone.
> Among the complicated birds and flowers they
> seem a generation carved in stone. (Heseltine, 282-83)

The full impact of these lines is felt only if one is aware of the appearance of these typically Australian trees. Cycads are palm-like plants of very ancient lineage, reaching back to Mesozoic times. One variety, the Macrozamia grows on Tambourine Mountain in Queensland, and surviving specimens are believed to be thousands of years old. Cycads grow to a considerable height, and produce brilliant red flowers. To visualize the scene evoked by the poem, therefore, would explain why Wright makes the cycads her symbols for timelessness.

The tension between the mortal, time-bound world and the realm of eternity, is brought out with tremendous effect in "Eli, Eli," in which the Biblical prophet is fated

> To see them go by drowning in the river--
> soldiers and elders drowning in the river,
> the pitiful women drowning in the river,
> the children's faces staring from the river--
> that was his cross, and not the cross they gave him. (Hall, 201)

The graphic picture of death and destruction carries echoes of Judith Wright's own memories of the horrors of the World War. Eli's concern is essentially humanitarian, but he knows that his message will not be heeded:

> To hold out love and know they would not take it,
> to hold out faith and know they dared not take it. (*Ibid.*)

However, he knows, also, one crucial fact which makes his cross bearable: suffering, like all else in the temporal world, is illusory:

> He watched, and they were drowning in the river;
> faces like sodden flowers in the river--
> faces of children moving in the river;
> and all the while, he knew there was no river.(*Ibid.*)

This vision of time as illusory is strongly reminiscent of Eliot's *Four Quartets*. The image of the prophet recurs in Judith Wright's poetry, as the symbol of the human ability to transcend the limitations of the present.

## III

Although the spiritual dimension becomes more pronounced in Judith Wright's later poetry, her prime concern always remains humanitarian, and the tensions generated by her poems are those of the here and now. Paradoxically, the vision of eternity only complicates her involvement in temporal conflicts. Change, the central principle of her poetry, represents process rather than stasis, and the flux of the temporal, rather than Eliot's "still point of the turning world."[16]

The desire for change stems, at least in part, from a refusal to be complacent about herself and her heritage. "Request to a Year" implicitly condemns the callousness of her own great-great-grandmother, who watches her own son drown:

> Nothing, it was evident, could be done;
> and with the artist's isolating eye
> My great-great-grandmother hastily sketched the scene,
> The sketch survives to prove the story by. (Hall, 202)

As the heir to this family history, Wright is, by implication, responsible. The ironic passage about "the artist's isolating eye" arouses unspoken doubts about the function of her own poetry: does it merely record human horror, without intervening to check it?

"At a Poetry Conference, Expo'67" describes the apocalyptic dream of the burning of poets, among whom Judith Wright herself is presumably included:

> Those burned-out sticks
> are radio-active, ticking like geiger counters,
> the spinal cords of poets, bright modullas
> and clever cortexes. Hang them on your walls.
> They'll do to mark your time. (Hampton, 70)

The need for change in the type of poetry produced in Australia is, characteristically, conceived in the image of a time-bomb.

The principle of change is thus associated with Judith Wright's own lifelong quest for poetic perfection. In the earlier volumes such as *The Moving Image* (1946), *Woman to Man* (1949), *The Gateway* (1953) and *The Two Fires,* Wright feels that she has made a complete statement about herself and her environment. Far from creating complacency, however, this leads to a search for change, and a new beginning. In the volume called *Alive* (1973), Wright breaks out of the traditional format of her earlier poems, to experiment with free verse-forms. The lines on the page now appear in irregular arrangements, and the images, such as the furniture in "Habitat," are unconventional. For Judith Wright the urge for innovation is the only impulse that can save poetic creativity from the dangers of stagnation. As Rodney Hall points out, it is incorrect to "Place" Judith Wright as a poet of the forties because she has continued to experiment with new kinds of poetry throughout her career.[17]

The desire for self-improvement is combined with the plea for social change. The land of Australia, so precious to an environmentalist like Wright has been ravaged by mechanization:

> The earth must be made a new Eden
> with central heating, domesticated animals
> mechanical harvesters, combustion engines,
> escalators, refrigerators,
> and modern means of communication.
> ("Eve to her Daughters," Hamptong, 76)

The irony here conveys the poet's anger more succinctly than any open tirade could have done. In the world outlined here, it is impossible to promise a child a secure future:

> Why try to give
> What never can be given--
> Safety, a green world?
> It's mined, the trip-wire's waiting. ( "Letter," Hampton, 72)

The operations of officialdom are also singled out for scathing criticism, as in "Report of a Working-Party":

> Ladies and gentlemen, we have returned
> from our foray into the future.
> Our report is appended.
> The final peaks are impossibly steep . . .
> We finally had to turn back
> because we were starting too many avalanches.
> We feared for your safety below.
> Frankly we don't think you'll ever make the top. (Hampton,
> 74)

The report is a record of the failure of the party, and of their despair for the future of humanity. The feeling repeatedly evoked in these poems, is of a present terribly distorted, and a future equally bleak, unless something drastic is done to change it.

That such a change can be effected, remains, however, one of the strongest assertions of Judith Wright's poetry. This is demonstrated in the poem called "The Trap," in which the child who captures a parrot becomes himself a prisoner of negative feelings:

> Cunning and will undo us. We must be
> their prisoners, boy, and in a bitter cage
> endure their lifelong rage.
> Look around you. See, the chains on everyone. (Hampton, 75)

In taking away the freedom of others, we make ourselves the slaves of inhuman emotions. In Judith Wright's scheme of things, however, it is not too late to rectify this state of affairs:

> Quick, save yourself! Undo
> that door and let him go. (*Ibid.*)

Determinism is rejected: the child can choose to change his destiny.

The motif of the child as the inheritor of the past and the symbol of the future recurs in the poems of Judith Wright. In the child is located the potential for change. In "Letter," for example, the mother acknowledges the bleakness of the world inherited by the child who threatens to become a drop-out after succumbing to drugs. The mother insists, however, that the search for values in a disintegrating world, is itself a reason to live:

> Keep searching.
> Dance even among these
> poisoned swords: frightened only
> of not being what you are--
> of not expecting love
> of hoping truth;
> of sitting in lost corners

ill-willing time. (Hampton, 73)

Resignation, and "opting out," are not viable solutions to the erosion of humanitarian values in the modern world. Active quest for love is the basis of Judith Wright's positive vision of change.

The idea of change carries feminist overtones in "Eve to Her Daughters," in which Eve explains to her daughter the egoism of Adam:

> Perhaps nothing exists but our faults?
> At least they can be demonstrated.
> But it's useless to make
> such a suggestion to Adam.
> He has turned himself into God,
> who is faultless, and doesn't exist. (Hampton, 77)

Eve had allowed herself to be dominated by Adam, but to her daughters, she suggests the course of resistance, though their inherited faults will make this difficult:

> I would suggest, for the sake of the children,
> that it's time you took over.
> But you are my daughters, you inherit my own faults of character;
> you are submissive, following Adam
> even beyond existence.(*Ibid.*)

In this poem, Biblical myth, and the concept of original sin, are interpreted from woman-centred point of view, to suggest a feminist variation on the theme of oppression.

Instead of falsifying her poetry with native myth which she has failed to assimilate, Judith Wright, as a white Australian, uses the Christian myths she has inherited from her ancestors. This myth, however, is adapted to the context of modern Australia. Moses in "Bullocky" is an example of her attempt to interpret the native land through alien myth. "Eli, Eli," is another. That the myth and the context are integrated, is a mark of Wright's special genius.

Judith Wright's call for reform makes the idca of change an essential part of her values. Love and compassion are seen as alternatives to the world of war and hatred which she rebels against.

In "Habitat," for example, even items of furniture become repositories of tender, almost maternal, love:

> Furniture: humble, dependent,
> asking for nothing
> except to be there, to be used,
> to be let stay around,
> like an ageing aunt
> waiting to hold the new baby. (Hall, 202)

In "Woman to Man," the unborn child is the product, as well as the symbol, of erotic love;

> This is our hunter and our chase,
> the third who lay in our embrace . . .
> This is the blood's wild tree that grows
> the intricate and folded rose. (Hall, 200)

"Tableau," which depicts the poet's encounter with a cancer patient on the street, presents love in the larger sense of brotherhood:

> I drank our strange ten minutes of embrace,
> and watched him whiten there,
> the drenched poverty of his slender face.
> We could have been desperate lovers not too late. (Hall, 206)

The moment of compassion is Judith Wright's answer to the ruthless mechanization of modern life, defined in "Habitat" through the images of

> The juggernaut machines,
> the blue drifting gases,
> the crashing air craft! . . . (Hall, 205)

The sense of brotherhood extends, in some poems, beyond the human world, to include the whole of creation:

> Our love is so natural
> the wild animals move
> gentle and light on

the shores of our love . . .
Bird and beast are at home,
and star lives in tree
when we are together
as we should be. ("Our Love is So Natural," Heseltine, 283)

This idyllic vision of the universal harmony, for all its peaceful tone, is inspired by the poet's anger at the destruction of the natural environment by the colonizers.

Love as a value enters the metaphysical sphere as well. In "The Harp and the King," the King fears eternity:

Once I thought there was a truth in time
while now my terror is eternity. (Heseltine, 285)

The harp, however, insists on the redemptive power of time:

Yet it is time that holds,
somewhere although not now,
the peal of trumpets for us; time that bears . . .
incredible redemptions--hours that grow,
as trees grow fruit, in a blind holiness,
the truths unknown, the loves unloved by us. (*Ibid.*, 286)

In love lies the promise of redemption, and this is the source of hope for the future.

The connection between time and love is perhaps most emphatically articulated in "Clock and Heart." Clock-time is a treacherous trap which draws the child inexorably towards death:

Its hidden teeth of circumstance
that draw the child into the clock
upon the cogs of tick and tock. (Heseltine, 287)

A further level of imprisonment occurs when the poetic impulse isolates the poet from other human beings:

The solitude of poetry
locked me within its second shade. (*Ibid.*)

Release from this double captivity is offered only by love:

> To light that shade and set me free
> no flame had power but human love. (*Ibid.*)

Through love, the poet escapes from "clock time." She is

> Set free at last in human time. (*Ibid.*)

which binds man to man, instead of acting as a force of annihilation. This poem, perhaps more than any other, confirms our feeling that, to Judith Wright, the lived experience of "ordinary love" is perhaps the greatest human challenge to the stranglehold of "clock time."

## IV

As this analysis demonstrates, Judith Wright's highly individualized formulations of time and change are the product of her own sensitive response to the social situation in Australia, and the sense of disorientation caused by the geographical location of the continent. Her experiences as a woman, and as a white Australian unable to fully assimilate native attitudes, lend added intensity to her exploration of these themes. Her best poems, however, are never polemical. Grappling with the problem of depicting native reality in a foreign tongue, Wright's superb linguistic experiments transmute the different layers of experience into pure poetry. Her struggle with the problem of time and change, therefore, is remarkable not only for its ideological force, but also for its mode of articulation, which raises her poetry from the level of political rhetoric, to the status of fine art.

## NOTES

1. Judith Wright, "Typists in the Phoenix Building," *The Penguin Book of Australian Verse*, ed. Harry Heseltine (Ringwood: Penguin, 1972), p. 288.
2. Judith Wright, taped commentary, quoted in James McAuley,

*A Map of Australian Verse, The Twentieth Century* (Melbourne: Oxford University Press, 1975), p. 164.

3. Judith Wright, "The Upside-down Hut," *Australian Letters*, 3, No.4 (1961), p. 30, quoted in James McAuley, p. 164.
4. Interview with Rodney Hall, New Delhi, 3 February 1990.
5. Judith Wright, interviewed on film by James Murdoch, "Judith Wright" (Film), *The Writers* (Archival Film Series: Australia Council, 1987).
6. *Ibid.*
7. Judith Wright, "Australia 1970," *The Collins Book of Australian Poetry*, ed. Rodney Hall (Sydney: Collins, 1981), pp. 206-7.
8. Judith Wright, interviewed by James Murdoch.
9. *Ibid.*
10. Henri Bergson, quoted in Bertrand Russell, *A History of Western Philosophy* (1946; London: Unwin, 1979), p. 759.
11. T.S. Eliot, *Four Quartets* (1944; Delhi: Oxford University Press, 1962), p. 13.
12. *Ibid.*, p. 44.
13. Judith Wright, "Eve to Her Daughters," *The Penguin Book of Australian Women Poets*, ed Susan Hampton and Kate Llewellyn (Ringwood: Penguin, 1986), p. 77.
14. Judith Wright, interviewed by John Thompson, "Poetry in Australia: Judith Wright," *Southerly*, 27, No.1 (1967), p. 38, quoted in James McAuley, p. 165.
15. Judith Wright, *Selected Poems* (London: Angus and Robertson: Australian Poets Series, 1963).
16. T.S. Eliot, p. 15.
17. Interview with Rodney Hall.

# Australian Drama: Major Trends

S. RAMASWAMY

Douglas Stewart, the Australian playwright, speaking of drama's importance in the creation of national identity says:

> The playwright, I think, creates the myths by which the people live: the heroic, gigantic, legendary figures, fathers of the race, ancestors, spiritual or actual, to which the living man can point and say, "That is what I am made of; that is what makes us different from other people; that is what I believe in; those are my gods and my devils." If you were a Greek you needed to know about the valour of Achilles and the crimes of Oedipus; if you are English, you must know the dreadful folly of Macbeth, the darkness and splendour of the kings, the enormous substantiality of Falstaff, gross, rich, and stable as the earth itself. In Australia--[1]

As if to take up the cue, Louis Esson, another Australian playwright, who was strongly influenced by W.B. Yeats and the Irish Abbey Theatre, wanted to do to Australian drama what had been the aim of the Abbey in Ireland:

> I would like to get a new movement started, with no connection with any repertory society. We can't do everything; and personally I have nothing but local and original works, however inadequate they were, a kind of Folk-Theatre. . . . I can see the plays clearly; they should be lively, simple, with plenty of colour, non-intellectual, without "middle-class" sentiment and drawing room ethics.[2]

This certainly was a good beginning and this playwright who wrote more than sixteen plays in the early decades of this century set the ball rolling with his *The Time is Not Yet Ripe,* a lively satirical political comedy. Playwrights like Vance Palmer and Sydney Tomholt, Katherine Susanna Prichard, Betty Roland, Locke-Elliot, Alan Seymour, Jack Hibbard, Barry Humphries, Hal Porter, Rodney Millgate, John Romeril, David Williamson, Alexander Buzo and Dorothy Hewett have enriched the Australian dramatic scene. However, what is attempted in this note is to take note of a few major trends in defining the achievement of Australian drama, with particular reference to three playwrights--Douglas Stewart, Ray Lawler and Patrick White.

In the initial statement quoted at the beginning, Douglas Stewart mentions how the playwright "creates the myths by which the people live" through "legendary figures." It is in this context of myth and legend in Australia that Stewart's own plays have to be examined. In perhaps the best known Australian play, *Ned Kelly* (1943), Douglas Stewart has created a "legend" out of the life of his outlaw hero--Ned, which is a dramatic presentation of the Kelly gang as a quintessentially Australian legend. However, this trend is found as early as 1829 in the play *The Bushrangers* by David Burn who is considered the first Australian playwright of significance. While *Ned Kelly* is a powerful stage-play, Stewart's *The Fire on the Snow* and *The Golden Lover* are excellent radio plays exploiting to the maximum the possibilities of speech and sound. *The Fire on the Snow* is a documentary about the British Antarctic Expedition of 1910. It was first performed in 1941. The source of the play was Scott's Diary and Apsley Cherry-Gerrard's *The Worst Journey in the World.* The characters in the play are Captain Falcon Scott, leader of the Expedition, Edward Adrian Wilson, Chief of the Scientific staff, Captain Laurence, Lieutenant Bowers and Petty Officer Evans. In addition to the five characters there is an Announcer. The play is prefaced by a Prologue to be spoken in a different voice from that of the Announcer in the play. It is this emphasis on the "Voice" throughout the play that makes it an admirable radio play. While *The Fire on the Snow* had to be "realistic," being a documentary, *The Golden Lover* is pure fantasy. Naturally the emphasis is on poetry in the play which helps in creating an atmosphere of romance and myth. It represents another trend in Australian drama--taking into account as it does the picturization of the Aboriginal--but with a difference. While in *The Bushrangers* David Burn had presented the Aboriginal in very theatrical terms as mentally inferior and unable to understand white morality or political concepts, Douglas Stewart gives a delightfully lyrical free interpretation of the story of Tawhai and her golden lover Whana which is told in James Cowan's *Faery Folk Tales of the Maori*. Tawhai was a young Maori woman and Whana was one of the "people of the Mist," the fairies of the Maori legend, thus reinforcing the myth and legend aspect helping in national identity--in this case, the Australianness. The light bantering tone so suitable to comedy is maintained throughout the play, *The Golden Lover*. The story of Tawhai, Ruarangi her husband and Whana the "golden lover" is told with classic simplicity and unsullied tenderness and feeling for the simple eloquence of the naturally gifted unsophisticated people. The poetry that wells forth straight from the heart lends a natural dignity to the homely utterance of these children of nature. The play has a dreamlike ethereal quality about it which has a hold on our hearts.

While Douglas Stewart emphasized myth, legend and poetry in his plays, Ray Lawler put the Australianness of Australian drama on a firm footing by his powerful play of social realism--*Summer of the Seventeenth Doll*. It is basically a play to be dealt with as contributing to Australian national consciousness and cultural identity. This is not to deny its universal significance and its tragic dimension. It is true that the stereotypically Australian behaviour and character are re-interpreted in terms of tragic inevitability involving time and change beyond human control. However, this does not diminish the authentic Australian atmosphere of the play. It represents an important trend in Australian drama--the naturalistic play in a working class milieu. From the achievement of Lawler in *Summer* (1955) it is possible to look both before and after in Australian drama. Louis Esson's *Drovers* (1920) anticipates the form of tragic deadlock as in *Summer* with its Australian setting of a remote, outback droving camp, the cattle stampede etc. and Dorothy Hewett's *This Old Man Comes Rolling Home* (1966) set in the working class environment of Redfern in Sydney, in spite of using a "Greek" chorus, is basically naturalistic in the manner of *Summer*. Kenneth Tymann, reviewing the London production of Ray Lawler's *Summer of the Seventeenth Doll* in 1957 wrote:

> One of Her Majesty's subjects turned up with a play about working people who were neither "grim" nor "funny," neither

> sentimentalized nor patronized, neither used to point a social moral nor derided as quaint and improbable clowns. . . . The play that pulled off the feet is *Summer of the Seventeenth Doll* and if Ray Lawler, its Australian author, is aware of the magnitude of his achievement, I shall be the most astonished critic in London.[3]

Though Ray Lawler may not have been "aware of the magnitude of his achievement" immediately after writing it, the present writer feels that Lawler was not entirely unaware of what he was attempting to achieve when he wrote the play. Lawler himself wrote:

> There is a central theme to hold the pieces together, that the unbearable nostalgia and bewilderment felt by a group of people when an enchanted private world, built almost entirely on a physical basis, crumbles away under the stress of years and changing circumstances. It is meant to be the tragedy of the inarticulate who feel far more than they rationalize or express.[4]

The "tragedy of the inarticulate" concerns the cane cutters Barney and Roo and it is their "private world built almost entirely on a physical basis" that crumbles. As Emma puts it at the end of the play:

> You and Barney are two of a pair. Only the time he spent chasin' wimmen, you put in being top dog! Well, that's all very fine and a lot of fun while it lasts, but last is one thing it doesn't do. There's time for sowing and a time for reaping and reapin' is what you're doing now.[5]

After sixteen summers, suddenly in the seventeenth summer, Barney and Roo realize that they are not young any more and that they must learn to move away from the limelight and make room for the younger generation. The effective dramatization of this none-too-easy-to-accept human predicament is what has made Ray Lawler one of the most significant playwrights of our time. Lawler's later plays *Kid Stakes* and *Other Times* are companions to the *Summer of the Seventeenth Doll* and they together form "The Doll Trilogy" which reinforces his contribution to the Realistic/Naturalistic trend in Drama.

From this trend in Australian drama we can move to the trend which is exactly its opposite--the "foray against Naturalism," in Patrick White. Though White is primarily a novelist, his plays are of great significance in any survey of trends in Australian theatre. Whereas his *Season at Sarsaparilla* is a "Charade of Suburbia" as he himself puts it, his *A Cheery Soul* is a reworking of one of his short stories into a play and his *Night on Bald Mountain* is an apocalyptic vision of a social world, it is his *Ham Funeral* that must concern us here because that was the play that deliberately flouted the conventions of Realism/Naturalism through its symbolic use of stage space. The first speech of the play *The Prologue* places it immediately in the Non-realistic convention, drawing our attention to the plasticity of the modern theatre technique which transcends the photographic realism in art. Going beyond the customary constrictions of chronology, the set, set in four main sections, the special lighting technique that is used and even the dialogue which is the opposite of the sort found in a conventional well-made play--these are some of the features which made *The Ham Funeral* a trend-setter and an avant-garde play when it appeared on the scene. It was because it set a new trend that it had to remain unproduced for fourteen years. As H.G. Kippax puts it:

> Why did *The Ham Funeral* remain unperformed for fourteen years? One reason, no doubt was that 1948-49 saw White's removal back to Australia to a small farm at Castle Hill near Sydney, where (to quote his friend Geoffrey Dutton) for the next five years he "struggled with goats, schnanzer dogs, fowls, asthma and *The Tree of Man.*" A second reason was that the theatre was ready for it neither in England nor Australia. Experiment in England until the mid 1940s was associated, so far as the professional theatre was concerned, with the verse dramas variously fashioned by Ronald Duncan, Christopher Fry and T.S. Eliot. Much of this experiment sought its effect in whimsy. Brecht was virtually unknown. Expressionism had never made converts in England even when used by so popular a playwright as J.B. Priestley and was regarded after the war as dated. Even in Paris the dates indicate the audacity of White's foray against naturalism: Ionesco's *The Bald Prima-Donna* and Adamov's first plays

> were not staged until 1950 and Beckett's *Waiting for Godot* not until 1953. It is not surprising that in far away Australia those producers who read *The Ham Funeral* received at the best with caution amounting to inertia.[6]

This long quotation has been given here not only to make the point about the new non-naturalistic trend that was set by Patrick White but also to place Australian drama in the more familiar perspective of British and European dramatic trends in contemporary theatre world.

While this brief survey of the major trends has taken into account only the Documentary, Poetic Drama/Radio Play, Realistic/Naturalistic Theatre and the Revolt against it, it must be remembered that Australian drama has much more to offer. Some of the Australian themes are connected with elements of colonial life, like bush ranging, vernacular speech, social mobility in Australian life, changing patterns of sexual and social behaviour in the younger generation, the power of bureaucracy, violence and racism, the generation gap, economic competitiveness and culture shock, etc. The theatre activity connected with Cafe La Mama Theatre established by Betty Burstall in Carlton, on the model of Ellen Stewart's off-off Broadway La Mama Theatre in New York, the Nimrod Street Theatre in Sydney and the Little Theatre activity of the small alternative theatres of Melbourne and Sydney--these further define the major trends in Australian Drama.

## NOTES

1. Douglas Stewart, "The Playwright in Australia," *Australian Theatre Year I* (1955-56), pp. 9, 27. As quoted by Terry Sturm in *The Oxford History of Australian Literature* (New York: Oxford University Press, 1981), p. 226.
2. Louis Esson, quoted by Terry Sturm, p. 213.
3. Kenneth Tynan, *Curtains* (New York: Atheneum, 1961), p. 179.
4. Ray Lawler, Letter to Leslie Rees, quoted in *The Making of Australian Drama* (Sydney: Angus and Robertson, 1973), p. 266. As quoted by Terry Sturm, p. 205.

5. Ray Lawler, *Summer of the Seventeenth Doll* (Fontana, 1953, pp. 112-13.
6. H.G. Kippax, Introduction to *Four Plays by Patrick White* (Melbourne: Sun Books, in association with Eyre and Spottiswoode, London, 1967), p. 4.

# Introduction

**DAVID KERR**

By my bedside table I have a copy of Rabindranath Tagore's *Gitanjali*, a slender volume of song offerings from your greatest modern poet. My wife was introduced to his work at the Anantapur conference in March this year, a few short months ago. We also have acquired a copy of his *Selected Poems*, and have regular recourse to both works for pleasure and enlightenment. We are latecomers to this enthusiasm for Indian Literature in translation and Indian Literature in English, but nonetheless admirers despite our tardiness. A glance at the printing history of *Gitanjali* emphasizes how many readers there are for this writer, and the interest being shown by Penguin and Macmillan in contemporary Indian writing demonstrates that there is a large and growing interest in Indian writing in English throughout the English-speaking world.

Tagore has a universal appeal: his themes touch us all. Is there, however, something in Indian literature that touches Australians in a special way? Is there a mutuality of concern between these two nations? Elsewhere in this volume Ian Copland of Monash University has commented on this question with the voice of an historian. Let me adopt a more personal note. When crossing India by train earlier this year (we did it several times: Delhi-Varanasi; Varanasi-Bombay; Poona-Bangalore and Anantapur-Delhi being our longest journeys) I was put in mind of the vastness, the semi-aridity and the heat of parts of outback Australia. There was a major difference, of course. The land is marginally more hospitable than ours, and even in the arid areas supports numbers of people that leaves an Australian shaking his head in amazement.

Incidentally, I am often asked about Australia's population, which for the whole continent is roughly that of Calcutta. The answer can be divided, for simplicity, into two parts: India has a fairly reliable monsoon which makes crop agriculture feasible throughout the Deccan as well as in the river valleys and coastal plains; and owing to the chances of history, possesses a totally different pattern of life and distribution of wealth.

But the land is harsh in each place, and despite our short history there are already signs here of the power of the land to overwhelm human initiatives, which pushes our imaginations to encounter larger themes:

> Their children saw Earth itself as the great ruin: was she not the contracted wreck of chaos? and of the Spiral that is primal Order? They walked her final patina. Travelling, delving, they found themselves everywhere in it. . . . Ruins and tribes and wildernesses merged thereafter and all the trusted creatures. Earth became the Great Museum whose other, more secret name is Noble Conquest.[1]

These images might equally apply to either India or Australia--in some ways, because of its longer history of permanent settlement, it reads more as a poem on India than on Australia. In other words, we are each responding, according to our culture and history, to similar underlying forces.

A second piece by Les A. Murray might illustrate what I mean. It is from a poem called "The Grassfire Stanzas."

> It's the sun that is touched, and dies in expansion, mincing, making the round dance, foretelling its future, driving the frantic lives outwards. The sun that answers the bark tip is discharged in many little songs, to forestall a symphony.
>
> Cattle come, with stilted bounding calves. They look across the ripple lines of heat, and shake their armed heads at them; at random, then, they step over. Grazing smudged black country they become the beasts of Tartarus. Wavering, moving out over dung-smouldering ground still covered with its uncovering.[2]

I need not labour the point more.

Culturally Murray also sees a connection. Australians are, he points out, as Indians are, cattle people. We graze herds and depend on them. But the cultural differences are larger than the similarities, and that, too, is an attraction. India, with its eastern sense of time, place and pace, offers us something sadly lacking in our own society, a strong spiritual awareness.

Our society is less complex than yours, at this point in history, and less threatened. We are geographically located at a safer distance from some of the more difficult political realities of a perilous world. We are not, as Ian Copland's article points out, sufficiently sensitive to some of the problems you face.

## II

As co-editor of the Australian contribution to the magazine I have received contributions that might trouble some of you. I am referring to the articles about *The Satanic Verses* by Salman Rushdie. I need hardly here rehearse the furore that this book has caused among our Moslem friends. I respect their feelings. Nevertheless, I feel the book merits dispassionate analysis and commentary. The article I was invited to write sets out to ask, from the position of an outsider to Islam, how Rushdie's treatment of Islam appeared to me. I hoped that, by even-handed analysis, I could respond as a westerner to what Rushdie had done. I am in no position to discuss the nature of the novel's offence. Simply, as a general reader, I hoped to show some of how it impacted on me. In order to do this I needed to read some Islamic material. I need hardly add that I did not expect to uncover the full complexity of the allusions or their significance. As the study developed, it became an exploration of Rushdie's treatment of the theme of migration and alienation from one's heritage. I do not seek to judge Rushdie either way. I hoped merely to cast a glimmer of light on the subject. The second contributor, David Myers, has offered something far more scholarly. His study of the novel as an account of the tragic and universal battle between good and evil is an impressive piece of writing, and it deserves a hearing. If what Rushdie has written is fallacious or mischievous it will not survive scrutiny. Only through open discussion will the truth be revealed.

The above passage represents an encounter--limited and halting as it is--between an Australian and an Indian perspective. For some it may represent a certain kind of difficulty that may emerge when communication between cultures is attempted. We should not be afraid of that. The key word is "encounter." It is a process that is fraught with the chance of misunderstanding, but at the same time is capable of yielding great depth of understanding, of building friendship, and enlarging vision. I know that has been my experience. Coincidentally, I am at the moment glancing at the introduction to a publication entitled *Encounters: Selected Indian and Australian Short Stories*. It was edited by Alur Janaki Ram and Bruce Bennett, with the assistance of Ashok K. Jha. It was published by Pointer Publishers of Jaipur in 1988.

I quote a brief piece from the introduction:

> The encounters forming part of the material of the stories of this volume are of varying kinds: they basically involve facing up to interesting or challenging situations at home or in the lands of adoption . . . immigrant experiences marked by a sense of exile or an awareness of dual or multiple cultural heritages and exposure to newer and unfamiliar areas of awareness. (x)

We all stand to gain from this kind of experience. May this volume contribute positively to that process.

## NOTES

1. Les A. Murray, "The Romantic Theme of Ruins," *The People's Otherworld* (Angus and Robertson, 1983), p. 21.
2. *Ibid*., pp. 4-5

# Beyond the Mirage: Reflections on the Indo-Australian Relationship

IAN COPLAND

On 24 April this year, at the height of the Indo-Pakistani war-scare over Kashmir, the Australian Defence Minister, Senator Robert Ray, announced that a contract had been signed with Pakistan for the sale of 50 Mirage fighter aircraft which were surplus to Australia's requirements. The contract was worth AUS $36 million, hardly these days a gigantic sum. (Ironically, it was almost identical to the sum which Australia had set aside in the 1989 budget for humanitarian aid to India.) Nevertheless the Defence Department presented the sale to the media as something of a coup: the planes were old, idle, and we had got them off our hands. Unfortunately, no one in Canberra seems to have bothered to establish, beforehand, the likely attitude of the Government of India. Either the Defence Department kept the Department of Foreign Affairs in the dark, or, if it did consult, it got bad advice. Hence, when India a few days later lodged a "vigorous" protest over the sale, Canberra was taken aback. Some time later the Foreign Minister, Senator Gareth Evans, admitted that India had placed a virtual freeze on bilateral relations, postponing high-level trade and investment talks and cancelling the visit of an Indian delegation to Canberra to discuss the details of Australia's AUS $ 35 million aid allocation.[1] Belatedly grasping the seriousness of the situation, the Australian Foreign Minister hastened to the subcontinent on what was described as a good will tour but was in fact a damage-limitation exercise. Following talks with his Indian counterpart, Inder Gujral, Evans announced hopefully that "we have cleared the air."[2] But the distrust generated by the incident remains, and the Indian press has been uncharacteristically sharp recently in its criticism of Australian policy, the *Times of India* suggesting that Canberra was running a "campaign aimed at giving the wrong impression" about india's naval buildup.[3] However as things stand now, it would be fair to say that April 1990 marked a low point in the 43-year old history of Indo-Australian diplomatic relations.

It is easy to be wise after the event; but the fact is, the sale should never have been contemplated, let alone pursued to the point where contracts had been exchanged. That it was points not merely to a failure of bureaucracy, but to a lack of imagination and basic understanding. It reflects the Australian popular media's stereotypical perceptions of Indian society and culture. It reflects our widespread indifference to what goes on in the South Asian region. Australian commentators have long remarked on the necessity of our coming to terms with the "near north"; and in more recent times governmental rhetoric has focused on the need to make the Australian school-population "Asia literate."[4] But when one examines this rhetoric and the structures set up to implement it, it becomes crystal clear that what is meant by the "near north" does not include, except in the most marginal sense, *South Asia*. Broadly speaking, India and China are comparable countries. But nowhere near the same effort has been expended during the past 20 years on developing relations with India as has been put into cementing ties with the Peoples Republic, which Prime Minister Hawke acknowledged in 1984 were "central to Australian foreign policy."[5] There is still no Indian equivalent, for example, of the Australia-China Council. Despite the signature of an Indo-Australian cultural agreement in 1971, Australian-sponsored cultural activity in the region is small compared with programmes of this nature mounted in China, Japan or Indonesia. In 1989 the Prime Minister and the Department of Foreign Affairs, Defence and Trade jointly commissioned Professor Ross Garnaut of the Australian National University to enquire into the implication of developments in *Northeast* Asia for the Australian economy. The Garnaut Report[6] was warmly endorsed in Canberra. No similar document has been commissioned for South Asia. Another recent high-level initiative--the Ingleson enquire into the study of Asia in Australian tertiary institutions--was notable for having no South Asian specialists among its members. Predictably, its report[7] gave negligible attention to India.

It is the same with language policy. About 350 million people speak Hindi, but the language is taught at only a couple of Australian universities (only at the A.N.U. to degree standard) and not at all in state secondary schools. Moreover, while other Asian languages like Mandarin and Japanese are prioritized by the government for development funding, Hindi alone of Indian languages, is considered worthy of support. Indeed, it was only as the result of a sustained outcry by concerned academics that Hindi was belatedly added to the "second tier" (along with Thai, Korean and Vietnamese) of the Government's National Language Policy. However, it is not surprising that the powers that be have been reluctant to fund, or encourage, initiatives in this area. Out in the community, there is apparently little demand for South Asian language acquisition. In May 1989, a McNair opinion poll commissioned by the Department of Foreign Affairs asked 2000 people what languages they would like to see taught more widely in our schools. Thirty-six percent nominated Japanese, 20% Chinese, 14% Indonesian, 7% Vietnamese and 6% Korean. The languages of the Subcontinent were conspicuous by their absence.[8]

All this would be understandable if India were far away or insignificant. But it is neither. Australia and India look out on to the same ocean, and the most far-flung of India's territories--the Andaman and Nicobar Islands in the Bay of Bengal--are as close to the populous parts of southern Australia as Thailand or the Philippines. And India is manifestly a major power. With 1.2 million men and women under arms, its ground forces are the world's third largest. It has the largest navy, outside of China and Japan, in Asia, and in terms of effectiveness its naval capacity is probably second only to Japan's. With a GDP of around AUS $ 230 billion in 1986-87, it is presently the world's 11th largest industrial economy, and if current growth rates (6-7% during most of the 1980s) are maintained, it is likely to soon overtake 10th-placed France. Last but not least, demographers predict that by the year 2020 or thereabouts, India will supplant China as the world's most populous nation.

In addition, Australia appears to have much more in common with India than it does with most other countries in our region. Unlike some of the latter, India is a true democracy. It has regular and free elections, an independent judiciary and a vigorous press. Internationally, India and Australia have often stood together on third world issues such as apartheid, and more recently India has backed our stand on Antarctica. We are fellow members of the Commonwealth. At an elite level, we share a common language--English. And at a popular level, we share a devotion to that most idiosyncratic of outdoor games--cricket.

Historically, too, the fortunes of India and Australia have been closely linked as a consequence of the imperial connection. Botany Bay was founded as a British penal colony about the same time (1788) as the English East India Company was imposing its authority on Bengal and establishing a base at Penang; and for the first 30 years or so of its existence New South Wales was something of a satellite of the Company Raj in Bengal, the Anglican Church there being until 1835 a part of the Diocese of Calcutta. Indeed, the foundation of New South Wales and the rise of the English East India Company's power in Bengal have been seen by some scholars as two aspects of the same broad historical process--the British "swing to the East" which followed the loss of the American colonies.[9] From the outset, moreover, matching economic needs drew the two colonies together. In the early years, New South Wales found itself heavily dependent on Bengal for defence, essential supplies, and news from "home." Later, as their wool, wheat and sugar industries took off, the Australian colonies became substantial consumers of Indian tea and jute; while the Indian Army became a major purchaser of Australian horses, some 350,000 making the Indian Ocean crossing between 1861 and 1931. However, perhaps the most important and lasting links which were forged during this period were human ones. During the earlier part of the 19th century, a number of retired Indian civil servants and Army officers migrated to Australia to start life anew as "squatters." Australians often holidayed in India en route to England.[10] And in the period 1860-1901 (when further non-white immigration was ruled out by an Act of the Commonwealth Parliament), thousands of native Indians came to Australia as labourers, camel drivers and prospectors.[11] Today, these colonial connections with India are commemorated in two names (Burra, Mangalore), in the profusion of Lucknow Streets in our capital cities, and in the quaintly-named "Ghan" express-train which plies between Port Augusta and Alice Springs, broadly following the route mapped out last century by Indian ( "Afghan")-driven camel teams.

If Australia's relationship with India down to 1947 was to some extent a bi-product of British imperialism, it was still a close and flourishing one, and all the signs pointed to it being maintained and strengthened in the post-imperial era. As one of the architects of Australian federation, Alfred Deakin, wrote after an extended visit to India in the 1890s:

> the future relations of India and Australia possess immeasurable potencies. Their geographical proximity cannot but exercise a very real and reciprocal influence upon the forces of national life in each. [12]

But that is not how it has turned out. Despite a promising start in the late 1940s, Indo-Australian relations have remained, for much of the last 40 years, cool and low-key. For instance, there was not a single head of government visitor (on either side) between 1959 and 1974. Why has the promise of the colonial period not been fulfilled?

At the root of the matter lies the problem of insularity. Australians (like most people, perhaps) are fundamentally parochial, far more interested in what goes on in their own neighbourhoods than in what takes place overseas. Curiously, this applies even to the children of "ethnic" families whose parents, presumably, are still concerned about their homelands. At one Sydney school, a determined effort was made a few years ago to add to the number of pupils studying a foreign language. The school has a high proportion of "ethnic" (especially Italian) students. Yet even attempts to introduce Italian proved unsuccessful. The same school also put on several costly extra-curricular tours to Malaysia in a bid to raise the students's awareness of Asian cultures; but these served, in the estimate of the teacher in charge, merely to reinforce their "narrowness" and to expose "their sense of cultural superiority and racist biases."[13] Moreover, to the extent that Australians look overseas they look West, to the Europe that most of them came from. Speaking as one who has laboured for years to push the cause of Asian studies in Australian schools, I can testify, from personal experience, that most teachers--and certainly most educational administrators--in this country still see such studies as exotic and peripheral, rather than as an integral part of the core curriculum. A decade ago, Professor Stephen Fitzgerald, a prominent Sinologist and former Ambassador to Beijing, ruffled the feathers of some colleagues by suggesting that there was an "Asian studies crisis" in our schools. He went on to offer this observation:

> I have yet to come across one course in a secondary college

> in which the total attention devoted to all Asian countries amounts to anything approaching parity with that which is devoted to the countries of Europe.[14]

And what was true then remains true now. Indeed the Ingleson enquiry found that the number of Australian university students taking *South* Asian subjects had actually fallen by one third during the period 1984-1989.

India, then, is not unique in being ignored by the majority of Australians; however for several reasons it does not get even the limited public attention that East and Southeast Asia receive. For one thing, it has always attracted negative stereotypes: India is poor; it is agricultural; its bureaucracy is clogged with red tape; its people are religious fanatics whose gaze is fixed on the next world; its birth rate is out of control. When Morarji Desai became Prime Minister, our newspapers devoted less space to his political views than to the fact that he drank his own urine. Likewise, local coverage of the "N.T.R." phenomenon focused almost exclusively on the Andhra leader's god-roles in popular movies. Accepting many of these stereotypes at face value, the majority of Australian businessmen see India either as a relatively small market (because of its "poverty"--they seem not to realize that India has at least 80 million well-heeled middle-class consumers) or one that is too hard (because of bureaucratic controls) to penetrate. Even a well-informed economist with the ANZ Bank admitted recently:

> Doing business is not easy, and it is quite on the cards that Australian businessmen may view India as a potential market and then run into almost a brick wall because they find that they have to deal with multiple government departments, each of which has its own aspirations. [15]

Certainly, our businessmen (and tourists) are favorably impressed by the fact that many Indians can speak and write English. Yet even this very obvious selling-point is not, perhaps, the advantage it appears to be on the surface, for it tends to engender unreal cultural expectations. As Dr. Robin Jeffrey of La Trobe University told the Senate Standing Committee on Foreign Affairs, Defence and Trade at a recent hearing in Melbourne:

> The fact that the elite in India speaks English leads to expectations that India wili function like Australia. When India does not, frustration and exasperation often result on the part of people trying to deal with the Indian bureaucracy or Indian business. Australians do not have such expectations about China--noone ever expected [people in] China to behave the same way [we do]. . . . [There is thus an] immediate perception that life is bound to be different, and we must [therefore] be rather more patient and show rather more stamina in dealing with China.[16]

China gets our attention, Jeffrey thinks, precisely because it seems strange and forbidding; India, he believes, suffers neglect because it looks, at least at the elite level, comfortingly familiar.

So what has all this to do with the formulation of Australian foreign policy? Several things. To the extent that it is the job of politicians to articulate, rather than shape, community attitudes, the Australian Government has probably done all that could be expected of it in the way of developing closer relations with the Subcontinent. There is clearly no popular mandate for change. Secondly, because immigrants from South Asia represent only a tiny fraction (less than 1%) of Australia's total intake, there is no visible Indian presence in the community in the sense that there now is of Chinese and Vietnamese. According to the 1986 census there were just under 48,000 people of Indian origin living in Australia--a substantial rise from the 3,000 or so who lived here in the 1950s; but in the last 15 years we have taken in at least 150,000 people from Indo-China, a sizeable number of them war-ravaged refugees. It is no wonder that in recent years Vietnam has come to assume a high profile in the minds of our policy-makers. Thirdly, for reasons canvassed earlier, neither of our two countries has a significant economic stake in the other. In 1987/8, Australia accounted for only 1.4% of India's total overseas trade, while India accounted for just 0.9% of Australia's total overseas trade. To put it another way, Australia was only 19th on the list of India's most valued customers, and India a woeful 25th in the rank order of Australia's trading partners (behind Kuwait, Indonesia, Malaysia and New Guinea). Fourthly, although Australia is patently an Indian Ocean country, the nation's political centre of gravity lies in the southeast, which is much more Pacific-orientated. Characteristically, the two frigates which represented Australia's contribution to the Persian Gulf blockade had to be dispatched from Garden Island, Sydney, as there is till (after 50 years of discussion) no major naval base on the west coast. Finally--and this is a sad commentary on the way we look at the world--India has not figured largely in Australian calculations because it is not reckoned a significant threat. At the start of the Cold War, Australian eyes turned to China, the home of the Red Menace. In the early 1960s, we became paranoid about the intentions of Indonesia (and Indonesian language study boomed!) A bit later, we sent troops to Vietnam, and suddenly Indo-China found a place on our cultural map. India, on the other hand, with its policy of Panch Shila, was a country that we could safely ignore. It is no coincidence that recent editorial comment in Australia on South Asia has focussed mainly on India's growing military capacity.[17]

Indo-Australian relations have never been acrimonious. On the contrary, apart from the unfortunate Mirage episode, our countries have managed to get along rather well. However, while relations have been friendly they have not been close, and this, it is argued, has been to Australia's disadvantage. Geographically, economically, and militarily India is a country of manifest importance to Australia and should figure much more centrally in our perceptions of the world than it currently does. Can things improve? So far, the political will (on both sides) has been lacking. But in recent days there are some encouraging signs, in Australia at least, that official opinion is beginning to shift. For the past year, a Senate Standing Committee has been taking submissions and hearing evidence from business people, academics and policy-makers on the future direction of Australian-Indian relations; and in July it published its report. Concluding that the existing state of knowledge of India in Australian government and business circles was "not adequate," the Committee called for the establishment of an Indian Studies Centre for advanced academic study of the Subcontinent, with appropriate government and private sector funding, the provision of incentives for employers in relevant areas to upgrade the "expertise about India of their employees," "the immediate establishment" of an Australia-India council along the lines of the Australia-China Council, and better cooperation among government departments responsible for the shaping of South Asia policy.[18]

These sensible recommendations are long overdue. It is to be hoped that they will receive the prompt and sympathetic consideration of the Australian Cabinet.

## NOTES

1. *The Age* (Melbourne), 26 Apr. 1990 and 2 Aug. 1990.
2. *Ibid*, 2 Aug. 1990.
3. *The Times of India* (Bombay), 1 Aug. 1990.
4. The term was first used by Prime Minister Hawke in a speech to the Asian Studies Association of Australia in Canberra in January 1988.
5. Senate Standing Committee on Foreign Affairs, Defence and Trade: *Australia-India Relations: Trade and Security* (Canberra, AGPS, 1990), p. 7.
6. *Australia and the Northwest Ascendancy* (Canberra, AGPS, 1989).
7. John Ingleson, ed., *Asia in Australian Higher Education: Report of the Inquiry into the Teaching of Asian Studies and Languages in Higher Education* (Asian Studies Council, 1989).
8. Murray Goot, "Speaking in Tongues: Surveys of Opinion on the Teaching of Asian Languages," *Australian Cultural History*, No. 9 (1990), Table 2, p. 124.
9. The debate over Australia's place in the "swing to the East" is summarized in Ged Martin, ed., *The Founding of Australia: the Argument About Australia's Origins* (Sydney, 1978).
10. See, for example, Helen Routledge, ed., *A Season in India: Letters of Ruby Maddern: Experiences of an Australian Girl at the Great Coronation Durbar, Delhi 1903* (Melbourne, 1982).
11. In 1903 the Tehsildar of Vilyatpur, in Jullundur District, noted that 35 men from the village had gone to Australia: this was something like one-third of the adult male population! Tom G. Kessinger, *Vilyatpur 1848-1968: Social and Economic Changes in a North Indian Village* (Berkeley, 1974), p. 92.
12. Alfred Deakin, *Irrigated India* (London, 1893), p. vi.
13. Peter Young, "Plain Views of a Sydney Teacher," *Asian Studies Association of Australia Review*, Vol. 3, No. 1 (July 1979), p. 37.

14. Stephen Fitzgerald, "The Asian Studies Crisis," *ASAA Review*, Vol. 2, No. 1 (July 1978), p. 3.
15. Evidence of Margaret Stoneman, Senior Economist, Interntional, ANZ Bank, to the Senate Standing Committee on Foreign Affairs, Defence and Trade enquiry into "India-Australia Relations," Melbourne, 16 May 1989, Hansard Official Record, p. 274.
16. Evidence of Dr. Robin Jeffrey, *ibid*, p. 354.
17. See, for example, *The Age*, editorial of 25 May 1989 entitled, "Easy Does It Mr. Gandhi."
18. *Australia-India Relations: Trade and Security*, pp. x-xi.

# Mode: Comedy, Type: Rakshasa, Author: R.K. Narayan

S.C. HARREX

Some foul play, somewhere.
A Breath of Lucifer

In a 1984 conference paper[1] devoted to the first-generation modern masters of Indian English fiction--Mulk Raj Anand (b. 1905), R.K. Narayan (b. 1907), Raja Rao (b. 1909)--I attempted to identify and differentiate their distinctive or typical narrative modes. The argument I presented, with tangential reference to some of their novels, examined a small sample of short stories by each writer. It later provided the basis of an article for a special issue of *World Literature Today* commemorating Raja Rao as the 1988 Neustadt Prize Laureate,[2] as well as the present essay on Narayan. Both essays are predicated with a few cultural assumptions in company with some theoretical propositions concerning "typology" and "fictional modes."

Two cultural assumptions I begin with, as an outsider *vis-a-vis* India and Indian literature, are, firstly, that to foreigners like myself the fictional worlds of Indian writers are usually inflected by Indian patterns of perception and behaviour which comprise a distinctive psychology, sociology, iconography and mythology; and, secondly, that such patterns when they are not explicit or interpreted with textual candour (often an awkward device) are implicit within a scale of accessibility which at one end diminishes into Inscrutability (for which, as all outsiders know, the East has a deserved reputation).

To varying degrees, the works of many Indian writers are consciously addressed to a heterogeneous audience of Indians and non-Indians both of which groups can be divided into two subgroups: cultural insiders and cultural outsiders. (Insofar as we assume it possible that a non-Indian can become a cultural insider, we may wish to consider on the one hand Kipling's achievement in *Kim* which many Indians commend, and on the other the exchange in Raja Rao's *The Serpent and the Rope* between Ramaswamy and his European wife:

> "One can never be converted to Hinduism."
> "You mean you can only be born a Brahmin?"
> "That is--an Indian," I added, as an explanation of India.[3]

Some writers have designed narrative strategies to appeal to the widest possible cross-section of a potential audience, and this has raised questions concerning cultural and literary "authenticity." English is therefore a privileged language for Indian writers to use insofar as they reach, because of it, audiences which are pan-Indian and/or semi-global.

Throughout his writing career R.K. Narayan has appealed to this kind of multi-cultural audience. Like other Indian-English authors, he has contrived many strategies for reminding his readers that his work is pervaded by a culturally distinctive fact, a socially inclusive reality: namely that by writing as an Indian in and of India, he does so within a mythopoeic tradition and within a society in which secular and religious life, mythical past and historic present, are simultaneous and synthetic rather than irreconcilable and divorced. This revelation in the main is implicit in Narayan's fiction and explicit in his other prose works, an example of the latter being his popular book *God, Demons and Others* (1964) in which he recreates stories from *Mahabharata, Ramayana* and other Sanskrit classics. Entitled "The World of the Storyteller," Narayan's introduction to this collection of stories describes the place of traditional mythological literature, and the role of the Pandit as oral story-teller, in village culture. In this essay, Narayan alerts his readers to cultural archetypes like the *rakshasa* (demon) and the institutionalized narrator (village Pandit or itinerant story-teller), and in so doing directs our attention to prominent typologies (narrator-protagonist and rakshasa-antagonist, for instance) in his own novels and short stories. In relating the term *typology* to Narayan's narratives, then, I do so in reference to those of his major characters, including the internal narrators, who are individuals reiterating specific characteristics in the manner of symbolic figures and pre-determined types.

The term *typology* can thus apply to archetypal personalities who have well-defined cultural roles and values, and on occasion Anand, Rao and Narayan have used them as models of characterization. This practice in Indian literatures, of course, has a venerable history, a popular and impressive example being the personifications--an evolution from sacred to erotic--of Krishna and Radha in love poetry.[4] But *typology* also provides a preliminary context for my discussion with respect to the critical literature concerning *types* of "fictional forms" (i.e. *modes*). This has produced the "modal approach" as postulated by Robert Schoolers[5] and Ulrich Wicks. Wicks defines this approach as "a concept of modes as ideal fictional types . . . or primitive narrative forms," and summarizes its main elements as follows:

> A world fictionally rendered can be (1) better than the world of experience, (2) worse than it, or (3) more or less equal to it. . . . Fiction can give us, then, the heroic world of *romance*, the degraded world of *satire*, or the mimetic world of *history*, respectively. These three models are the middle and end points of a spectrum of fictional possibilities which have seven modes in all: satire; picaresque; comedy; history; sentiment; tragedy; romance.[6]

In the context of this spectrum, the prominent development in Raja Rao's fiction is from "history" to "romance," from the political to the metaphysical novel. A constant in his work, as it is in Narayan's, is an attachment to Indian--especially Hindu--*tradition*. At the same time they are very difficult writers, typologically and stylistically. The difference, also, is manifestly modal, with Raja Rao's major mode being "romance" and Narayan's "comedy" as these terms are defined and perceived within Wicks's modal "spectrum." Thus, even though Raja Rao defines *The Cat and Shakespeare* (1965) generically as "metaphysical comedy," its comedy *per se* (a kind of Indian divine comedy) has much more affinity with the mode of romance than that of conventional comedy. Narayan, on the other hand, is a master of the latter without restricting himself to it entirely. Indeed, in nearly all Narayan's fictions he combines with comedy important elements of the history mode, while in some of his sombre works--for instance, *The Dark Room* (1938)--or in some darker nuances within individual works he may introduce a tragi-comic tone. He has also written one novel--his least characteristic work, *The English Teacher* (1947)--which is the least modally consistent being a combination of history, comedy, tragedy and romance, as well as a quasi-autobiography.

In the present essay, however, I want to confine my attention to some very characteristic features of Narayan's use of the mode of comedy with particular reference to the short story "A Breath of Lucifer" in *A Horse and Two Goats* (1970).

The above comparison of Raja Rao with R.K. Narayan legitimately suggests that these two authors, so starkly different in their style, technique and fictional preoccupations, are comparable in their commitment to traditional cultural values. The similarity and difference is well demonstrated typologically; both make contemporary artistic use of traditional narrative method and ideology, but each specializes in an entirely different fictional mode. Narayan's mode of *comedy* is close to *history* because of the humanism of his implied point of view, as well as the credible psychology of his characters. Whereas Raja Rao's compulsion is to elevate metaphysical theory above human compassion, the reverse happens in Narayan. And whereas Raja Rao relies on lyrical monologue or poetic erudition to shape his subject, Narayan relies for the same purpose on comic irony.

In Narayan's work, the traditional elements which form and inform his fictional modes include some of those he has identified in "The World of the Storyteller." "Each tale," he writes, "invariably starts off when an inquiring mind asks of an enlightened one a fundamental question."[7] Narayan's adaptation of this strategy is often pregnant with parodic and ironic possibilities. Thus his novel *The Vendor of Sweets* (1967) opens with the following exchange:

> "Conquer taste, and you will have conquered the self," said Jagan to his listener, who asked, "Why conquer the self?" Jagan said, "I do not know, but all our sages advise us so."
>
> The listener lost interest in the question; his aim was only to stimulate conversation, while he occupied a low wooden stool next to Jagan's chair. Jagan sat under the framed picture

> of the goddess Lakshmi hanging on the wall, and offered prayers first thing in the day.[8]

This vertical composition of the social setting--a hierarchy from ignorance through enlightenment to godhead, from listener on the lowstool, Jagan in his chair, sages, and Lakshmi on the wall--introduces the historical myth-bound milieu in which a comedy of life is to be enacted. The cultural themes are also postulated. This is typically Narayan.

Similarly, his short story "A Breath of Lucifer" begins with another variation of the formula. The narrator is the questioner and the enlightenment he seeks concerns the appearance and character of his male nurse whom he cannot see because his eyes are bandaged following an operation:

> Sam was only a voice to me, a rich, reverberating baritone. His whispers themselves possessed a solid, rumbling quality. I often speculated, judging from his voice, what he might look like: the possessor of such a voice could be statuesque, with curls falling on his nape, Roman nose, long legs able to cover the distance from my bed to the bathroom in three strides although to me it seemed an endless journey. I asked him on the very first day, "What do you look like?"
>
> "How can I say? Several years since I looked at a mirror?"
>
> "Why so?"
>
> "The women at home do not give us a chance, that is all. I have even to shave without a mirror." He added, "Except once when I came up against a large looking glass at a tailor's and cried out absent-mindedly, 'Ah, Errol Flynn in town!'"
>
> "You admired Errol Flynn?"
>
> "Who wouldn't? As Robin Hood, unforgettable; I saw the picture fifty times."
>
> "What do you look like?"
>
> He paused and answered, "Next week this time you will see for yourself; be patient till the bandages are taken off."[9]

That this story also opens in the comic fictional mode should be self-evident. We are offered comedy of situation in that the answer by the "enlightened one" to the "inquiring mind" frustrates the questioner in an amusing parody of a literary convention. Also the introduction of the "enlightened one" as comically egocentric is a promising aberration, and the reader's curiosity synchronizes with that of the narrator. As the story unfolds, the character of Sam conforms with Narayan's idea that, in the traditional story, the central interest resides in "outstanding personalities" and "typical figures." "I believe," says Narayan in "The World of the Story-teller," "that, though circumstances and details may vary, it is personality alone that remains unchanging and makes sense in any age, or any idiom, whether the setting is 3000 B.C. or 2000 A.D." (9) Like most of Narayan's protagonists, Sam is the consequence of a question we can imagine Narayan asking as he fleshes out his characters: "What makes an ordinary, anti-heroic person eccentric or outstanding?" In the case of Raju in the short story "Trail of the Green Blazer," his outstanding quality is an abnormal contradiction in his character which leads to an abnormal, comically ironic contradiction in the action he performs. Raju is a talented pick-pocket, proud of his accomplishments in a vocation which he thinks of as an honourable profession. He enjoys job satisfaction, but is aware that the life of a petty criminal--and by extension his family dependents--is precarious. But contradicting his normal cautious attitude, on the occasion narrated in the story, is his involuntary susceptibility to moral impulse; his compassionate imagination compromises him. Having skilfully relieved the man in the green blazer of his purse and its legal tender, he realizes he has also stolen the balloon that "Green Blazer" had said he was buying for his motherless boy. So overwhelmed is Raju by remorse at the disappointment he will cause his secondary victim, he decides on an ingenious moral compromise. He will keep the money, put the balloon back in the purse, and surreptitiously restore the purse to its owner. He is of course caught in the act, his behaviour totally misinterpreted. Raju's truthful defence that he was trying to put the purse back is laughed out of court. This is grand comic irony.

Sam likewise is an engaging rascal in whom imagination and disaster, attentive compassion and assertive egoism, are curiously mixed. As the narrator's attendant, he is meticulously professional, caring and reassuring; imaginative and resourceful; absolutely efficient, devoting his ego totally to his job. But in response to the patient's curious inquiries about his past and present situations, how he became a male nurse and so on, Sam is enigmatic, evasive and offers contradictory accounts of his personal history. We begin to suspect that he is capable of manufacturing for himself a rich fantasy life in keeping with his earlier Errol Flynn posture. Allegedly he acquired his skills as a nurse performing heroic surgical and medical deeds, under the command of his Colonel, in various unspecified and moveable wars. He is similarly vague about an alleged extra-marital affair by which he has been plagued. The denoue ment of the story, of the uncertain revelation of Sam's character, is the crisis of his last night in attendance prior to the removal of the patient's bandages the following day. The celebration party organized by Sam ends disastrously. He becomes drunk on soft drink laced with alcohol, hallucinates, claims the hospital is on fire, and takes his blindfold bewildered patient out into the hospital grounds where the latter spends an anxious, uncomfortable night until he is discovered in the morning and returned to his bed. The narrator's convalescence has suffered a painful setback, while Sam of the demon drink has vanished. The story ends with a postcard from Sam several days later:

> I wish you a speedy recovery. I do not know what happened that night. Some foul play, somewhere. That rogue who brought me the Coca-Cola must have drugged the drink. I will deal with him yet. I pray that you get well. After you go home, if you please, send me a money order for Rs. 48/-. I am charging you for only six days and not for the last day. I wish I could meet you, but my colonel has summoned me to Madras to attend on a leg amputation . . . Sam. (130)

Despite the narrator's suffering, there is something comic about Sam's outrageous claim to innocence and his affectionate impertinence. To the narrator in a world without sight and whose point of view is restricted by sensory deprivation, Sam must seem on the night of the imaginary fire to be an agent of the devil. This psychologically valid point of view is reinforced by a typological technique of characterization. For Sam can also be viewed as an incarnation of the rakshasa type, or demon, to whom Narayan refers in "The World of the Storyteller"; a traditional literary persona that provides an explicit model for Narayan's portrait of Vasu in *The Man-Eater of Malgudi* (1961). Sam's personal history comically qualifies him for the role. A Christianized Indian, Sam used to revel in playing Lucifer in his church's dramatic troupe; his bishop,

Sam claimed with pride, regarded him as the best Lucifer "anywhere." In real life, in the story, the narrator gets an inkling of his true demonic personality when he smells the alcoholic "breath of Lucifer." And Sam on the fateful night reveals his Satanic identity, attempting to subvert truth with illusion. The chief effect of such characterization is comic and ironic.

There is comic logic in Narayan's tactic of adding Lucifer to the fraternity of Indian rakshasas. Further comic ironies are to be found in the juxtaposition of the story, with its chaotic crisis, and the serenity of the "Prologue" which Narayan wrote as an introduction to the story proper. Narayan's personal account of temporary deprivation of sight following his own cataract operation describes the experience as an inward-turning vision akin to yogic self-development; by activating the "visual memory," it in turn creates delightful scenes in mythological time and space. The outer life of doctors, visitors etc., by contrast, is the "unreal world in which they live." The narrator, on the other hand, experiences the dimension of demonic nightmare during his otherwise parallel blindfold convalescence. Moreover, the discrepancy between illusion and reality which Sam is responsible for brings disruption and consternation, in which *Maya* prevails, in contrast with the peace and illumination of inner reality which Narayan describes and endorses in the "Prologue."

Considered in terms of typology, fictional mode, and narrative technique or point of view, "A Breath of Lucifer" is a subtle narrative structure. The dual narration provides a thematic comprehensiveness, balancing the Prologue's vision of the ideal and sublime with the story's example of reality as disruption and nightmare. At the technical level, we are given a juxtaposition between extrasensory perception (Narayan's experience) and severely limited perception (his narrator's experience). Connecting the romance mode of the former with the psychological history mode of the latter is the all-encompassing mode of comedy underscored with irony. The story's basic structure, its thematic ground plan of Maya versus Truth and its rakshasa concept of personality, is an adaptation of traditional narrative.

As in the case in "Trail of the Green Blazer," the plot of "A Breath of Lucifer" utilizes the "moment of crisis" device for which short stories especially are renowned. Sam and Raju are similar characters in that they belong to the ubiquitous rogue class, but they are different Narayan types: Sam is the antagonist whose personality combines the uniqueness of individual personality with the typical in the form of the rakshasa, while Raju is the protagonist of outstanding but ordinary personality whose fate is determined by an unusual comic flaw. The comic irony with which Narayan adapts traditional literary conventions, and which is his narrative forte, is typified in "Trail of the Green Blazer," by his effective use of the ending with a moral:

> He told himself, "If ever I pick up something again, I shall make sure I don't have to put it back." For now he believed God had gifted the likes of him with only one-way deftness. Those fingers were not meant to put anything back.[10]

The ending of "A Breath of Lucifer"--Sam's postcard communication quoted above--eschews the closure of finality (the demise of the rakshasa) with which Narayan rounded off his mythological comedy in *The Man-Eater of Malgudi*. Instead, the more open or transitional closure here serves to return us to the end of the "Prologue":

> Within the confines of this existence I feel snug and contented. Its routines are of the utmost importance to me. I am so much at home within it that I suspect I shall feel a regret when it ends. (115)

This image of harmonious convalescence is also an appropriate closure for the mode of comedy which is, after all, a healing form of art. And Narayan, we are convinced, is on the healing side of humanity.

## NOTES

1. "Towards a Typology of the Indo-English Short Story," Second International Conference on Indian Ocean Studies, University of Western Australia, 5-12 Dec., 1984.
2. "Typology and Modes: Raja Rao's Experiments in Short Story:," *World Literature* Today, 62 (4), Autumn 1988, pp.

591-95.
3. (London: John Murray, 1960), p. 336
4. See, for example, *Love Songs of Vidyapati*, trans. Deben Bhattacharya, ed. with an intro., notes and comments by W.G. Archer (Delhi: Hind Pocket Books, Orient Paperbacks, 1963).
5. "Towards a Poetics of Fiction: An Approach Through Genre," *Novel*, 2, 1969, pp. 101-11.
6. "The Nature of Picaresque Narrative: A Modal Approach," *PMLA*, 89, 1974, pp. 240-49.
7. (Mysore: Indian Thought Publications, 1965), p. 7.
8. (Harmondsworth: Penguin, 1983), p. 5.
9. *A Horse and Two Goats* (Mysore: Indian Thought Publications, 1982), pp. 116-17.
10. *Malgudi Days* (Harmondsworth: Penguin, 1984), p. 121.

# From Satiric Farce to Tragic Epiphany: Salman Rushdie's *The Satanic Verses*

DAVID MYERS

The literary reception of Salman Rushdie's *The Satanic Verses* has so far focussed either on a metafictional interpretation of the work as a series of fantasies, satires and pastiches featuring surrealism, black humour, world-lit parody and witty blasphemy[1] or on an idealistic defence of the work's right to be published based on freedom of speech and liberation from censorship.[2] The theological reception of the novel has focussed on the right of one of the world's major religions to have its sacred articles of faith protected from the public ridicule of an agnostic. For these reasons, the literary reception has been positive and the theological reception negative. But perhaps the evaluations of both groups have been premature and are derived from a misunderstanding of the work's ultimate thrust.

No critic as yet seems to have considered the possibility that *The Satanic Verses*, notwithstanding its manifest cacophony of intellectual farce and the grotesque, is nevertheless a novel which could be praised both by aesthetes and by liberal theologians alike as a work which culminates in the moral vision and unorthodox spirituality of a contemporary tragedy.

To comprehend the plausibility of this approach, it is essential to realize just how high Rushdie has set his ambitions in this novel. He has attempted to capture the authentic moods of four different social cultures which are caught up in the throes of change. Firstly there is England, conservative, white, imperial, vainglorious England sinking into a bedlam of squalor, poverty and racism. Secondly there is the power-struggle of Mahound (a fictional simulacrum for Mohammed) as he strives to transform seventh century Jahilia from venal, idolatrous and lecherous trading centre to the stern puritanism of monotheistic Islam. Thirdly there is the re-birth of Islamic fundamentalism either under the dictatorship of the Imam in 20th century Iran or under the suicidal leadership of the butterfly-saint Ayesha in 20th century rural India. Fourthly there is the picture of contemporary metropolitan India trying to re-establish a national culture but finding itself trapped between slavish imitation of the English conquerors and a commercial cheapening by the mass entertainment media of both its Hindu and its Islamic religious cultures.

This is an extraordinary task to be accomplished in one novel and it is not surprising that Rushdie's main characters of necessity assume parodistic-mythological dimensions so that they can act out on a grand scale the public issues and conflicts of these four cultures. The major themes emerging from their often farcical enactment of public conflicts are the failure of our age of mass commercialism to achieve spiritual depth and the consequent vacillation of uprooted individuals between vanity and self-indulgence on the one hand and self-destructive doubt and guilt on the other hand. Rushdie concedes that the price paid by contemporary Western civilization for liberty and some measure of egalitarianism is that the solace of religious faith has been lost in a maze of agnosticism and materialism. The closure of *The Satanic Verses* argues that the only way out of this maze is a quest for commitment to a community, but not through religious dogma and imposed conformism but rather through unorthodox, mystic faith or intellectually open discussion in a framework of altruistic socialism.

The heated debate of the last year[3] has taught us that it seems impossible to find any compromise between the Western, intellectual quest for elusive truth through philosophy and art and the insistence of Islam that the absolute truth has already been revealed by Mohammed's Recitation in the Koran. Absolute freedom of speech cannot coexist with the taboos of absolute faith. Western intellectuals prize liberty and individualism as the hard-fought for basis of creative, multicultural civilization, a basis achieved to some extent by such satirists as Montaigne, Voltaire and Swift, all of whom were accused in their lifetimes of defaming religion. The followers of Islam, by contrast, prize the submission of the faithful and insist that religious conformism is essential in order to protect the Islamic religion from what they perceive as the schisms and declining social authority of contemporary Christianity.

The culture-clash unleashed by Salman Rushdie's *The Satanic Verses* is intelligible in these terms. Western intellectuals need to concede that faithful Muslims feel hurt and insulted by Rushdie's satiric attack on the moral perfection of the Prophet, on the divine infallibility of the Koran, on the sacred authority of Gibreel as the messenger of God, and on the fundamentalism of the Imams. Muslims on the other hand need to understand that Rushdie is not a gratuitous blasphemer being used by the Western media to discredit the Islamic faith. Rushdie is a passionate intellectual searching through the medium of literature for a tenable intellectual position in matters both of the soul and of social justice. His satire on racism in Thatcher's England is considerably more trenchant than the irony and irreverent whimsy through which he attempts to give a human all too human context to the official dogma of Islam.

While it is true that the dominant tone of *The Satanic Verses* is that of satire and black humour and that the many plots are developed from the remote point of view of a metafictional narrator playing with farce and the grotesque, I would nevertheless contend that *The Satanic Verses* is far from being merely a religious satire. A character study can prove that Mahound, the fictional simulacrum of Mohammed, emerges as a dedicated, patriarchal and even heroic figure particularly when contrasted with the novel's clownish antiheroes, Gibreel Farishta and Salahuddin Chamcha. Furthermore, an analysis of the significance of the novel's title together with a textual examination of the leitmotif that is derived from it indicates that Rushdie is setting up a number of serious religious propositions concerning the existential relationship between good and evil. Finally, a stylistic consideration of the novel's closure demonstrates that Rushdie succeeds, quite improbably, in transforming the novel's final thrust from satiric farce to tragic epiphany, with either fairytale-mystic or moral-utopian overtones. The closure of *The Satanic Verses* is a self-denial of the remote, supercilious narrator and a neo-romantic yearning to create meaning through the rediscovery of authentic self and the opening out of this self through irrational faith and commitment to the other.

The surreal, mythical fall of the two central figures, Salahuddin Chamcha and Gibreel Farishta, at the beginning of the novel is parallelled by their tragic, personal fall at the end of the novel. The words tragic and tragedy here are used deliberately and are meant to indicate a number of defining features of a kind of tragedy that is still possible as a genre in the 20th century. These features include a fall or failure of the main characters which produces in the reader an overwhelming sense of a dream destroyed, of a life wasted, of futility.

The inner conflicts of these individuals and their potential for greatness have been revealed to the reader by the narrator with such force that the reader has a decisive insight through empathy into the inevitability of human failure and suffering. The failure is commonly associated with the death of the character and this death is evoked in a solemn, exalted tone. Such is the death confession of Gibreel Farishta. If the character does not experience physical death, then he/she experiences something akin to spiritual death and rebirth. This spiritual death is brought on by the individual's admission of total moral failure and the resolution to start afresh. Such is the experience of Salahuddin Chamcha.

Paradoxically the physical or spiritual death of the main characters may also be the moment in which they achieve through suffering their nobility and possibly their epiphany. This provokes in the reader a moment of inspiration and joy at the greatness of the human spirit. This moment is the tragic moment and it is still to be found, in spite of metafictional techniques and in spite of post-modernism and deconstruction, in contemporary fiction, as it was once found, in a culturally different form, in classical Greek tragedy. This is the experience of Ayesha the butterfly saint and Mirza Saeed the atheist who are mystically united in death.

The emergence of mystic epiphany and tragic inspiration at the end of *The Satanic Verses* from an unpromising morass of farce and satire can be found best exemplified in the ultimate fates of Gibreel Farishta, Salahuddin Chamcha, Ayesha and Mirza Saeed. The spiritual inspiration which their tragedies provide is derived from three sets of religious propositions which are central to the novel's theme. These propositions are religious in an existential sense of the word but are often anti-institutional in their independent approach to the dogma of Islam.

The first set of religious proposition suggested by *The Satanic Verses* states that no one, whether prophet or saint or artist or simply an average individual, has an easy path to salvation, because no one is absolved of the quality of being human, all too human. Further, it is not possible in this novel for the atheist or the agnostic simply to ignore the religious dimensions of life and death. The challenge of faith is harrowing and all-pervasive. Finally, there is no path to salvation except through the tormented admission of personal failure and experiencing the suffering of hell. In applying this proposition to his interpretation of Mahound, the fictional simulacrum of Mohammed, Rushdie knew that he would incur the wrath of the Mullahs who are claiming the same inspired moral perfection for Mohammed as Christians claim for Jesus Christ.

The second set of religious propositions suggested by the novel states that the only cure for the anguish of cosmopolitan uprootedness and intellectual agnosticism is to reconcile oneself with some form of the community which one has denied in one's youth. The prodigal son must renounce the vanity of his ambition for fame in exile and return to his father's fold in order to seek a redefined community in his native land. He must cease to ape the imperial conquerer in a self-denigrating culture-cringe and instead look to an unorthodox renewal of the traditions of his own native land as a positive framework for individual self-definition.

It is the third set of religious propositions in *The Satanic Verses* which is the most ostensibly irreligious and controversial. Rushdie implies that from a human point of view the traditional distinction between God and Satan is unprovable; the providence and destiny have long since been replaced by chance and chaos; that the Archangel Gibreel, who dictates the Recitation to Mahound, is a medium for both the truth of the Recitation and the falsehood of *The Satanic Verses* ( "it was me both times, baba, me first and second also me"); and that the mythical fall of Gibreel Farishta and Salahuddin Chamcha is an "angelicdevilish fall" in which the diabolic horns and the halo are distributed at random. These propositions are regarded as shocking and insulting by the Mullahs of Islam, but when you think about it they are little different in essence from the religious propositions advanced by Franz Kafka in his allegorical novel *The Castle* and in his mystic aphorisms. Rushdie's religious propositions in *The Satanic Verses* are those of a post-modernist agnostic who feels driven to part-playful and part-anguished metaphysical speculation as a compensation for his loss of faith. As Rushdie himself says:

> Dr Aadam Aziz, the patriarch in my novel *Midnight's Children*, loses his faith and is left with "a hole inside him, a

> vacancy in a vital inner chamber." I, too, possess the same God-shaped hole. Unable to accept the unarguable absolutes of religion, I have tried to fill up the hole with literature. The art of the novel is a thing I cherish as dearly as the bookburners of Bradford value their brand of militant Islam.[4]

In this article I shall argue that Rushdie's three sets of unorthodox religious propositions are realized in tragic epiphanies in the novel's closure. A tragic epiphany is defined as the sudden transformation of a character either by an agonized realization of failure, waste and futility and/or a revelation of ultimate, existential truth accompanied by a total commitment to an ideal or a community. This epiphany is ultimately granted to Gibreel Farishta, Salahuddin Chamcha, Ayesha and Mirza Saeed. But each epiphany has a different emphasis.

At the moment of his death by suicide Gibreel Farishta experiences what might be termed a negative epiphany. He is overwhelmed by his guilt and by his inescapable mental sickness and breaks through into tragic but liberating honesty with his confession of the evil that has been caused by his narcissism, his facile self-aggrandizement and his hysterical obsession with sex and jealousy. (He could also have confessed to the cynical commercialization of religion in trashy pseudo-theological films for the masses.) His confession is written in a style that is antithetical to metafictional play; the tone is elevated, serious and tragic. *The Satanic Verses* has abruptly changed its tone from surreal farce to tragedy. We experience empathy and admiration for him in his moment of honesty and self-accusation. We feel, as is the case in classical tragedy, that there is no way out for him except death.

Salahuddin Chamcha's epiphany comes as a decisive insight into the soul-destroying phoniness of his whole life which has been misspent denying his Indian heritage and toadying to the English overlord. In trying to become more English than the English, Salahuddin has become a nobody, an uprooted, cosmopolitan mimic without a true identity or the authenticity of soul that comes from being true to the original self of childhood and family tradition. Salahuddin's reunion with his dying father is the moment when his farce is transformed to a tragic admission of waste and alienation from himself and from others. He has spent his life shutting himself off from others. At his father's deathbed he experiences a Saul to

Paul conversion and understands that he must seek for fulfilment not in England but in India. Through the proselytizing (and energetic erotic influence) of Zeenat Vakil he then begins the process of conversion to Indian patriotic communism. The conversion is a little utopian and smacks of convenient ending for a novel that has at last run out of ideological steam and is looking for a conciliatory ending. The stylistic tone, however, leaves no doubt that Rushdie means it very seriously.

Ayesha's epiphany is a beautifully told and quite anachronistic fairy-tale of mystic faith. When she is given her otherworldly blessing of butterflies, she wins the power to convert erotic passion into caricative love and she radiates the certainty of absolute faith which is the only romantic cure for the self-inflicted wound of the agnostic. Ayesha is meant to stand in incongruous contrast to the 20th century mood of this novel--that is, to atheism (or agnosticism), to parodistic pastiches of the religious myths, to materialism and to spiritual shallowness. All the qualities of spirit which 20th century Western intellectuals lack, and know they lack, are incorporated in the saintly Ayesha. Ayesha is the age of faith and miracles reborn. Her ultimate miracle in defying death by walking with her fellow-pilgrims across the bed of the Arabian Sea to Mecca is told from a narrative perspective in which bemusement is outweighed by wistful yearning for the impossible made real in fiction.

Mirza Saeed's epiphany is of a traditional, tragic kind. First he falls (in peripeteia) from his princely estate, losing his subjects, his wife, his wealth, his home and his sanity. His tragic fall has been brought about by his character flaw, that is by his clinging obstinately to rationalism and atheism and by his ugly mockery of Ayesha and her pilgrims. In the depths of his despair and at the moment of his death he is suddenly granted a vision of perfect love. His guilty, adulterous yearning for Ayesha is mystically fused with a spiritual love. His earthly life had inevitably become flat and meaningless because he had dedicated it to a mean-spirited, self-protective closing-in of his egoistic self against the other. In death he discovers the ecstasy of opening up and being subsumed into the other. This opening-up is an act of faith and love and, as Salman Rushdie presents it in *The Satanic Verses*, in the 20th century secular equivalent of the love of Jesus and Mahomet for the revelation of the living God.

It is, however, in the self-contradictory nature of Rushdie's divided soul that at the moment of his character's yearning to return to the community and the faith of their childhood in India (or Arabia), he himself as narrator cannot relinquish his mischievous urge to satirize the very traditions to which he now feels drawn. His intellectual pride derides his irrational soul. *The Satanic Verses* has, predictably, infuriated the communities of Moslem believers[5] even though some of the novel can be read as a homage both to the humanly flawed greatness of Mahound and to the tragic joy of Ayesha's faith.

Rushdie wilfully contributes to the misunderstanding of his novel by orthodox religious readers when he includes a passage in his work which implies that all literature is the work of the Devil and that Rushdie sold his soul (or his life) to the Devil in order to win the inspiration necessary in order to write *The Satanic Verses.* He had Gibreel Farishta say:

> A book is a product of a pact with the Devil that inverts the Faustian contract . . . Dr Faustus sacrificed eternity in return for two dozen years of power; the writer agrees to the ruination of his life, and gains (but only if he's lucky) may be not eternity, but posterity at least. Either way . . . it's the Devil who wins.[6]

This is a witty conceit, but probably no more than that. Rushdie causes trouble for himself because he cannot resist a facetious, well-turned phrase. As an intellectual, post-modernist writer he is so interested in deconstructing the Romantic notion of the artist as inspired by God that he grotesquely overstates the opposite case purely for the sake of a clever metaphor.

His self-deprecating irony plays into the hands of those who doubt the value of uncensored art, of free speech and of individualism by implying that an artist is in the employ of the Devil, trapped by the vanity of his lust for fame. Rushdie could have said, with just as much justification, that the post-modernist artist compulsively crucifies himself on a cross of his own making. This cross is made out of the artist's monastic dedication to art and also out of his apparent inability to commit himself in faith to any public ideology or religion. Certainly one does not finish reading *The Satanic Verses* with the feeling that it was written in order that an atheist might make mockery of a religious community.[7] Rather, the closure of the novel indicates the grotesque failure of the atheists and rationalists and the spiritual triumph of the unorthodox existentialists, though not necessarily in this life.

The very name which Rushdie decided to give to his fictional simulacrum of Mohammed reeks of easily misinterpreted irony. In metafictional play with the tensions surrounding faction and fiction, Rushdie does not call his character Mohammed ("he-for-whom-thanks-should-be-given") nor does he give him his nickname Moehammered ( "he-who-goes-up-and-down-old-Coney" mountain). To use Rushdie's words on this crucial point:

> Here he is neither Mohamet nor Moehammered; has adopted, instead, the demon-tag the farangis hung around his neck. To turn insults into strengths, whigs, tories, Blacks all chose to wear with pride the names they were given in scorn; likewise, our mountain-climbing, prophet-motivated solitary is to be the medieval baby-frightener, the Devil's synonym: Mahound. That's him. Mahound the businessman, climbing his hot mountain in the Hijaz. The mirage of a city shines below him in the sun. (93)

This passage makes clear that Rushdie has not chosen to insult Mohammed's memory by calling him Mahound. Rather he is trying to capture the prophet's proud and steadfast espousal of a great revolutionary idea in the years when the idea was derided by the establishment of Mecca and Mohammed himself was scorned and ridiculed. Mahound becomes an epitaph of greatness of soul in the vital years of struggle for recognition.

There is similar irony in Rushdie's decision to focus on the apocryphal satanic verses as the moment of temptation for Mahound, the moment when it appears that with an apparently small compromise he can at last attain public recognition for his God, Allah. Devout Moslems were of course offended by this focus on an event whose historicity has never been verified. But for Rushdie the novelist this event is the structural foundation stone on which he builds his fictional edifice.

Rushdie is nothing if not an honest intellectual and he refuses to paint a facile halo for the saints and the prophets. He is determined to show their potential weakness, the moment when they come perilously close to compromising their whole mission by succumbing briefly to temptation. But this is not done in a mood of cackling, vengeful atheism, but rather as a moment of quiet insight into the way that humans actually work and history is created. Mahound ultimately triumphs by rejecting the temptation of political power and returning to the purity of his vision of monotheism. But he has been made human and credible for modern readers precisely because of his single moment of weakness. Rushdie then transposes this conflict between our need for faith on the one hand and our vanity and lust for fame on the other hand into the chaos of our 20th century world.

The structure of *The Satanic Verses* invites us to compare Mahound's successful fight against temptation in the 17th century with Gibreel's and Salahuddin's succumbing to temptation in the 20th century. Mahound's steadfast faith and the dedication to his community is contrasted with the spurious, shoddy pseudo-religion which Gibreel offers his community through his cheap theological films and with Salahuddin's arrogant denial of his father's Bombay community by self-imposed exile in London. Rushdie uses this comparison and contrast in order to evoke some of the great problems of our age in the Western world: cynicism, materialism and loss of faith; tragic uprootedness of the cosmopolitan artist; spiritual homelessness and the need to break out of the sterile circles of narcissistic pride and find a new community; the recognition that this new community of the faithful can only be attained after passing through trial by ordeal and surmounting the impasse of intellectual doubt.

The self-disciplined strength of Mahound is contrasted in the novel's structure with the self-indulgent weakness of Salahuddin and Gibreel. The greatness of Mahound's concept of God and religion is contrasted with the farcical, surreal fantasies and febrile delusions of grandeur from which both Gibreel and Salahuddin suffer.

Rushdie has chosen to focus on the satanic verses not in order to jeer at the human, all too human imperfections of Mohammed, but in order to illuminate the crucial moment when a great idea is either watered down and lost or takes its place on the stage of world history. This dramatic insistence on the purity of an idea or vision is given further structural significance in the novel when it is re-created as a leitmotif in the story of Ayesha the mysterious butterfly saint in 20th century India. Repeatedly Rushdie asks the question which is the theological foundation of this novel: *"What kind of idea are you?"* (500) To this question the saintly Ayesha replies: *"I was tempted, but am renewed; am uncompromising; absolute; pure."* (501)

It is the way of most revolutionary ideas, implies Rushdie, that their prophets compromise when challenged and that their ideas sink into the maelstrom of human chaos. Of the prophets who do not compromise, many are butchered by the powers of the status quo and forgotten. Only a select few remain to have an enduring influence on the human condition. Rushdie suggests in his novel that the prophet Mahound did yield briefly to the political temptation to compromise in his early days in Jahilia (Mecca). Nevertheless, he withdrew swiftly from this compromise in order to maintain the purity of his revolutionary monotheism and this purity gave rise to the Book of Recitation and the religion of Islam.

The other question which Rushdie asks in order to evaluate the revolutionary idea or vision is: *"What kind of idea are you at the moment of triumph?"* By this he means: is the prophet of the idea vengeful and vindictive when he finally assumes power or is he generous and forgiving? Upon his return to Jahilia, Mahound proves himself to be stern and authoritative, but also forgiving to his enemy the Grandee, to the Grandee's treacherous wife Hind and to the general population who had hounded and ridiculed him into exile a decade earlier. The thrust of this section of *The Satanic Verses* is therefore not to denigrate the religion of Islam but rather to re-affirm, from an unorthodox, unbeliever's point of view, the greatness of Mohammed and his revolutionary idea or vision.

There is of course a mischievous inclination in Rushdie to tease and to mock at the same time as he is declaring his admiration. This ironic schism is not untypical of the intellectual and may be seen as a way of preserving the independence of the intellect when confronted with the phenomenon of uncritical adulation. It is because of this ironic schism within Rushdie that *The Satanic Verses* is a novel that ranges from light-hearted satire to tragic spirituality. Rushdie's ambiguous perspective is most apparent in his character portrait of Mahound.

In this character portrait Rushdie deliberately plays down the political, commercial, diplomatic, military and legal dimensions of Mohammed's career. In fact Rushdie's novel has nothing to do with an historically objective assessment of Mohammed's statesmanlike and worldly-wise leadership of the squabbling Arabic clans. Instead Rushdie has chosen to construct what he must have known would be a provocative psycho-biography. He has not hesitated to take liberties with history, partly in order to create dramatic fiction and partly in order to emphasize the human aspect of Mohammed's struggle for a revelation from the divine spirit. For example, Rushdie has invented the promiscuous, power-mongering Hind as the wife of the Grandee of Jahilia. Hind seem to have much more to do with the figure of Queen Jezabel in the Biblical tale of Naboth's vineyard. Rushdie has also fused the two main historical opponents of Mohammed in Mecca, namely Abu Jahl and Abu Sufyan, into one figure, the Grandee of Jahilia, Abu Simbel.

More importantly, Rushdie has decided to emphasize the spirituality of Mohammed by making a parallel between him and Jesus Christ. He calls Mahound's religious movement a revolution of the poor, a "revolution of water-carriers, immigrants and slaves" (101) and to lend credence to this interpretation he invents the figures of Khalid the water-carrier, Salman the Persian immigrant, Bilal the slave and Baal the satirist as Mahound's disciples.

Rushdie bases his psycho-biography of Mohammed--his attempt as an artist to bring Mohammed's largely unknown inner life to expression, on two controversial incidents which he views as vital turning points in the prophet's life. Both incidents are shaped and expressed in terms of the antitheses which determine the structure of *The Satanic Verses*. These antitheses are: political intrigue versus spiritual purity; the fickleness and venality of the unconverted masses versus the unwavering vision of a great leader; the mockery of materialists and doubters and the submission of the faithful.

The two incidents are: the so-called satanic verses in Mahound's early years and his alleged twelve wives in his late years. It has been suggested that both incidents have been deliberately chosen by Rushdie to slander the origins of the Islamic religion. I consider this to be an unfair allegation which can be refuted by an objective textual analysis of the novel.

It must be noted that on the whole Mahound is not negatively depicted in *The Satanic Verses*. There is perhaps some ironic humour in the depiction of Mahound's surreal nocturnal wrestles with Archangel Gibreel (or Shaitan the devil) in the quest for a divine revelation, but this humour is the inevitable result of a rationalist writing about a religious miracle and could for example be compared with Thomas Mann's humorous evocation of Christian mythology in *Der Erwaehlte (The Holy Sinner)* and *Joseph und seine Brueder (Joseph and his Brothers)* and of Hindu mythology in *Die vertauschten Koepfe (The Transposed Heads).* Mann maintained that this humour resulted from the incongruous mingling of sacred myth with rational psychology and this point could be made with equal validity for Rushdie's humour. Certainly Jean Paul Sartre's attack on God and religion in *The Flies*, if we can take this example, has a vitriolic intensity which is quite lacking in Rushdie's *The Satanic Verses.*

There is no question of Mahound being depicted by Rushdie as cowardly, deceitful or hypocritical in his Recitation as the Messenger of Allah, just as there is no question of his being bloodthirsty in his rule over Jahilia or lecherous in his attitude towards women. On the contrary. He emerges as dedicated to his religious and legal revolution, courageous, resolute, prepared to face martyrdom, dignified and wise. He is shown as achieving the highest self-realization: that is, he is acknowledged both as the determined prophet of the monotheistic idea and also as the religious and secular leader of his people. Though Rushdie's work is undeniably irreverent about Islamic dogma, it is nevertheless positive, in human all too human terms, about our need for a guiding vision, whether mystic or moral.

The depiction of Mahound's achievements in *The Satanic Verses* is all the clearer if we compare and contrast Mahound with his character-foils in this novel. Rushdie lampoons himself and his profession as poet in the devious figures of Salman the Persian and Baal the satiric poet. Salman and Baal are seen as weak, treacherous and susceptible to the fleshpots. Their weakness is perceived to stem partly from their status as outcasts, from their inability to draw spiritual strength from solidarity with the faith and customs of community and homeland. Salman is an uprooted cosmopolitan in exile and Baal is so narcissistically in love with the cleverness of his verses that he has no concept of his own pitifulness.

There is a similar structural contrast between Mahound and the other lesser characters of the novel in the matter of sex. Mahound eschews the lechery of Hind and enters into his twelve marriages as a way of forging a statesmanlike confederation of the clans of Jahilia and Yathrib. By contrast Gibreel Farishta and Salahuddin Chamcha become hopelessly enmeshed in the intrigues of their lust, their dishonesty and their jealousy in other sections of the novel.

There is no question of Rushdie accusing Mahound of lechery. On the contrary. It is the satirist Baal and the brothel madam of Jahilia who try to undermine the authority of Mahound (and make some quick money) by dressing up twelve whores as facsimiles of Mahound's twelve wives. But Mahound protects the dignity of his Islamic revolution by having the whores stoned to death and Baal beheaded.

Mahound thus subordinates sexual desire and erotic love to his religious mission whereas Gibreel is guilty of self-indulgent promiscuity and subsequently descends into a hell of sexual jealousy and Salahuddin misuses sex and marriage as a way of escaping from being Indian and of gaining entry to British society. It is only when Salahuddin is rejected by his British wife Pamela and by the British people during the London race-riots that he slowly begins to realize that he must return to his family in Bombay in order to rediscover himself in a community of his own people.

It is also noticeable in these character contrasts that it is not Mahound who loses touch with the traditions of his homeland or the needs and directions of his people. It is Gibreel and Salahuddin. Gibreel commits childish and compulsive blasphemies against religious lore (after having made fame and fortune by the cheap commercial exploitation of theological movies for the masses) and Salahuddin intellectually denies the religion of his childhood in order to help make himself more British than the British. Their uprootedness is the source of their shallowness, their lack of commitment and their pusillanimity. Mahound on the other hand retains his roots in the traditions of his society even as he is transforming that society with his revolutionary idea. Mahound draws his inner strength and his sense of purpose partly from his inner vision and partly because he combines this revolutionary vision with his otherwise conservative and diplomatic leadership of his community.

Mahound's arch foe, Shaitan (Satan), on the other hand, suffers the eternal damnation of uprootedness, of not-belonging. Rushdie expresses this interpretation of Satan's suffering in the epigraph to *The Satanic Verses:*

> Satan, being thus confined to a vagabond, wandering, unsettled condition, is without any certain abode; for although he has, in consequence of his angelic nature, a kind of empire in the liquid waste or air, yet this is certainly part of his punishment, that he is . . . without any fixed place, or space, allowed him to rest the sole of his foot upon. (Daniel Defoe, *The History of the Devil)*

We have to ask ourselves why Rushdie chose this epigraph for his novel. Clearly this particular characterization of Satan as homeless and without community has to be reflected in the themes of *The Satanic Verses.* And so it is. In contrast to Satan, Mahound the prophet and Ayesha the saint retain their roots in their community at the same time as they are demanding a sacred revolution of its purpose. They have a fixed place to which they belong, namely Mecca (Jahilia) as the spiritual centre of Islam.

On the other hand neither Salahuddin, nor Gibreel, nor Salman the Persian nor even Baal the satirist have a fixed abode or a community to which they belong. As artists or intellectuals they are uprooted from their community and they suffer in the pride of their isolation. Salahuddin lives in self-imposed exile in England and scorns the community of his childhood in India: Salahuddin's metamorphosis as Satan with horns and tail is a symbolic expression of his being lost and damned as a homeless vagabond.

Gibreel abandons his movie-making community in Bombay and blasphemes against Islam by stuffing his face with pork. He suffers such delusions of grandeur in his uprootedness in England that he feels compelled to announce the Day of Judgement by blowing on a trumpet he has bought from a pawn shop. He is ridiculed and threatened with an insane asylum precisely because he has lost touch with his community. It is a sign of his uprootedness that he drives his Indian mistress, Rekha Merchant to infanticide and suicide and then subsequently destroys himself in his passion for the English woman Alleluia. Finally, there is Salman the Persian (a parodistic self-portrait in cameo by Rushdie) who is a slippery, devious immigrant from Persia, consumed by doubt and incapable of giving loyal, long-term support to any community.

All of these characters are represented negatively by Rushdie and all of them are contrasted with the triumphant life of Mahound. There also seems little doubt that Rushdie is giving ironic, part-projections of his own suffering in self-imposed exile when he depicts the sufferings of Salahuddin and Gibreel in England. This is why those parts of the novel set in 20th century England are satiric and grotesque, whereas the deeply moving, spiritual climax and conclusion of the novel are set in India. Rushdie is projecting a wish-fulfilment for himself in this climax and conclusion, namely his desire to escape from self-imposed exile, from the very lack of belonging to a community, with which he characterizes the punishment of Satan.

Another way to prove the spirituality of *The Satanic Verses* is to examine the function of the various satanic verses which function as a leitmotif in the structure of the novel. Let us therefore now examine the quite separate satanic verses of the slimy, professional versemaker Baal in 7th century Arabia, of the blasphemous and obscene Salahuddin Chamcha in the late 20th century London, and of atheistic Mirza Saeed in the late 20th century Western India.

In the plot of *The Satanic Verses* cowardly Baal is blackmailed by the Grandee of Jahilia, Abu Simbel. Baal is hired to belittle Mahound the Messenger's proclamation of Allah and monotheism. Baal chooses to ridicule Mahound's religious movement as a ludicrous "revolution of water-carriers, immigrants and slaves." (101) Baal writes the facile satire of a propagandist:

> Messenger, do please lend a careful ear. Your monophilia, your one one one, ain't for Jahilia. Return to sender. (106)

But Baal's mockery is of no real significance. He is too spiteful and petty to comprehend a positive vision and he represents only the licentious whoredom of Jahilia. Mahound struggles against far more powerful foes and conquers a much more insidious temptation. The Grandee of Jahilia offers to deliver to him the religious allegiance of every soul in the city if he will compromise his monotheistic idea and publicly recognize the ancient trio of goddesses, Al-Lat and Uzza and Manat as also worthy of worship. Mahound wrestles in agony all night on deserted Mount Cone seeking truth from a being whom he wrongly identifies as the Archangel Gibreel. He returns to Jahilia the next day in order to announce his political compromise in the contentious Satanic verses. Mahound is so determined that his proclamation of monotheistic Allah should emerge from obscurity and ignominy that he fails to realize until later that he has been lured into compromising the purity of his revolutionary idea. Temporarily he wrongly believes the verses to be the word of God speaking through Gibreel. When he perceives the political and theological enormity of his error, he retracts these verses as the work of Shaitan (Satan) and returns to the purity of his idea of monotheism.

Moslem fundamentalists regard the allegations about Mohammed succumbing temporarily to compromise and announcing *The Satanic Verses* of Al-lat and Uzza and Manat as both historically unverifiable and slanderous of the divine origins of the Koran.[8] This is understandable insofar as pious Moslems are entitled to regard Mohammed's sacred Recitation in the same reverential light as Christians regard the Gospel of Jesus. And look how passionately devout Christians reacted to Martin Scorsese's film *The Last Temptation of Christ* (based on Nikos Kazantzakis's novel of the same name) in which Jesus was portrayed as having an all too human sexual weakness for Mary Magdalene.[9] These protests by religious fundamentalists in Christianity and in Islam raise the unsolved socio-political issue of the sanctity of faith on the one hand and on the other hand the right to freedom of speech and freedom of belief which are essential if a multicultural society is to protect itself from domination by a single Church or a single creed.

From the point of view of creating Mahound as a great hero with a slight, human flaw, *The Satanic Verses* is splendid writing. If Rushdie had eulogized his fictional simulacrum of Mohammed as a plaster saint, this would hardly have been of interest to any but the most devout Moslem. In an electrifying scene in the poets's tent in Jahilia, Mahound announces his satanic verses: "They (Al-Lat, Uzza and Manat) are the exalted birds, and their intercession is desired indeed." (114-15)

This scene is electrifying precisely because we realize that the puritanical but otherworldly Mahound has made the mistake of compromising his faith for a short-term political advantage. He has been successfully tempted. It appears at first as though Mahound's political compromise has been overwhelmingly successful when first the Grandee and Hind, and then the entire population of Jahilia, make their obeisance to Allah. But this is a hollow victory and is contrasted with the scalding tears of shame shed by Mahound's most faithful disciple, the humble water-carrier Khalid. (115) Khalid senses and we the readers know that the revolutionary power of an idea can only be maintained if the idea is kept pure and uncompromised.

We feel the despair and yet also the fierce determination of Mahound to wipe out this false step as he trudges through the desert in order to wrestle on the mountain with Archangel Gibreel in pursuit of a renewed revelation from God. We are enthralled by the courage shown by Mahound when he returns to Jahilia and delivers a public abrogation of the Satanic verses. (124) At this moment, even for unbelievers, Mahound becomes a true hero. This is the stuff of inspiring fiction, inspiring regardless of whether or not the incidents are historically verifiable.

The leitmotif of the satanic verses re-occurs in two other passages in this novel in quite separate contexts. The main character of the novel, Salahuddin Chamcha, concocts "little, satanic verses" (445) in order to take an obscene revenge on the man who has betrayed him, his fellow Anglo-Indian actor, Gibreel Farishta. Gibreel is suffering through bouts of insanity (schizophrenia dementia), believing himself to be the Archangel Gibreel (Gabriel) and also sick with the crazy jealousy of an Othello for his mistress, Alleluia Cone. Salahuddin makes anonymous phone calls to him, whispering obscene jingles such as:

> When she's down at Waterloo
> She don't wear no yes she do
> When she's up at Leicester Square
> She don't wear no underwear (445)

This trivial jingle is satanic in its context because it represents the betrayal of friendship and a fiendish determination by Salahuddin to exploit Gibreel's mental sickness and thus destroy both his love and his sanity. Salahuddin has become the voice of the Devil, just as Baal had before him. In the spiritual mythology that determines the narrative structure of *The Satanic Verses*, it is highly significant that at the end of the novel Gibreel rewards Salahuddin's evil with kindness. He saves Salahuddin from certain death in the fiery furnace of London's race riots. Salahuddin is therefore not punished according to the Old Testament idea of an eye for an eye and a tooth for a tooth. Instead he is saved by Gibreel's mercy and forgiveness.

There is a similar structural pattern on the third and final occasion when the satanic verses re-appear in this novel. The verses are spoken by atheist and village leader, Mirza Saeed Akhtar. Mirza has been following a dedicated group of faithful Muslim foot-pilgrims (his former villagers and his wife who is dying of cancer) in his Mercedes-Benz. The pilgrims are inspired and led by a beautiful teenage girl called Ayesha. Naked Ayesha has been blessed with a miraculous garment of living butterflies. Her only food is butterflies. A cloud of butterflies points the way for the foot-pilgrims to Mecca (an Islamic Padyatra, 489). The pilgrims have been assured by Ayesha that the waters of the Arabian Sea will part in a miracle which will enable them to walk to Mecca. The mythical parallels with Moses leading the Jews out of Egypt and into the Promised Land are clear. Indeed Ayesha is called "Bibiji--the name of the long ago saint" (482) and refers to herself as "a messenger" (483) in a mythical echo of Mohammed as the Messenger of Allah.

As part of his tempting of these pilgrims, Mirza undermines their faith in their odyssey by telling them tales, tales which implicitly parallel their saintly leader Ayesha with the evil enchantress Circe. Circe bewitched people and turned them into pigs, he tells the pilgrims. He also implicitly identifies Ayesha with the vengeful Pied Piper of Hamelin "who lured a town's children into a mountain-crack" (484) whereupon they were never seen again. He then quotes Browning's poem about the Pied Piper and the verses become Satanic in the new context of the smearing and slandering of Ayesha as a contemporary Pied Piper who is destroying the lives of a whole village by luring them on this senseless pilgrimage.

> Hamelin town's in Brunswick
> near famous Hanover City.
> The River Weser, deep and wide,
> washes the walls on the southern side. . . (484)

These are the verses with which Mirza Saeed begins his propaganda, tempting the villagers to give up this painful madness and to return to their deserted village. To this implied slander artfully disguised as entertainment for pilgrims a la Canterbury Tales, Ayesha responds in anguish:

> Those who listen to the Devil's verses, spoken in the Devil's

tongue . . . will go to the Devil in the end. (484)

Later in the novel Ayesha provides a magnificent, spiritual climax when she leads her pilgrims through flood and a Hindu mob's sectarian violence to the Arabian Sea. Her pilgrimage is a strange anachronism in our age of cynicism, materialism and irreligionist. Irresolute followers who have deviated from Ayesha's strict leadership are left floundering and almost drowning in the Arabian Sea, but the select bank of faithful pilgrims is seen by the rejects walking serenely along the bottom of the Arabian Sea towards Mecca. It is a haunting vision of the certainty of faith.

In a mythical (and structural) echo of Mahound the Messenger, Ayesha answers the leitmotif question:

> *"What kind of idea are you?"* with the response of the pure at heart
> *"I was tempted, but am renewed; an uncompromising; absolute;, pure."* (500)

In a glorious coda to this supernatural tale of Ayesha--a coda which is nothing if not mystical--Mirza Saeed the atheist and Satanic tempter is forgiven and accorded salvation at the hour of his death by fire. His beloved Ayesha steps "miraculously out of his wife's body." (506-7) Mirza's rationalism and materialism, which have made him proud and have closed him off from the community of the humble, are overcome at the moment of death by the force of his erotic love for Ayesha. But secular love is here miraculously transformed into caritative love in a scene that has mythical overtones of Gretchen's intercession for sinful Faust at the end of Goethe's cosmic drama *Faust II*. The lines with which this miracle is expressed in *The Satanic Verses* are a model for the powerful expression of a spiritual epiphany without melodrama:

> He was a fortress with clanging gates.--He was drowning.--She was drowning, too. He saw the water fill her mouth, heard it begin to gurgle into her lungs. Then something within him refused that, made a different choice, and at the instant that his heart broke, he opened. His body split apart from his adam's-apple to his groin, so that she could reach deep within him, and now she was open, they all were, and at the moment

> of their opening the waters parted, and they walked to Mecca across the bed of the Arabian Sea. (507)

These lines constitute one of the stylistic and spiritual climaxes of *The Satanic Verses* and proclaim Rushdie as a mystic. But if this novel is a work of mystic vision, why has Rushdie given it the title of *The Satanic Verses*? The title is an open invitation to misinterpret the work and to claim that it is a work of vanity, a work of Shaitan the devil (cf. Gibreel's definition of a novel as a pact with the devil [459]), potentially as wrong-headed as the verses of Baal, the theological error of Mahound the Messenger, and the temptation of Ayesha by Mirza Saeed? Certainly the title has sensational value, but then Rushdie hardly needs to adopt such commercial tactics when he is already acknowledged as one of the greatest living authors in the world today.

I believe that the title is deeply related to one of the great themes of the novel. This theme is that there is no re-birth or reincarnation without first experiencing death. There is no idea which can claim absoluteness and purity without first having undergone the temptation of Shaitan. There is no faith, no love and no salvation which can claim to be genuine which has not suffered the agony induced by the lure of the satanic verses. Rushdie hints at the hell through which he has suffered in conceiving and writing this masterpiece about humankind's contradictory yearning both for individual freedom and also for salvation, both for an independent quest for truth and also for loyal commitment to a community. We should not be deceived by the novel's irreverence and playfulness. This is a serious and ultimately a tragic work.

Gibreel, for example, who has lived through hell several times over--having been through the experiences of denying Allah, of dying and being reborn in a mythical fall, of deluding himself that he has been reincarnated as the Archangel Gibreel, of recognizing that he is afflicted with schizophrenia dementia and is ravaged by uncontrollable fits of Othello-type jealousy--Gibreel can find no release from the sickness of his life except in suicide.

In suicide Gibreel atones for having driven his Indian mistress, Rekha Merchant, to her hideous child-murder and self-destruction at the beginning of the novel, and for having repeated this crime at the end of the novel by pushing his loyal lover, Alleluia, to her death from the very same building. The erotic passion of Rekha,

Gibreel and Alleluia could of course be analyzed as farce, but even if so, it is farce which culminates in tragedy. The tragedy is not contained in the physical deaths, but in Gibreel's last haunting confession that he is incurably insane and that he has murdered the one person who has loved him loyally in spite of everything. It is Rushdie's linguistic mastery that transforms this confession into tragedy (see pp. 544-45). Rushdie is able to adapt his style to express from the inside Gibreel's horror at himself and his unbearable remorse. Gibreel's suicide brings him release from the torments of insanity and guilt, but it is a release without transcendence.

The question is: does Gibreel's co-actor in this cosmic drama of earthly love, spiritual love, archangels and deluded devils,--in short this contemporary recreation of Goethe's *Faust*--does Salahuddin himself find salvation and transcendence in the concluding pages of *The Satanic Verses?* Certainly he expects to be murdered by Gibreel for having driven Gibreel back into insanity with his obscene, satanic jingles and he does not find this "death-sentence unjust." (546) But first through the forgiving kindness of Gibreel and then through the enduring love of his dying father, Salahuddin gets another chance in life. Finally he is loved and encouraged to join in a community of intellectual communists by his Indian mistress, Zeenat Vakil. These moments of love and forgiveness at the conclusion of *The Satanic Verses* are the moral climaxes of the novel and the epiphanies of the work as tragedy.

Zeenat Vakil inspires the proud, self-seeking Salahuddin to repent. To repent of his toadying to England and of his denial of his own true self in scorning the people and the customs of India. Zeenat inspires Salahuddin to join in a human chain that stretches across Bombay in a peaceful Communist Party demonstration of people's communal love and concern. The human chain is ignored by the capitalist mass media of India as unworthy of reporting. But the community which the stand-offish Salahuddin finds in this demonstration--a community with a very different faith and a very different ideology from Mahound and Islam--is nevertheless meant to provide a structural parallel in the novel with the community of the Moslem foot-pilgrims which the likewise stand-offish Mirza is finally permitted to join at the moment of his death through the mystic intercession of the saint Ayesha.

*The Satanic Verses* is about the damnation of self-seeking

pride and uprootedness and about the romantic salvation that is, in an utopian sense, to be found in the communal faith, commitment and resoluteness of the humble. Those who have "closed themselves off"--to use Salman Rushdie's metaphor--punish themselves in the hell of their isolation. Those who "open themselves up" to love and community, are on a self-challenging pilgrimage to heaven. Salman Rushdie is a free-thinking mystic.

## NOTES

1. See John Leonard, *Australian Left Review*, No 110, May/June 1989, p. 36.
2. See Robert Haupt, *Sydney Morning Herald*, 4 March 1989. Contrast Shipp's argument for the "sanctity and security of life, social harmony, tolerance and protection from unjustifiable discrimination." George Shipp, "The Rushdie Affair--The importance of being consistent," *The Current Affairs Bulletin*, April 1989, vol. 65, no. 11, p. 30.
3. The yearlong debate is thoroughly summarized from all points of view in the excellent anthology, *The Rushdie File*, ed. Lisa Appinganesi and Sara Maitland (Syracuse University Press, 1990).
4. Rushdie, *Observer*, 22 January 1989. As quoted in *The Rushdie File*, p. 62.
5. Moslem protests quoted in *The Rushdie File* range from the Fatwa of the Ayatollah Khomeini and the book-burning by the Moslem communities of Britain to the more measured response of Dr Ali A. Mazrui (who nevertheless compares *The Satanic Verses* with *Mein Kampf!)* to defences of the freedom of literature by Fadia A. Faquir and Egyptian Nobel Prize winner Naguib Mafouz.
6. Salman Rushdie, *The Satanic Verses* (Viking, 1988), p. 459.
7. See especially such impassioned defences of *The Satanic Verses* as those by Carlos Fuentes and Michael Foot in *The Rushdie File*.
8. Patrick Parrinder claims that "the majority of Western translations of the Islamic scriptures argue that the Koran as a whole is a forgery." *The London Review of Books*, 19.09.88, p. 11.

9. Garry Wills ridicules Christians who claimed that Scorsese's film *The Last Temptation of Christ* was blasphemous. *The New York Review of Books*, 13.10.88, pp. 8-10.

# Migration and the Human Spirit in Salman Rushdie's *The Satanic Verses*

DAVID KERR

Salman Rushdie's *The Satanic Verses* has had more critical attention than generally occurs within the first year from publication, mostly owing to the political and personal crisis the work has provoked. John Leonard, for example, has said of *The Satanic Verses*, that it

> is one of those go-for-broke "metafictions"--a grand narrative and a Monty Python send-up of history, religion and popular culture; Hindu cyclic and Moslem dualistic; post-colonial identity crisis and modernist pastiche; Bombay Bombast and stiff-upper-liposuction; babu baby-talk and ad agency neologism; cinema gossip, elephant masks, pop jingles, lousy puns, kinky sex . . . which the sly-boots Author-God tip-and-twinkletoes away with a cannibal grin.[1]

Rushdie's latest novel is both breathless and breath-taking as it jousts with History, Time, language and the foundations of religion--specifically Islam, though the challenge he mounts has wider application. Peter Craven, in his defence of the beleagured Rushdie, speaks of "its intermingling of surrealist and fabulist strains, the confident rhetoric of its 'magic realism'."[2] In his *Scripsi* article Craven is concerned to examine whether the offence taken by Muslims has a substantial basis in the text. Consequently, he concentrates his attention on the overtly Muslim passages, commenting almost as an afterthought, "The novel is least successful where it presents myth usurping the modern foreground of Thatcher's Britain."[3]

Possibly. There are certainly moments when invention flags.

Yet the miracle is that Rushdie has invented a shape that accommodates wildly divergent materials--the fantastic worlds of Bombay, London and Jahilia, the city of sand, and the Indian village of Titlipur. His underlying theme is migration, specifically as it affects Indians and Pakistanis in London, and more generally as it affects the spirit of mankind. The starting point for Rushdie's fiction has generally been his own life, considered as *representative* of the lives of Modern Indians. In this case the specific stimulus was that of being an Indian immigrant, destined to carry the whole baggage of the ancient modern subcontinent into inner London, where one perforce lives in a permanent state of seize among the bigoted tribe of Thatcherite England.

It is a tall order, giving *prima facie* substance to Leonard's charge that, "Somewhere along the line . . . Rushdie lost control of his novel." (36) So perhaps this writer will be excused for following the path of oversimplification in the hope that in so doing the underlying structure of the work may be revealed. I must emphasize that I am not adopting a merely sociological view of migration. In Rushdie's work migration becomes symbolic of the human condition. It is historically true that Rushdie was himself a migrant, first (unwillingly) from Bombay to Karachi, subsequently from Pakistan to London. While the personal element in this writing is heavily disguised through the blending of the mythic and fantastic into the real world, central experiences in his life keep pushing through, in the process being transformed to expose new possibilities.

I propose to concentrate on *The Satanic Verses*, in which I want to argue that the structure of narrative has been determined by metaphor. A note on his two earlier novels may illustrate the point. Take, for example, the death of Saladin Chamcha's mother in *The Satanic Verses* and compare it with what appears to be the equivalent incident in *Midnight's Children*. In *Midnight's Children* he writes:

> But I was still in the street in the midnight shadow of the mosque when it came, plummeting towards the illuminated windows of my father's idiocy, death whining like pie-dogs, transforming itself into falling masonry and sheets of flame and a wave of force so great . . . [that] . . . within the house of my aunt's great bitterness my father mother aunt and unborn

> brother or sister who was only a week from starting life, all of them all of them squashed flatter than rice pancakes.[4]

The loss of the mother-figure in *The Satanic Verses* is altogether different, taking the form of bathos rather than the tragic liberation experienced by Saleem.

> That night, for the last time, Saladin Chamchawala played his old role of doorman, dressed up in an English dinner-jacket, and when the guests came--the same old guests--. . . . They were all trying to hide their fear of the war, *dangers of air-raids*, the radio said. . . .
>
> Late that evening the sirens sang and the guests ran for cover, hiding under beds, in cupboards, anywhere. Nasreen Chamchawala found herself alone by a food-laden table, and attempted to reassure the company by standing there . . . munching a piece of fish as if nothing were the matter. So it was that when she started choking on the fishbone of her death there was nobody to help her . . . even Saladin, conqueror of kippers . . . had lost his nerve. Nasreen Chamchawala fell, twitched, gasped, died, and when the all-clear sounded the guests emerged sheepishly to find their hostess extinct in the middle of the dining room . . . finished off for no reason, gone for good. (46)

The prose tumbles and runs as before, always threatening to collapse under its own complications. But the long sentences (Rushdie must surely average much higher than the "seven to eleven word sentence" that Mulk Raj Anand refers to in the first number of *The Commonwealth Review* [p. 13]) have a cooler quality in *The Satanic Verses* than in *Midnight's Children*. Rushdie has distanced himself from his circumstances, and to an extent has replaced the sense of shocked horror of the earlier book with bizarre comedy in which it seems that human pain is somewhere else.

However, it is the treatment of migration across the three works that best illustrates the transformation that is occurring. Migration, let me concede, is not a central issue in *Midnight's Children*, despite reference to the largest single migration the world has ever known. (357) In *Shame*, however, the pain of forced transitions finds its way into a significant explicatory passage:

> I, too, know something of this immigrant business. I am an emigrant from one country (India) and a newcomer in two (England, where I live, and Pakistan, to which my family moved against my will). And I have a theory that the resentments we *mohajirs* engender have something to do with our conquest of the force of gravity. We have performed the act of which all men anciently dream, the thing for which they envy the birds; that is to say, we have flown.
>
> I am comparing gravity with belonging. Both phenomena observably exist: my feet stay on the ground, and I have never been angrier than I was on the day my father told me he had sold my childhood home in Bombay. But neither is understood. We know the force of gravity, but not its origins: and to explain why we become attached to our birthplaces we pretend we are trees and speak of roots. . . .
>
> The anti-myths of gravity and of belonging bear the same name: flight. . . . To fly and to flee: both are ways of seeking freedom. . . .
>
> When individuals come unstuck from their native land they are called migrants. . . . What is the best thing about migrant peoples. . . .? I think it is their hopefulness. . . . We have come unstuck from more than the land. We have floated upwards from history, from memory, from Time.
>
> I may be such a person.[5]

This passage acts as a precursor for the opening of *The Satanic Verses*, where two men, Gibreel Farishta and Saladin Chamcha, fall from the sky (a terrorist bomb has exploded in a place) and make a soft landing in snowy marshes near Hastings, England. The symbol has been given flesh, set in motion!

For an Indian migrant to live in Thatcher's England calls for a deliberate act of continuous recreation. As Gibreel Farishta sings, floating, with the gift of anti-gravity, to earth on the opening page of the novel, "To be born again . . . first you have to die." From that point on the writing conjures with the transformations in both Farishta's and Chamcha's lives. Farishta, Bombay film actor, plays Deities, and when at the height of his fame, suffers an illness where he oozes blood. He attempts to bargain with God for his life, only to conclude that "he was talking to *thin air*, that there was nobody there at all." (30) His recovery comes when he reaches the point "that he no longer needed there to be anything to feel." (30)

Chamcha's transformations are, to begin, more in the realm of social and physical possibility. His background closely parallels Rushdie's own--Bombay youth, English education, living "without a god of any type," and determined to become "the thing his father was-not-could-never-be, that is, a goodandproper Englishman." (43) He creates himself by a deliberate act of will, thus becoming "unnatural, a blasphemer, an abomination of abominations. . . . Or consider him sociopolitical: most migrants learn, and can become disguises. Our own false descriptions to counter the falsehoods invented about us." (49)

This note recurs throughout the novel, acting as a kind of touchstone for the transformations that take place in its pages. When Saladin is picked up by the immigration officers he has become transformed into a goat-like creature. How does it happen? The manticore explains it to Chamcha: "They describe us. . . . That's all. They have the power of description, and we succumb to the pictures they construct." (168)

However, there is a deeper spiritual question implied in the separation from the father which emigration completes. Rushdie links the separation from the physical father and the loss of faith in him with his loss of belief in the invisible God. He also charges his father with the denial of history and the stopping of time, the same charges that he levels at the Imam (a caricature of the Ayatollah Khomeini). To his father he says, "*I accuse him of inverting Time.*" (41) That is, by sending his son to England after India has achieved independence and escaped that influence of the Raj, his father forces him to return to the womb that nurtured that world.

At the same time he is at odds with India, a country which, as the fictional poet, Bhupen Ghandi says, must face the fact that its deepest shame is of its own making--"We are all guilty of Assam. . . . Each person of us. Unless and until we face it, that the children's deaths were our fault, we cannot call ourselves a civilized people." (56)

The underlying question here is the same one which faces all migrants, who by definition are seekers, searchers for the truth about themselves, about life. On what do I base my sense of worth? How do I place a value on my soul, when on all sides I am devalued and debased. The contemporary social significance of the migrant in London gains universal significance in the novel through two lines of connected development--the exploration of the relationship between Good and Evil, and the search for a sense of personal worth, each of which becomes implicated in the dramatization of the mythological foundations of Islam.

The problem of accounting for the existence of Evil lies buried, so Rushdie seems to suggest, in the mystery of the human heart. The story of Saladin Chamcha and Gibreel Farishta, both masters of disguise and consequently out of touch with their individual reality, shows evil arising from a core of dissociated feeling. For example, each betrays the other and each has the opportunity to save the other. Chamcha uses his skill at adopting disguised voices to fuel the jealousy simmering between Gibreel Farishta and his wife Alleluia Cone. His action springs, so he tells himself, from resentment felt when Gibreel Farishta did nothing when he was arrested by the immigration officers. Neither, in the end, is absolved from evil, for as the novelist says: "Let's rather say an even harder thing: that evil may not be as far beneath the surface as we like to say it is.--That, in fact, we fall towards it *naturally*." (427)

Rushdie's fictional version of the foundation of Islam is designed to give an historical dimension to his enquiry by sheeting home the awkward question of responsibility to its source. He pursues the ambiguity at the heart of Gibreel's revelations to Mahound--seeking to uncover the key to differentiating the good from evil in one's own soul. Islam, to Gibreel, appears to offer clarity--that, at any rate, is what he wants to believe. Hence Gibreel's challenge to England, which offers "ambiguities, . . . Biblical-Satanic confusions" (353) which he proposes to strip away by creating a hotter climate without fogs!

It may be necessary to point out to western readers that, if one sets aside the dramatic reconstruction of Mahomet's personal life, Rushdie has drawn the main elements of theological controversy from versions of the Quran known to have existed. For example, Mahomet's concession to heathenism, the recognition of the exalted virgins, Al-Lat, al-'Uzza and Manat, is explicitly stated in a version of the Quran quoted by Alfred Guillaume,[6] but appears in a different form in the version of the Quran translated by N. J. Dawood for Pelican Classics. Rushdie quotes the initial verses--the supposed "Satanic Verses" and the repudiation. The justification for Rushdie's concern may also be found in the Quran (22:51):

> Never have We sent a single prophet or apostle before you with whose wishes Satan did not tamper. But Allah abrogates the interjections of Satan and confirms His own revelations. . . . He makes Satan's interjections a temptation for those whose hearts are diseased or hardened. . . . Allah will surely guide the faithful to a straight path.
>
> Yet the unbelievers will never cease to doubt it until the Hour of Doom overtakes them unawares or the scourge of the Woeful Day descends upon them.[7]

Rushdie pushes the issue back a step further from Prophet to Archangel, by creating in the dream-world of Gibreel Farishta an archangel who knows "one small detail, just one tiny thing that's bit of a problem here, namely that *it was me both times, baba, me first and second also me*. From my mouth, both the statement and the repudiation, verses and converses, universes and reverses, the whole thing, and we all know how my mouth got worked." (123)

The historical repudiation of the Satanic Verses led to Mahomet being forced to leave Mecca and seek sanctuary elsewhere, and, after a time be invited to Medina by a group of pilgrims who had heard him preach. The migration is equally important to Rushdie, for in addition to being part of history, it chimes in with his underlying theme of migration and loss of identity in alien societies.

In Jahilia Rushdie has created a symbolic city, based on the historical Mecca, which is offered implicitly as both contrast and parallel with modern London.

> The city of Jahilia is built entirely of sand, its structures formed of the desert whence it rises. It is a sight to wonder at: walled, four-gated, the whole of the miracle worked by its citizens, who have learned the trick of transforming the fine white dune-sand of the forsaken parts,--the very stuff of inconstancy,--the quintessence of unsettlement, shifting, treachery, lack-of-form,--and have turned it, by alchemy, into the fabric of their newly invented permanence. These people are a mere three or four generations removed from their nomadic past, when they were as rootless as the dunes, or rather rooted in the knowledge that the journeying itself

> was home.
>
> Whereas the migrant can do without the journey altogether; it's no more than a necessary evil; the point is to arrive. (93-94)

The comparison between Jahilia and London is that both are effectively entrepots; the contrast, that one has managed to transform the stuff of impermanence (sand) into permanence, whereas the other (London) is unfocussed until Gibreel turns up the heat. At that point the forces of evil are unleashed, just as they are in Jahilia when Mahound repudiates *The Satanic Verses*--"The lion is loose. Peace will have to wait." (116) At the climax of the passage we read: "Djinns, houris, demons populate the city on this night of phantasmagoria and lust." (117) The parallel with London during the fires and riots at Brickhall (a name hinting falsely at solidity and stability) is clear.

> Fire, falling fire. 'This is the judgement of God in his wrath,' Gibreel Farishta proclaims to the riotous night. . . .
>
> The towers stand up on stilts, and in the concrete formlessness beneath and between there is the howling of a perpetual wind, and the eddying of debris. . . . [In response to Gibreel's trumpet]. . . . Little buds of flame spring up on the concrete, fuelled by discarded heaps of possessions and dreams. There is a little rotting pile of envy: it burns greenly in the night. (461-62)

In this passage Farishta dreams that he is the avenging angel, Azreel, the scourge of evil. At the climax of the passage he is confronted by the "arch-friend," Saladin Chamcha, pinned by a beam in a collapsed building, and threatened with imminent immolation. The question that poses itself is: "*When your enemies are at your mercy: how will you act then*?" (467)

As it turns out, the Farishta who vowed he was finished with England-induced ambiguities chooses to rescue the arch-fiend, Saladin Chamcha, his "old chumch." As Rushdie rhetorically asks, "Does he have a choice?" The answer is presented as a "small redeeming victory for love"--but not, I suspect, for clarity! In the end the ironies redouble. Chamcha, who resents Farishta's inaction as the immigration police drag him off, is powerless to prevent a distraught Farishta from blowing his brains out.

> *He's hidden a gun inside*, Salahuddin remembered. "*What is your wish? I am the slave who holds the lamp.*" What a limiting thing is a weapon, Salahuddin thought, feeling oddly detached from events.--Like Gibreel when the sickness came.--Yes, indeed; a most confining manner of thing. . . . How the universe had shrunk! The true djinns of old had the power to open the gates of the Infinite, to make all things possible . . . how banal, in comparison, was this modern spook. (546)

Chamcha's modern scepticism ventures nothing at the critical moment, whereas in Chamcha's own extremity Farishta assumes the powers of the djinns by causing the smoke to divide like the waters of the Arabian Sea, providing Chamcha a pathway to salvation. The generosity of his act is underlined by his realization, not moments earlier, that Chamcha of the many voices has been the source of his jealous fury against Alleluia Cone, that he is totally evil--"now there is nothing left of Saladin but this, the dark fire of evil in his soul, consuming him as wholly as the other fire . . . is devouring the screaming city." (463)

But it is this totally evil man who risks his life to save the lives of others he imagines to be threatened by the fire, causing Rushdie to write: "Is it possible that evil is never total, that its victory, no matter how overwhelming, is never absolute?" (467) His action, let it be said, is unreflective, impulsive, which is not characteristic of the "translated man,"[8] Saladin Chamcha. Gibreel, on the other hand, is untranslated, and as John McLaren points out, he is not the author of his own narrative. Except, perhaps, at this one critical point when he has the power--when the choice is his alone!

Because of Farishta's miraculous exhalation:

> the fire [parts] . . . like the red sea it had become . . . until there lies before them a clear pathway to the door;--whereupon Gibreel Farishta steps quickly forward, bearing Saladin along the pathway to forgiveness into the hot night air; so that on a night when the city is at war, a night heavy with enmity and rage, there is a small redeeming victory for love.

(468)

The Fall which opens the novel has ironically led to redemption for the undeserving Chamcha and self-destruction for the tortured Angel, Gibreel Farishta. The one who is destroyed has been beset by visionary delusions throughout--"It was so it was not in a time long forgot" (544)--whereas the other has remained sceptical, with agnosticism largely undisturbed by the ambiguous last moments before his father's death: chilled by the "dawning terror," reassured by the final smile. (531)

They are, as Rushdie points out early, an ambiguous pair--perhaps, from the spiritual point of view best considered as the two halves of one whole. He refers to them as--"Gibreelsaladin Farishtachamcha, condemned to this endless but also ending angelicdevilish fall," (5) thereby underlining the complex unity of life in which all the elements mutate to produce both beauty and terror, indeed, every quality and its opposite.

Or is it unity? The novel argues that point, as it does most central issues, several ways. For example, Otto Cone (Alleluia's father), rejects totally the suggestion that it all "adds up." (295) He argues for the incompatibility of life's elements, yet his daughter found that, when on Everest, "her father's daemon sounded banal, emptied of meaning." (296) His suicide at the age of seventy-plus, jumping into an empty lift-shaft is offered as reconfirming the possibility that great evil eventually triumphs--a possibility denied elsewhere.

The novel, then, consists of a merging of opposites. The migrant, imprisoned under the beam of public contempt, has nevertheless a larger, more complex view of his place in history, which is paradoxically liberating. The mutations through which Chamcha and Farishta pass are inherently unstable, as are the moral categories that might be applied in judging them. Chamcha descends to goatishness and emerges from it, but essentially lives within history, making up faces to fit prevailing circumstances: Farishta becomes angelic and suffers unwillingly from delusions of God-like power through which he both traverses and fashions history. By the novel's end he has acquired the sulphurous breath that denotes satanic contamination. Why? Possibly because he has abandoned the clarity of vision that Islam seems to suggest is available to us through the Prophet's teachings. Ironically, the redemptive act quoted above leads on to life for Chamcha, who has been humanized by hate, and self-inflicted death for Farishta, burdened as he is by the consequences of the fires of envy that were fanned in him by Chamcha's malevolent spite!

It is a fantastic world we live in, yet the novel in the end insists that the one we occupy, despite its bizarre and incompatible elements, somehow conveys to our collective unconscious what its natural limits are. We might be tormented by the problem of mortality, intrigued and baffled by the nature of good and evil, teased by the line dividing reality from illusion, we can imagine monstrous worlds, such as the nonsense of the *Aliens Show*, but we are never in real danger of believing them. We are alienated from our world, but not *that* alienated!

The difficult illusions are the ones that impinge on our Faith. No-one confuses the act of burning the waxen image of Thatcher (a three nights a week event at a certain waxworks) with destroying either the person or the "ism" she represents. Wish-fulfilment, it may be; actuality it is not.

The line becomes blurred with the migration of the village of Titlipur to the Arabian Sea where the miracle of the parting of the waters is to take place. Some claimed to see the event take place, others saw nothing.

> This was the testimony of Sarapanch of Titlipur, Muhammad Din: "Just when my strength had failed and I thought I would surely die, I saw it with my own eyes; I saw the sea divide, like hair being combed; and they were all there, far away, walking away from me." (504)

The final image of part VIII shows Mirza Saeed Aktar, who has denied the vision, at the point of death moving from his closed fortress state to the state of open acceptance of--even joy in death, which is replicated by the death of Chamcha's father in the final stages of the novel. For him the waters finally open.

> His body split apart from his adam's apple to his groin, so that she could reach deep within him, and now she was open, they all were, and at the moment of their opening the waters parted, and they walked to Mecca across the bed of the Arabian Sea. (507)

We are all migrants then, on a journey to death and self-discovery. The novel charts the perils of the journey, testing the stances taken by sceptics and believers of various kinds. Meaning is layered on meaning, image on image, structure on structure, linking past with present, east with west, suggesting an imponderable, shared destiny. The point is to choose a pathway, minute by minute. The problems involved in making choices are manifest and unavoidable. There is no blueprint, which is not to say that choice is a matter of indifference. On the contrary, the absence of precise rules for living places a heavier responsibility on each individual to live authentically--no matter how difficult that might be.

That is Chamcha's problem. He is acutely aware how much he lacks in the power to focus attention--probably because the self he has fashioned is artificially made in response to circumstances. When he returns to his dying father he feels "hourly closer to many old, rejected selves, many alternative Saladins--or rather Salahuddins--which had split off from himself as he made his various life choices." (523)

He too must open to his centre--his real world--which is not the world of fairy-tales. Yet in rejecting the visionary element in life by imputing childishness to it, as he does on the last page of the novel, this reader feels he has one journey still to make. In turning his back on the transformation of death--the last migration--and embracing life, he has done what he must do--as well as postponing what he must meet. When he cries out that the past must be bulldozed if need be to allow the future to emerge he is expressing his frustration at what he sees as the constraining influence of traditional values. His aggressive gesture, however, gives him away. He is only open to part of his future.

## NOTES

1. John Leonard, "Satanic Versions," *Australian Left Review*, 110, May-June 1989, p. 32.
2. Peter Craven, "Salman Rushdie, No Parenthesis," *Scripsi*, Vol. 5, no. 4, April 1989, p. 19
3. Salman Rushdie, *The Satanic Verses* (London: Viking, 1988),

p. 31

4. Salman Rushdie, *Midnight's Children* (London: Picador, 1982), p. 342.
5. Salman Rushdie, *Shame* (London: Jonathan Cape, 1983), pp. 86-87.
6. Alfred Guillaume, *Islam* (Harmondsworth: Penguin, 1954), p. 35.
7. *The Koran*, trans. N. J. Dawood (Harmondsworth: Penguin, 1956), p. 405.
8. John McLaren, "The Power of the Word: Salman Rushdie's *Satanic Verses*," *Commonwealth Studies Conference Paper*, Singapore, November, 1989 (copy on loan to the author).

# Tradition and Tragedy: Anita Desai and R.K. Narayan

PAUL SHARRAD

Compared to the more familiar writings of R.K. Narayan, Anita Desai's novels may seem both odd and depressing. Critical responses to the former have tended to emphasize the charming comedy of his traditionally-minded small-town community. Desai, by contrast, is often seen as a somewhat Western existentialist experimenter. Narayan's Austen-like satire of individual foibles is tempered by a warm human sympathy and a belief in the benign workings of fate for those who submit to the cyclic upsets and restorations of an orthodox Hindu world-view. This reading is described succinctly by Jaidev in a recent article:

> The pattern is comic in a classical sense; the individual is "infected" with self-consciousness, asserts his self, is isolated from community, suffers, but at last is reabsorbed in the stream of community. The deviant individual is clearly useful to the novelist, for it is his follies that become the subject of the comedy. The lesson of nearly all of Narayan's novels is identical: the individual's deviation suggests his sickness, perhaps his madness, and his recovery follows his submission to the healthy will of the community.[1]

As with most critics, Dev interprets this comedy in terms of traditional Hindu concepts of self-knowledge and detachment that allow one to be "in the world but not of it." If Narayan's irony is inclusive, integrating, accepting, Desai's is exclusive and destructive though equally corrective in its intent--one cannot be in the world and not be its creature; one may not go beyond the world and still function in the here and now as a human individual. The dividing line between Desai and Narayan can be sketched in by invoking the cliche that classical Indian literature has no tragedy, partly because the self is defined in pre-modern and non-Western terms wherein the possibility of conflict essentially does not arise (put extremely simplistically, *atman is Brahman*, whether you like it or not; ego differentiation is illusory).

I want to suggest here that Desai owes something to Hindu tradition as Narayan does to modernity-cum-Westernization, and that this area of overlap makes Narayan's work darker and more astringent than it may at first seem while leaving open possibilities for positive readings of Desai's tragic fiction. This is not to suggest that there are no differences: Desai, for example, seems to regard community as a constricting and hostile phenomenon from which escape is necessary for self-fulfilment (especially for women--a notable difference from Narayan's largely male-centred world); there are also the clear divergences in the authors's biographies. However, in Desai's work there is the same Narayan-like dynamic of tension arising from a separation of the individual from the social group. Indeed, it could be argued that Desai is more traditionally ascetic in her depiction of a necessary but dangerous solitude than the more overtly Hindu creator of Malgudi's worldly bustle, in which renunciation is never without a tinge of the worldly. Moreover, if the drama of Desai's fiction has something to do with her more modern outlook, then Narayan's novels also locate conflicts, however temporary they may prove to be, in the arena where tradition and modernity clash--a place of factories, big banks, movies, family planning and tourism.[2]

Let us take what is arguably Desai's most artistically achieved work and Narayan's ever popular *The Vendor of Sweets* as test cases.[3] In *Fire on the Mountain* , we have, admittedly, eccentric figures. One (Nanda Kaul, great-grandmother and former wife of a University administrator) is cut off from society by an act of will, another (Raka, the convalescing great-grandchild) is in retreat from emotional trauma, and the third (Ila Das, a poverty-stricken spinster) the world rejects out of sexist and class prejudices. It can be argued that in each case, in Narayanesque vein, there is a conflict arising from, and a corresponding retreat from modernity and Western influences. Nanda Kaul takes refuge from her husband's affair with a Christian teacher in an old colonial hill-station and a mental life of tales of ancient romance. Raka is threatened by a Western-style masked ball at the club, by the Pasteur Institute's mysterious alchemies, and by a family history of neurosis founded on the jet-setting life-style of the modern diplomat. Ila Das clings to memories of a genteel girlhood and is murdered for promoting government family planning schemes and opposing child marriages. Certain qualifications must be made, of course, to this comparison: the sources of Desai's dramatic tension are not as firmly located in modernity and the West, nor are the possibilities of refuge/resolution as clearly defined in terms of Hindu tradition (Nanda Kaul, for example, looks to tales of Marco Polo in China and *The Pillow Book of Sei Shonagon* from Japan; Raka's India, new and old, is an equal mix of promise and peril and registered as a physical immediacy of sense impressions). Although there are these differences, the general outline of establishing abnormal characters is nonetheless not unlike that of Narayan.

Carignano, Nanda Kaul's retirement house in the old hill town of Kasauli, is central to all three sections of the novella, so we are justified in taking its reclusive owner as at least the most foregrounded character of the three, if not the central one.[4] Her isolated world suffers a number of intrusions--first, a physical incursion upon the present in the shape of Raka, and secondly a figure from the past in the person of Ila Das. Each carries within the seeds of a personal tragic development, and both become logical representatives and agents of the old woman's private Nemesis or Karma. On the face of it, the brutal and sudden resolution of the novella bears little resemblance to Narayan's traditionalist harmonizing of conflicts. In Narayan's book, *The Vendor of Sweets*, it takes an extreme event such as the intrusion of an outsider to generate significant tension. Mali, though familiar as an indulged eldest son, is out of the ordinary because he lacks the usual extended-family controls, has no siblings and no mother. He sets himself apart from normal social institutions such as school and work, and having gone overseas is transformed into a demonic force of modernizing, technological energy (just like the taxidermist/ hunter/rakshasa of *The Man-eater of Malgudi)*. His irruption into Jagan's well-ordered world is the more extraordinary because of that other outsider, "that casteless girl" Grace, the part-Korean who accompanies him from America. Here is something traditional rituals and social structures seem unable to encompass. But, just as every statue has a saving flaw, so all humans are fallible, and the constraining balances of the cultural and social network reassert their subtle power over the individual. It is only within this harmonious set of relationships that eccentricities can be viewed with ironic tolerance and characters like Jagan can regain their fragile equanimity. Tradition encompasses all, and the comedy of *maya* as *lila* rules supreme. As the opening of the novel indicates, we can avoid radical questioning ( "Why conquer the self") by simple good faith ( "I don't need to know; the sages tell us we should.")

While the endings of the two novels are different, the problems producing them, and the modes of their conception are fundamentally the same. Both protagonists are seeking contentment through withdrawal, intellectually convincing themselves that this is validated by traditional precept. Jagan and Nanda Kaul invoke their age and the idea of the four *ashramas* (life phases) as justification for their distancing themselves from the problems of worldly existence.[5] Jagan has also used his association with Gandhiji's non-violent reading of the *Gita* to justify a prolonged avoidance of family responsibility.[6] However, the peace traditionally promised is not forthcoming because both he and Nanda Kaul misinterpret the principles involved and fail to admit to undercurrents of unresolved emotional tension, so that, despite apparent detachment, they are vulnerable to the disturbances of mortality and selfhood.

In Nanda Kaul's case, the conflict is more apparent. She has reached "this period of her life when stillness and calm were all that she wished to entertain," (17) but finds herself constantly "distracted" by the cares of the world, and has a personality described as intense, wilful and vengeful. (13, 47-48) Though she has aged well beyond the fulfilment of family obligations and is theoretically entitled to withdraw from the world, her discharging of her duties as "householder" is not complete because she has (for reasons we later discover) denied her children anything more than a conventional show of care, having taken resentful cover behind a busy round of social activity. Her submission to *dharma* has always only been ironic and is belied by her ramrod back and flashing eye. (11, 19, 30) Her claim on peace is therefore a false one. If the hills speak Sanskrit, (49) it is the Sanskrit laws that will keep her on the wheel of life, pulling her eagle-like aloofness back to the domesticity of the cuckoo--leaving her as a potentially violent changeling in the nest of tradition:

> An eagle swept over it [the plain], far below her, a thousand feet below, its wings outspread, gliding on currents of air without once moving its great muscular wings which remained in repose, in control. She had wished, it occurred to her, to imitate that eagle--gliding, with eyes closed.
>
> Then a cuckoo called, quite close, here in her garden, very softly, very musically, but definitely calling--she recognized its domestic tone.
>
> She gave that ironic bow again, very, very slightly, and went to the kitchen to see what Ram Lal had for her lunch and tell him about the great-grandchild's visit. (19)

This kind of symbolic writing might be used to mark a distinction between Desai and Narayan. Certainly the latter deals in conventional significance within a social ritual that rehearses cyclic patterns of mythic tradition. Desai's symbolism is employed in a less determined, more privately suggestive manner. Nonetheless, the symbols themselves are often the same and, by their nature, are similarly ambiguous in both types of writing. Fire, for example, purifies and destroys: it is warmth and light and cooked food and smelted metal, but is also violence, passion, heat, drought, epicurean faddishness and industrialism's satanic mills. In *The Vendor of Sweets*, the smoke from frying *jalebi* mingles with the smoke of devotional incense, (7) the homely lights of Jagan's compound are dimmed by glowing visions of Mali's factory for story-writing machines which inflame the passions of would-be millionaires and would-be saints alike. Desai's book matches the polluting furnaces of the Pasteur Institute (producing both rotting carcasses and healing serums) with the smoke from the fire that will sweep the mountain clean.

In the conventional world of Narayan's Malgudi, the gap between ideal and human practice--between one possible symbolic meaning and another--is accepted as a natural part of creation. We are born into ignorance and our lives are infected with illusion, especially during the first two phases of our bodily existence. The novel explicitly refers to the *Bhagavad Gita* whose truths all the characters take to be axiomatic, often without understanding them or seeing how they conflict with their commercial activities.[7] The *Gita* lets them see that their failings are a natural part of life and that they are ultimately removable. *Fire on the Mountain*, on the other hand, works through imagistic patterning and associative cues, but creates characters who resist any such uncertainty. The book's tensions are therefore of a different order than those in Narayan's work, even though they may arise from exploitation of the same material. Desai's technique plugs into a more radical level of symbolic meaning unconstrained by the everyday, so that, without actually mentioning any traditional text, it directs our thoughts to fundamental metaphysical considerations. Any conflict between these and the lives of individuals is likely, therefore, to have a more drastic outcomes. Unlike Narayan's fictional society, the isolation in *Fire on the Mountain* of Kasauli from the world and of Nanda Kaul from Kasauli leaves her bereft of controls and protections other than the ones she can generate herself. When her personal equilibrium is upset, there is nothing for her to fall back on. The gap remaining between transcendent forces and individual cares is so great that only something dramatically tragic can fill it. In this, however, there is not necessarily anything that is especially modern or Western. In fact it is possible that Desai is being more uncompromisingly traditional within a Hindu frame of reference than Narayan.

In the *Bhagavad Gita*, we are instructed that the three constituents of nature "appear to limit in finite bodies the liberty of their infinite Spirit." Fire (*rajas*) "is of the nature of passion, the source of thirst and attachment. It binds the soul of man to action." Work performed with *rajas* dominant will result in pain and rebirth on a wheel of greed, unrest and lust. *Rajas*, however, is an intermediary state, "a level path." *Tamas* (darkness) is born of ignorance, produces dullness and leads downward to rebirth amongst the irrational creatures. *Sattva* is light. It is pure and leads to wisdom and rebirth amongst the seekers of truth, but it also binds the soul to "earthly happiness and lower knowledge." (Mascaro, 103-5) The hillside world of Nanda Kaul and Raka is infused with all three elements. Their intensity produces a chiaroscuro effect that leads our mind towards the necessity for spiritual release, even as it stresses the reality of the material settings.

Narayan's writing can function in the opposite way: by making the religious allusions specific and overt, it ironically places emphasis on the material, human side of life. Thus, when Jagan comes to his crisis-point, he has a private vision the importance of which is signalled by mention of the supreme moment in the *Gita*.

Krishna's self-revelation in his multi-faceted divinity is, however, presented from effacing the *comedie humaine* of the book; it is rather irreverently connected to the more sordid changeable nature of Mali, Jagan's errant and recently arrested son.

The Charioteer's apotheosis is not referred to in Desai's work, but can instructively be applied to it. Krishna defines himself as the epitome of all attributes: he is both "radiant sun" and "of radiant spirits . . . fire." Fire here appears in the context of monsters and god of destruction (it is wind which is the primary element of purification). The major monster--interestingly so in Jagan's case--is the lord of wealth, and the epithet juxtaposed with the fire reference runs, "among high mountains [I am] the mountain of the gods." (Mascaro, 86-87) *Fire on the Mountain*, then, can be read as exploiting at least echoes of the *Gita*, that traditional repository of symbol and meaning.

If Narayan operates through ironically counterpointed situations, characters and conversations, Desai's writing functions through its orchestration of sensory images. Her world at Carignano is contrasted to the world the postman brings to her gate. She asks "to be left to the pines and cicadas alone." But her world of nature is as full of active alliteration and assonance as the postbag is full of "messages and demands." An effect of busyness contradicts the abrupt ending of the opening paragraph, just as the final sentence opposes its own meaning--peace is to be attained by action continuing:

> Nanda Kaul paused under the pine trees to take in their scented sibilance and listen to the cicadas fiddling invisibly under the mesh of pine needles when she saw the postman slowly winding his way along the Upper Mall. She had not gone out to watch for him, did not want him to stop at Carignano, had no wish for letters. The sight of him, inexorably closing in with his swollen bag, rolled a fat ball of irritation into the cool cave of her day, blocking it stupidly: bags and letters, messages and demands, requests, promises and queries, she had wanted to be done with them all, at Carignano. She asked to be left to the pines and cicadas alone. She hoped he would not stop. (3)

It is consistent from the outset that the self-contained retreat at

Kasauli--the "quiet house" and her "cool flowering of relief" will see only "intrusion and distraction." Contemplative renunciation is offset by the force of Nanda Kaul's "cold and piercing stare from the height" and the insistent drive of the forms of the verb "to want" along with those other expressions of desire: "ask, wish, hope." Already we suspect that her physical withdrawal is not replicated at a spiritual level; fires of unconsumed passion fuel the withering scorn she pours on the bovine postman.

Nanda Kaul imposes limits on her quest for peace that are at once excessive and short of a proper ideal. "To be a tree, no more and no less, was all she was prepared to undertake." This is to opt for a less than sage-like suspension, a stasis which is represented in the continual expression of things in the negative. Wishing to be a tree suggests the lowest state of the soul, *tamas*. Moreover, to be a tree in the world of Kasauli promises not calm, but uprooting and burning (23, 28):

> Sighting her, grey and only faintly stirring under the three pine trees that stood by the gate in their exaggerated attitudes as of men going up in flames with their arms outstretched, charred, too, about the trunks, the postman felt something ominous hover in the heavy summer light.(12)

Here we can see Nanda Kaul caught in a self-destructive blaze. *Rajas* produces action, and at the close of the book, she officiously sweeps up the path to their house "like an aroused snake" to confront the telephone "in two divided halves." In the final scene her head droops while the telephone receiver dangles and the flames rise on the hillside. The contrast reproduces the up-and-down movement of the initial chapter, but this is not a closed cycle; it is lacking in harmony and incomplete. Passion rescues Nanda Kaul from the mindless melancholy of *tamas,* but it condemns her to a rebirth (perhaps metaphoric, since we are characteristically left unsure whether she is actually dead or not) in which she may acquire true self-knowledge and peace.

By holding *The Vendor of Sweets* against *Fire on the Mountain*, we may begin to see that Jagan's story is one of psychological complexity (of the kind otherwise associated with a modern and perhaps Western literary outlook) as well as being an affirmation of a traditional Hindu world view. Certainly his inconsistencies, so long as they are contained within social and cultural bounds, give rise to no great tragic drama--wry banter and amused tolerance are typical attitude in Malgudi. There is even a slightly approving tone attaching to Jagan's ritual of counting the day's takings. Though we are meant to see the irony of his elevating material enterprise to the level of religious practice, we are also, I think, free to appreciate that he takes his trade seriously and is ritualizing his profession, distances himself properly from its baser involvements. (Even though he has bent the law to dodge tax, he seems to show a genuine indifference to wealth when his savings disappear). There is a point, though, beyond which the sweet-vendor's terror of his son and his disturbing loss of self control on two occasions ( "but I am a poor man!" he wails to the importunate Mali, echoing his outburst at the death of his wife, [106,44]) moves outside of social and traditional limits and becomes something very like Nanda Kaul's deeper, more personal torment. Desai herself comments that Nanda Kaul's yearning is not for immortality, but for detachment, and that this goal is sought not for its own sake but because "only in such a state can her illusions survive intact."[8] Much the same can be said of Jagan until the resolution of his crisis.

When the old lady cries, "I want no more! I want nothing! Can I not be left with nothing?" (19) she raises the possibility that nothing is exactly what she will be left with. This extreme annihilation is perhaps something Jagan courts, since he too plays the role of ascetic renouncer. He is respected for his outward show of austerity and altruism, even if most people understand the compromised intentions behind it. The cousin's ingratiating comment, "You have perfected the art of living on nothing," (11) reflects nothing as extreme as Nanda Kaul's wish, as we know that he is aware of Jagan's prosperous business. Both he and Jagan appreciate the fact that one must have something in order to renounce it; one must be wealthy to practise charity. So the old man makes gestures of saintliness while accepting the need to "go on working and earning, taking all this trouble." (11) Hence we see the superficial appurtenances of sanctity: the diet, the book, the *khadi* spinning, the half-hearted giving away of sweets.

There is no doubt that Jagan is sincere in his adherence to the teachings of Gandhi and the *Gita*. His imprisonment and beating during the Independence struggle cost him his standing in the family (169) even though they also led him to a career whereby he could reestablish his position. In fact, it is the degree of genuine commitment to ideals that allows Jagan to delude himself about his real condition. He cannot move into a proper renunciatory phase of life until he has resolved the unfinished business of his personal life. It is not the social duties, but the solitary wrestlings with private care which push him into a similar state to that of Nanda Kaul.

Jagan is also something of a loner. His personality has tended towards the gormless (as we see when his family have to supervise his wedding arrangements). His impressionable nature absorbs Gandhi's example and he uses it as an excuse for his failure at college (32) and to avoid having to cope with the demands of marriage. He and his wife grow apart until she dies. It is at this point that his carefully maintained persona collapses. (44) He remains prone to "mental strain" (56) that is brought on by an indelicate reference to sweat or the sight of children lingering at his sweet-stall. (11, 86) His characteristic way of dealing with problems is to avoid them until they become so pressing as to provoke a crisis in his life.

Now if we take the longest chapter (chapter 12)--the one beginning with the vision of Krishna (176)--we find that much of it is spent detailing Jagan's memories of his early married life. Here is the cycle in which this novel's drama is played out. The wider frame is from Jagan's youthful imprisonment to the recent arrest of Mali, an outward beginning and ending of worldly involvement and suffering for the father. But this external resolution through renunciation can only be fully realized once Jagan comes to terms with his personal past. Until then, all his devotional acts are made in bad faith, according to the mere letter of the law--non-violence is a mask for cowardice, flexibility is a cover for weakness, tolerance for confusion. It is probable that Jagan has to work through a lengthy and repressed state of grieving attachment to his wife that has been prolonged by feelings of guilt concerning his possible impotence, his heartless treatment of her illness, and his awareness that he disgusts her, (25) coupled with a fear of her strong personality. If Jagan has failed as a husband (and a father), how can he succeed as a saintly renouncer? The powerful complex affects his treatment of his son and produces compensatory ritual gestures that generate self-esteem for his fragile ego. Something of the same may be said in relation to Nanda Kaul's treatment of her great-grandchild.

As his private life becomes more desperate, things like his dietary habits become fads and then obsessions, just as the *Gita* shifts in status from a genuine holy text to a smoke screen for his mental disturbance. (71) The climactic meeting with his son leads Jagan to assert that "a wife must be with her husband whatever happens." "That was in your day," says Mali, with perhaps knowing irony. (151-52) It is only when Jagan stops avoiding false detachment--when he assumes a parental role, decides to marry his wayward children off, faces up to his marriage and the death of his wife that he finds the calm he has unsuccessfully been seeking. (165) Once Jagan admits, "I have let things drift too long," (111) and begins to set his affairs in order, he shifts from being unable to determine any truth, (107) to passing judgement on and making provision for both Mali and that most threatening outsider, Grace. The "casteless girl" becomes "a good girl" and what approximates to a "Western" or "modern" sense of tragedy assumes the familiar Narayan configuration of a comic restoration of equanimity. In Desai's book, Nanda Kaul, bereft of socio-cultural props, leaves her self-awareness until the very last moment, and by then it is too late to expect a return to harmony in this life. In Narayan the irony, ultimately, is that the *Gita* establishes its wisdom even through Jagan's distorted understanding of it, despite and even because of the image-maker's possible con-trick and Jagan's comic mix of asceticism and bank-accounts.

If we hold Narayan's fictional view of life up against Desai's, we can see how her characters try too hard for an absolute freedom and self-possession, becoming tragic figures as a result. The Vice-Chancellor's wife, having separated herself from family, having known only the depersonalized bureaucracy of Northern upper-class life, has opened the way to extreme states of mind and cut herself off from human defenses other than her own. She, like Jagan, tries to define herself according to traditional ideals, but lacks any moderating influence to temper her inevitable failure. The wheel of traditional law is not denied, but can only manifest itself in its fiercest aspect, and that is consonant with the harsh spirit of the mountains which are the home of gods rather than poor fallible human beings. The inbuilt ambiguities of symbols that function on the higher levels of mythic or metaphysical meaning, however, and the notion of rebirth through the three states of being as outlined above, permit a reading of *Fire on the Mountain* that is not entirely bleak, eccentric or Western Existentialist. Desai, with her part-European heritage and her trips abroad, may describe a modern condition using the artistic techniques of writers like Woolf and Joyce, but the result is not *entirely* different from work by the man who rarely sets foot outside of Malgudi.

## NOTES

1. Jaidev, "The Importance of Being a Child: a Note on Two Details in Narayan's *The Guide*," *Journal of Indian Writing in English*, 15 (2), 1987, p. 11.
2. The general point is made by Santosh Gupta, "Jagan's Experiment with Truth in *The Vendor of Sweets*," *Journal of Indian Writing in English*, 16(1), 1988, p.22; the examples refer to *The Financial Expert, The Vendor of Sweets, The Printer of Malgudi, The Painter of Signs and the Guide*.
3. Anita Desai, *Fire on the Mountain*, (1977, Harmondsworth: Penguin Books, 1981). R.K. Narayan, *The Vendor of Sweets* (1967: New york: Avon/Bard, 1971)
4. This qualification is made because the writer regards Ila Das as being central to the story. See Anita Das, "Feng Sui' or the Sense of Place," in Britta Olinder, ed., *A Sense of Place: Essays in Post Colonial Literatures* (Gothenburg: Gothenburg University, 1984)), pp. 106-7.
5. R.K. Srivastava comments on the use of the *ashrama* in Desai in the introduction to his collection, *Perspectives on Anita Desai* (Ghaziabad: Vimal, 1984), p. xxxvi.
6. Santosh Gupta mentions the "subtle subterfuge" whereby Gandhian ideals become compromised aids to self-deception. (pp. 24-26)
7. *The Vendor of Sweets*, for example, mentions the *Gita* on pages, 13, 47, 50, 65, and 115. References to the *Gita* apply to Juan Mascara's translation (Harmondsworth: Penguin Books, 1962; rpt. 1971).
8. "Anita Desai at Work: An Interview," in Srivastava, p. 223.

# Nayantara Sahgal's *A Situation in New Delhi*

TOM MULCAIRE

As a political novelist, Nayantara Sahgal is concerned with examining her country in the light of India's political and social changes during the post-war period. In *A Situation in New Delhi*,[1] she attempts to do this in 165 pages. This is ambitious, and not completely successful.

*A Situation in New Delhi*, is a novel very much based on fact. Its main character, Shivraj (never actually met in the book), is clearly a roman-a-clef of India's first Prime Minister, Jawaharlal Nehru. Sahgal is, in fact, the niece of Nehru.

The novel commences with an announcement of Shivraj's death in the English press. Michael Calvert an English biographer (based on Nehru's biographer, Michael Brecher) and former resident of India is moved enough by his friend's death to return to India and write Shivraj's biography. It is at this point that the reader can make certain assumptions about what is to follow. We are either about to embark on a retrospective journey of Shivraj's India through Calvert's eyes, or we are to see modern India (circa 1964) in the aftermath of Shivraj. It is in fact the latter, though not in the way we first imagined.

At this early point in the novel, the focus shifts from Calvert to Devi, Shivraj's sister. She is the Education Minister in the cabinet of the new Prime Minister (Nehru's sister, Vijaya Pandit, was a minister in the post-Nehru Shastri government). Devi feels politically impotent in the period following her brother's death and is seen to question the direction her country is taking. Her son, Rishad, a student at Delhi University, also seeing stagnation in the new government and its policies, is involved in a covert terrorist group whose aim is to undermine the social order through random acts of violence and terrorism. Their aim seems to be to create a new society from the ashes of the old. Before this central plot gathers momentum there is a feeling of ennui from the character of Devi that permeates the novel until this point. It is not until the activities of Rishad become clearer that we begin to feel a sense of involvement with the characters and their actions. At one third of the way through a 165 page novel, this takes far too long.

The "situation" in New Delhi is essentially the student unrest at Delhi University. A small group of students, clandestinely led by Rishad, is involved in acts of violence against the University in general and the Vice-Chancellor of the University, Usman Ali, in particular. Usman recognizes that part of the reason for the student unrest at the university is that every job requires a degree--thus there is outrage if any student is expelled or denied a place in a university. More importantly, from Rishad's point-of-view, there are gross injustices in India which are fuelled to a great extent by the caste system.

Within the socio-religious framework of India, strong divisive influences such as caste, the status of untouchability, and linguistic chauvinism operate. The influence of caste is a strong element in the novel. The character of Pinky, and the preparation for her arranged marriage, exemplifies, and to an extent satirizes, the caste system. Rishad suggests that, despite Shivraj, equality can never be attained in India while this system exists:

> They would never banish the contrasts, never in ten thousand years build an equal society. How could they, when they were products of the rot themselves, of caste, of vested interests and stinking old ideas? (67)

Usman also recognizes the problems of a caste system. He points to Shivraj's "pedigree"--Shivraj (and Nehru) was of the Brahman caste--and Usman suggests that this background must have ultimately influenced every political act that Shivraj had undertaken. Although this novel was first published in 1977 and should be seen to an extent as a reflection of this time, problems of caste are still an issue in India.

Sahgal suggests that India is a country in constant revolution. She also suggests that there are "good" and "bad" revolutions. The passive revolution of Shivraj is contrasted with the violent revolution of Rishad. It is when Usman assumes the mantle of revolutionary leadership left vacant by Shivraj that there is an indication of hope for the future. Rishad's tragic death suggests a movement that is doomed from the start--doomed because of its clandestine nature. The suggestion is that if a revolution is to be successful, it must be a popular groundswell led by a charismatic leader in the style of Gandhi or Nehru.

Sahgal shows us a country caught between two worlds--the ancient and the modern. Michael Calvert describes India as a "staggeringly old country"-- "old and settled and structured when Britons were painting their bodies blue." (107) The tribal fanaticism of Pinky's arranged wedding is contrasted by the worldly cynicism of the guests at her engagement party. Rishad describes India as being caught between "ancient myth and industrial present." The technological changes brought about by the policies of Nehru, and the assimilation of socialist principles cannot eradicate three thousand years of culture. This is why the revolution of Rishad must fail. Only that revolution which can work within the cultural framework of India and its social history can have any chance of leading its people to a greater equality. This is ultimately Sahgal's message.

## NOTES

1. (Penguin Books, 1988).

# The Need to Suffer: Crisis of Identity in the Fiction of Ruth Prawer Jhabvala

RON SHEPHERD

Ruth Prawer Jhabvala occupies a contradictory position in relation to Indian writing in English. On one hand her fiction clearly belongs to the growing body of Indian-English writing; indeed she can be counted part of the establishing movement along with writers like Mulk Raj Anand, R.K. Narayan, Raja Rao and Anita Desai. On the other hand, and despite Jhabvala's intimate knowledge and understanding of India and Indians, she herself is of German-Jewish origin and because of her marriage to a Parsee lived in India for a quarter of a century. It is fair to say that Jhabvala has posed something of a problem for critics and commentators who like to think that when they talk about "Indian writing" or "Indian-English writing" the meaning of these terms ought to be immediately clear and unproblematical. The easiest way to avoid problems when writing about Indian-English literature is to leave Jhabvala out altogether, which is in fact what has usually happened in many of the early critical works published in this field. The ironies inherent in this situation of a Jewish author who, despite her major accomplishment, suffers the crime of "not belonging" are manifold.

I use the word "suffers" intentionally because I think there is a side to Jhabvala's work which has not been properly recognized. Much has been written and said about Jhabvala's ironic method in her fiction, her authorial detachment, her use of nuance and of humour, and Yasmine Gooneratne's definitive study of Jhabvala's work covers much of this ground very thoroughly.[1] What is not so clear is the other side, or perhaps the "underside," of this author's work where the picture of Jhabvala as a modern day "Indian" Jane Austen needs some adjustment.

In a personal essay "Myself in India" which is included in two volumes of short stories, *An Experience of India* (1971) and *Out of India* (1987), Jhabvala has tried to say something of her own difficulty in coping with life in India. For anyone whose familiarity with this author is based on her fiction rather than on her autobiographical commentary (and this includes most of us), this essay comes as a revelation. Can this be, we wonder, the shrewd, composed satirist we know from Jhabvala's stories? In this essay it is not just the candidness, but more oddly the apparent failure of self-knowledge, of authorial omniscience, which takes us by surprise. Because after admitting that "something is wrong" and after attributing her distress to a variety of specifically *Indian* irritants, she not only fails to convince but displays all the signs of unawareness--remarkable in one so normally aware. To explain her distress, she blames the Indian climate, and India's overwhelming poverty which she discusses in a voice edged, one might say, with hysteria: "*Can* one lose sight of the fact?" she asks, "God knows, I've tried . . . after seeing what one has to see here everyday, it is not really possible to go on living one's life in the way one is used to." She continues:

> But there is no point in making a catalog of the horrors of which one lives, *on* which one lives, as on the back of an animal.[2]

And again:

> I feel lonely, shut in, shut off . . . all my moments are dull. Why? It is my own fault, I know. I can't quite explain it to myself but somehow I have no heart for these things here. It is because all the time underneath I feel the animal moving? But I have decided to ignore the animal.[3]

Throughout the essay the author sounds surprisingly like one of her own out-of-control characters, or else like someone in the stories of Anita Desai, or else like those numerous Western counterparts from the fiction of Margaret Atwood to the English Jewish author Anita Brookner. In this piece of self-dramatization she sees herself "shut in" and "shut off," an admission which is also connected, I suggest, with an imagery of incarceration which runs through most of her stories. She refers repeatedly to "the animal" which, in the context of her discussion, seems to mean the sheer physicality of India (though the misty indefiniteness surrounding this image seems to point to some deeper psychic enormity). Towards the end of the essay she speaks of herself as a misfit in India, unable to mix with either educated (Westernized) or uneducated Indians.

These are her reasons for discontent. Yet, as in the case of V.S. Naipaul who also grumbled about India, this only appears to be half the story. For it seems all too easy for India to become a surrogate for someone's personal problems. This is not to say that the difficulties listed by Jhabvala are not real or important. But that India seems to be able to heighten a foreigner's sense of instability and able to subvert any firm sense of identity (the principal theme, of course, in Forster's *A Passage to India* ). John Berger has told us that what we see is what we already know, and I imagine this to be particularly true of the foreigner's perception of India, that the nature of his/her experience depends on what he/she brings to India. For Jhabvala to claim that India is the problem would be like Philip Roth's Portnoy claiming that the U.S. was his problem, correct in one way but only half the story. In the pieces I have cited from Jhabvala's "Myself in India," the truth or something closer to the truth is, in fact, not too hard to see. She really knows only too well that her diagnosis is only part of a less visible problem: "It is (really) my own fault," she admits, and further confesses, "I can't quite explain it to myself," an admission important to what I am arguing.

For the purpose of this paper I want to talk about just one novel, Jhabvala's *Esmond in India*, which although published quite early (1958) does in many respects typify this author's writing, containing a large cast of assorted characters from East and West, low class and high class, educated and uneducated. The narrator is the detached observer familiar to us in all but Jhabvala's stories told in the first-person. The method used depends on close observation of motive and behaviour and employs ironic parallels. Here is the controlled omniscient observer at her best. But even here I think we can also see connections between the claustrophobia, indecision and uncertainty of her essay and some of the perhaps less obvious features of this novel.

Esmond is an Englishman who took an Indian wife Gulab because initially of a romantic view of India, and subsequently in the hope of legitimizing his Indian credentials in the eyes of an expat community of English ladies whom he serves in the role of sightseeing guide and expert. In part the novel traces Esmond's growing antipathy to his wife and to India, the two becoming virtually synonymous to him. But also involved are his wife's mother who rightly sees Esmond as a pretender and tries to get her daughter to leave her husband, and two other families whose troubles serve to bring out the themes of past compared with present, idealism compared with materialism, and male compared with female freedom. The one thing that most of these different people share in common is a sense of being trapped.

Esmond finds himself trapped in his marriage to Gulab, while Gulab herself, though conventionally faithful to her husband, feels that their Western styled apartment is like a chicken-cage compared with the roominess of her mother's Indian house.[4] Esmond's growing frustration with Gulab is one of the most interesting developments in the story. While he can use his wife's social reticence to impress the English ladies, he becomes increasingly sarcastic and finally vicious with Gulab; her social reticence, her lethargy, her lack of intellectual curiosity, and above all her smell and sensuality, repel him and he mentally contrasts her with the energetic and mentally alert English ladies. Esmond is not so much a cad as a rather stereotypical and very insignificant Englishman replete with all of the Englishman's familiar prejudices and blindnesses. Of special interest in this comparison of Gulab with Western females is the particular image which springs to Esmond's mind, the image of an animal:

> There were, he knew, many other incompatible marriages; he had much experience of them among his friends. But at least there was always some neutral ground on which the last two parties could meet. They could, occasionally and in between their quarrels, converse about indifferent subjects, if not like friends then at least like strangers shut up together in a railway compartment. Or they could sit and discuss their incompatibility, and so get some satisfaction out of rationalizing their unhappiness. He was longing to do that. But with Gulab? She could understand nothing; talk to her, and her eyes--her beautiful deep sad eyes, which once he had thought full of all the wisdom and sorrow of the East--remained what he had long since decided was a mere blank. It was like

> talking to an animal. An animal, he thought, I am married to an animal.(166)

Gulab's heavy Indian beauty, her lethargy, her smell, her sensuousness, her unwavering conventional deference to her husband as lord and master, add up to a sense of India which the foreigner finds threatening and oppressive, not just Esmond but, as her essay seems to suggest, Jhabvala herself. Esmond's image of the "animal" is not so very different from Jhabvala's in her essay "Myself in India." One gets a glimpse of just how much of herself goes into the lives of her characters.

Esmond and Gulab are not the only people trapped. Ram Nath, the head of one of the two families in the novel, was hailed as a great man during India's Independence struggle, and he is still revered as such by Har Dayal, friend and head of the second family. But those days when there was so much to do, when there was so much scope for heroic action, are long since receding into a mythical past leaving Ram Nath alone and mostly forgotten, shut up in his dingy rooms, his present poverty the result of past self-sacrifice. The story maps Ram Nath's growing awareness that he has allowed himself to withdraw from life and to exist in a mental cocoon. But what he can do about his predicament is not at all clear. His friend Har Dayal, on the other hand, never took the same central part in the freedom movement, never had to participate in the same self-sacrifice, and so is left comparably well-off, spending his days in social trivia and guilt. And if both these men are in their different ways trapped by the passing of time, their lives are further restricted by the demands of shrewish wives who feel that they need to exert their own pressure, press their own demands. There is very little, in Jhabvala's presentation of the Indian family, in the way of tolerance, fairness or collaboration.

If Ram Nath's past idealism is ironically contrasted with Har Dayal's materialism, this theme is further developed through Shakuntala, Har Dayal's dreamy-eyed young daughter who swears that the only life worth living is that life which is devoted to some great cause. Ironically Shakuntala becomes infatuated with Esmond whom she manages to see as a suffering Byron. She throws herself at Esmond's feet in an ecstasy of self-sacrifice, ironically paralleling Har Dayal's desire to humble himself before Ram Nath. Both instances, not to forget Gulab's stubborn submissiveness to her husband, amount to a gentle parody of the Indian need to worship, to express devotion through sacrifice.

In this, as in Jhabvala's other short and longer stories, it is true that the author demonstrates a mastery of ironic implication which is the art of an accomplished satirist. What is not so clear is the kind of correction which Jhabvala's satire advocates. Unlike the fiction of Jane Austen where there is a strong confidence in the remedial powers of intellect and where individual eccentricities can be measured against known and knowable norms of human behaviour, there seem to be no such consolations available in Jhabvala's world. All of her characters are trapped and no-one has the power to do anything about it. The most intelligent people find that they have made mistakes or else fall victim to deep and powerful impulses. The philosophical issues raised--whether idealism is preferable to material indulgence, whether traditionalism is preferable to modernity, whether heroism is in the long term of any real value. etc.--are never clearly sorted through. The ironies in her stories are generated through contrasting behaviours rather than through measurable deviation, for there is finally little that can be known with any degree of certainty. So that behind the apparent confident narrator one finds a failure of omniscience similar to that of her essay, "Myself in India."

It appears, then, necessary to rescue Ruth Prawer Jhabvala from the 18th century and reinstate her in the twentieth alongside her postmodernist contemporaries. Following such a reinstatement one possible way of explaining the sort of problems I have raised thus far would be to consider her fiction in the context of her family history and background. One may see parallels with other Jewish story tellers; for example, the persistent sense of frustration and entrapment in Kafka, Roth, Malamud, etc. In a volume called *Contemporary American-Jewish Literature*, we find this comment:

> For those who have lived through Auschwitz and Dachau, books that do not return us in imagination to the apocalyptic horror of the concentration camps must seem, at times, utterly irrelevant.[5]

Surely this could be significant in the case of the present writer who lost some of her family in the Nazi Holocaust. What I am really arguing is that Jhabvala's "India" is more a state of mind than a geographical reality. This confinement, this oppressive heat and dust, this nightmarish poverty which reduces humans to the level of animals, this anonymity which reduces personal identity to nothing, this "India" takes on the characteristics of another Auschwitz or Dachau or at the very least adumbrates the experience of the wilderness and of exile, a place of necessary suffering and privation, something necessary for spiritual atonement. The American-Jewish writer, it has been claimed, cannot help but betray a collective racial unconscious, "consciously or unconsciously celebrat(ing) traditional religious moments (exile, convenient, transcendence, etc.)."[6] In "Myself in India," Jhabvala says that only her marriage forced her prolonged stay in such an "unbearable environment." Yet it is clear from the last pages of her essay that India did also possess for her some less obvious attraction. For instance, speaking about Indian religion and devotional songs, she writes:

> I love listening to Indian devotional songs. They seem pure like water drawn from a well; and the emotions they express are both beautiful and easy to understand because the imagery employed is so human. The soul crying out for God is always shown as the beloved yearning for the lover in an easily recognizable way. . . . I feel soothed when I hear such songs and all my discontentment falls away. I see that everything I have been fretting about is of no importance at all because all that matters is this promise of eternal bliss in the Lover's arms.[7]

"All that matters" here is the promise of transcendence, an unambiguously religious idealism which must be set against those dominant images of exile. The trouble is, Jhabvala complains in her essay, she is not herself Indian, and so doesn't really belong. What I find interesting in all of this is the way this country afforded, in Indianized terms, the particular conditions for the free play of a fairly conventional Jewish consciousness--namely the rite of passage from ordeal to deliverance. Only in such an unbearable environment as this, she says in her essay, does religion become the one necessity of life. Like the various holy female questers in her stories Jhabvala seems to have needed some private rites, some Biblical wilderness for the purpose of suffering and atonement following the dispersal of the tribes in both Old Testament and modern Holocaust times.

In the same symbolic sense, perhaps deliverance came in 1975 when, after a sojourn of 24 years in a country she found unbearable, she turned her back on India to take up permanent residence in New York--though, it should be added, the nature of her several more recent "American" novels may well make us wonder whether New York turned out to be the longed-for "promised land."

## NOTES

1. Yasmine Gooneratne, *Silence, Exile and Cunning: The Fiction of Ruth Prawer Jhabvala* (Orient Longman, 1983).
2. "Myself in India," *Out of India* (Penguin, 1987), p. 14.
3. *Ibid.*, pp. 15-16
4. *Esmond in India* (Penguin, 1980; 1958), pp. 57-58.
5. Irving Malin, ed., *Contemporary American-Jewish Literature: Critical Essays* (Indiana Univ. Press., 1973), Allen Guttmann's "The Conversions of the Jews," p. 48.
6. *Ibid.*, p. 4.
7. *Ibid.*, pp. 29, 21.

# Hatterr and Bazza: Post-Colonial Picaros

HAYDN WILLIAMS

Barry ( "Bazza") McKenzie, outrageous comic anti-hero, is the creation of the Australian comic entertainer Barry Humphries in a series of comic strip cartoons, with drawings by Nicholas Garland, which appeared from 1963 onwards in the British satirical magazine *Private Eye*. Humphries is well-known (Notorious?) for his impersonations on stage and on TV of a range of Australian types including his (transvestiste) presentation of Dame Edna Everage as well as of the beautifully disgusting Sir Len Patterson.

Bazza McKenzie is, in my opinion, his finest and most complete comic creation. Though originally only the dialogue and narrative were Humphries's work, with Garland supplying the extremely droll cartoons (which incidentally cry out to be transferred to the cinematic medium as Cartoons, not merely as the feature films already made with "live" actors), Humphries's contribution can be easily detached as a separate comic novel in the picaresque tradition. In fact, the whole series of comic strips can be seen, especially when viewed in totality, as the Complete Barry McKenzie.[1] One's attention is constantly switching from the pictures of the "bubbles" of speech emanating from the characters and to the very droll pieces of narrative and plot-summaries. This in no way detracts from Garland's great skill; rather it illustrates how integrated were the two arts. It is easy to see why. Humphries was himself trained as an artist and he supplied abundant suggestions for Garland's drawings.

The character of Bazza McKenzie had already appeared under a different name in one of Humphries's cabaret acts which revolved around a buffoonishly comic Australian. As "Bazza," he became, with a few changes, the urban Australian "Ocker." Indeed it was Humphries who may be credited with popularizing this word which may be applied to both the crude "proletarian" Aussie (pace the

Marxists!) and his dialect. The male Ocker person enjoys a life that turns in popular mythology around drinking beer (regurgitated in regular even obsessive bouts of vomiting), leering at Sheilahs (women), watching cricket, deriding all foreigners and migrants (including the loved-hated "pommy bastard" British) and joining with fellow Aussie male mates in sessions of drinking, boasting, insulting and colourful bawdy colloquy.

Humphries's caricature was based on a tradition of historical Australian types presented in fiction, both British and Australian. The Australian bush hero had been ambiguously displayed brilliantly by Henry Lawson and other contributors to the Bulletin. He had been celebrated both heroically and comically in Australian popular verse. A song about a decidedly shady antihero--Walzing Matilda had become the Australian anthem in popular eyes. And there were numerous versions of Aussie comic buffoons and antiheroes, both bush and urban, in Australian Radio and popular journalism.

But Humphries's Bazza was also unique. To begin with he was stripped of glory by being presented as continually and unashamedly crude and gloriously ignorant. He was for example, a walking and talking encyclopedia of racial and sexual prejudice. He was an urban Australian and totally Anglo-Celtic (Scottish?) and Protestant. Humphries deliberately excludes from his picture the strong Irish and Catholic strain of previous "Ocker" types in life and art. Though Australia has a radical and socialist heritage, Humphries presents his young Ocker hero as a conservative, even down deep a royalist of sorts, with a blind and irrational fear of homosexuals of both sexes--perhaps more derision than fear. (Ironically, Humphries himself comes of British stock and is politically on the right.)

Thus Bazza lives up to a prototype largely invented by the Aussies themselves and by the British in a distorted and deprecating view of Australians who are regarded both as Colonial Britishers "accidentally" shipped to the Antipodes against their will or by misjudged migration, and also as "foreign" and cricketing enemies. They must then be loved and hated equally. This is common psychological dilemma for the colonial and the "mother country." Like the Jew, the Scot, the Irish and the Welsh, the Aussie provided convenient comic sideshow targets to be pelted at by comedians in music-hall or subsequently on Radio and TV. There was admiration and some affection no doubt hidden somewhere in this degradation.

The brilliance and wicked funniness of Humphries's version of this prototypical comic Aunt Sally lie in his extension of the satire to include the English themselves and by inference the pompously non-Ocker part of the Australian population to whom Bazza McKenzie was shameful caricature and a national disgrace.

Humphries's story takes Bazza to England in the early 60s--the England of "England swings," a post-imperial England "invaded" by migrants from former colonies (including Australia) and beset by hippies, rock-and-roll pop-performers, Soho strippers, Aldermaston anti-nuclear marchers, the radical chic brigade, and miniskirted nymphomaniacs. Bazza is already derisive of the "Poms" (the British) from the views held, back in Australia, of their appalling climate (in contrast to Oz sunshine), their alleged distaste for taking baths (unlike the shower-addicted Aussies), their truly dreadful warm beer served in dark pub interiors, their snobbish and rigid class-system (in opposition to Australian egalitarianism and mateyness) and the pervasive homosexuality of the upper-class males ( "pooftahs") (in contrast to boasted Australian manliness).

But now what does Bazza find? The situation is much worse than even he had expected. For the once stodgy, cold and proud British have become self-hating, self-denigrating radicals, running round after the latest lunacies imported from America or the East. British backbone has turned to jelly.

As the strip develops in the pages of *Private Eye*, Humphries however who had intended the satire to be chiefly on these allegedly effete British, found Bazza taking over. It is Bazza himself who now emerges, energizing the strip as the comic anti-hero. It is his exaggeration of Australian prejudices and myths and illusions which provide most of the real comic power and so the story revolved round Bazza's misunderstanding of British customs. The euphemisms, literary references and assorted subtleties of English speech from top to bottom of the social scale escape him hilariously like a foreign language. And his repeated misadventures as the victim of British wiles are compounded by his own stomach-churning alcoholic excesses, gourmandizing, and would-be sexual incontinence.

Humphries underlays all this inter-cultural humour with a more general type of satirical humour going back to Latin and

Shakespearean sources such as linguistic mishearings, malaprops, dialects, and the appearance of an identical twin. There is also the old stand by of anti-clerical comedy and the pillorying of puritanism in both England and Australia (something that goes back at least to Ben Jonson) which is in paradoxical harness with the attack on permissiveness.

However Humphries's real ancestors are Fielding, Smollett and Sterne--the grand 18th century begetters of the "comic epic poem in prose" that is the English novel. Bazza's predecessors are the peripatetic comic Scotsmen of Smollett (Peregrine Pickle for example) and the naive anti-heroes of Fielding--Joseph Andrews, Parson Adams, Partridge and Squire Weston. It is no surprise that Albert Finney's portrayal of Tom Jones on film should share the decade of the Humphries and Garland comic strip.

The "comic epic poem in prose" is the very apt description borrowed from Fielding which is given to Govind Desani's *All About H. Hatterr* by Molly Ramanujan.[2] Desani's Indo-British comic masterpiece appeared first in 1948[3] over a decade earlier than Bazza, and has remained a popular Indian English classic ever since.

Desani's is also a product of a post-colonial comic encounter--this time between the Indians and the British, though Desani, though writing in the aftermath of British withdrawal, cunningly places the action of *All About H. Hatterr* in colonial times. And he too makes great comic and satiric play out of prejudice and racial misunderstanding. There are curiously apt links between Desani's comic extravaganza and E.M. Forster's tragic portrayal of East-West encounter in *A Passage to India*. However, it is the Henry Fielding model of the novel which unites Desani and Humphries in their presentation of the comic clash between the colonized and the colonizing masters.

Garland drew Bazza wearing a double-breasted suit (rather a fashion in Australia long after it had become somewhat demoded in the UK) and significantly a tall hat based roughly on the Aussie bush model, which he never takes off, not even in Church preaching a sermon in lieu of his twin brother the Rev. Kevin (then incapacitated by drink and in the charge of the police suspected of being the phantom vomiter who has been regularly defiling streets in central London).

Hatterr meanwhile is called so after his tall hat modelled on that of his Scottish headmaster (a suggestive link with Bazza the Scot) and more remotely on the headgear of Lewis Carroll's Mad Hatter. Like Bazza, Hatterr's first name is a nickname--Hindustaniwallah--with its echoes of the Anglo-English culture of the subcontinent. Though the Hat plays no further part in the novel than its iconic reminder of the hero's British education and his progeneration in Victorian Nonsense fantasy, other items of clothing do, notably his trousers and various assortments of underwear which fall or are pulled down to expose his nakedness to a cruel and unfeeling world.

Desani's novel consists of a series of picaresque episodes--the picaresque in form and content lies behind the Fielding and Smollett model--in which Hatterr returns to India from exile in Britain seeking to pursue various goals men have held up as desirable: status, money, freedom, sexual satisfaction, holiness--some corresponding roughly to the four Hindu ashramas. Hatterr, ending in pratfalls and nudity minus trousers and dignity, is continually urged to further risks by the advice of his friend, the Anglophile Banerrji, who speaks almost entirely via quotations from English literature plus cliches. Hatterr's own language resembles Bazza's in being colloquial not "mandarin," occasionally bawdy though never crude and cloacal like Bazza's. Bazza too has his conning and misleading friends including his Aussie cheer squad of drinking mates and an assortment of exploitative or just naive Britishers who add Bazza to their list of gurus and wondermen from the ex-imperial colonies.

Humphries and Desani are linguistic comedians. Desani is the master of deliberate bathos and cleverly collates literary English with slang and with comic-sounding direct translation from Indian languages into English. Like Nabokov, another cross-bred literary genius, Desani revels in puns: a body borne to the grave is heralded with the cry: "Coming up, one corpus!" Hatterr is addicted to funny euphemisms especially for underwear (a Victorian hangover, perhaps). A nurse's see-through knickers are referred to archly as "indecent, Grecian reach-me-downs." Both Hatterr and Banerrji riot in dazzling varieties of English, and we are reminded of how many types of English flourish in the Indian subcontinent to this day.

Humphries makes Bazza the purveyor of "Ocker"--the slang of the Australian urban working-classes with its plethora of engaging insults-- "bastards," "poms," "drongos," "pooftahs"--and Bazza employs a whole range of hilarious but crude euphemisms for lavatorial, excretory, gastronomical and sexual experiences (mostly digusting) which are usually incomprehensible to the British, speaking their narrowly upper-class restricted Standard Received English, or the rival and odd Cockney or Cornish dialects--which Bazza himself in his turn finds equally incomprehensible. The English language in *Barry McKenzie* never succeeds in communicating to anyone except his Aussie mates; on the contrary the language deceives and divides; above all it acts as a Berlin wall between the British and the colonials they once ruled.

In Desani's novel on the other hand, English is endlessly and effortlessly communicative. The characters are enormously and creatively loquacious. Language is the link that unites the anxiety-ridden Hatterr with the strongly euphoric Bengali Banerrji. The "Englishes" of both books are rich, fantastic, and can be by turns poetic and startlingly vulgar and cloacal. Strangely enough English was like that in the Elizabethan Age, before Australia had been discovered by the Europeans or India ruled by westerners. Both Humphries and Desani supply a leg-pulling linguistic appendix listing the recondite words for the benefit of the English.

Disillusionment follows a search--this is a common theme of Humphries and Desani. Bazza's first visit to England ends in acute disappointment, but he returns impelled by the weird testamentary wishes of dead Anglophile relations. Most of his absurd encounters are with the English aristocracy fallen on bad times, plus grasping cabdrivers, sexual perverts, hippies, various members of the literary and artistic bohemia from swinging Soho or left-wing Hampstead--all of whom grate upon Bazza's populist conservatism and Australian derision from sham politics and idiot idealism. It is kind of pragmatic derision that extends to Christianity (never be found in Church, for example, is almost the Ocker male's motto) and to Communists and all artists. Hilariously Bazza's outrageous language provokes the admiration of hippy literary groups; his bawdy songs are taken up by left-wing pop groups; his crayon sketches for kids make him the new Grandma Moses; he is about to go on the air at the BBC to represent Australia at the behest of the gullible silly-billies of the British intelligentsia!

Ironically it is Bazza's naivety which shines out. He is essentially (like Joseph Andrews and Parson Adams) an innocent among sophisticates, the last simple colonial among British post-colonial decadents. A sexual boaster deep down distrustful of his potency, he brags of past sexual conquests but never seems to score many successes with English sheilahs. He excoriates the British for being unpatriotic--that is, for stupidly echoing his own criticism of them. This is typical of the stance of many ex-colonials. Like many educated Indians, the Aussies like the British as they once were. Nirad Chaudhuri is also famous for deploring the decline of the British.

Hatterr's disillusionment is different. He is not an Anglophile--unlike Banerrji. He first tries to be a sahib by aspiring to join that holy of holies, a British Club in colonial times. He is thwarted by his wife's infidelity and his own (an undignified amour with an Indian washerwoman which exposes him to the wrath of the English caste system). His deeper disillusionment is with Indian spirituality in an India what proves to be full of bogus holymen--and Hatterr is cruelly conned. This is a theme which has become more topical of recent years with the spread of Hinduism in the occident and New Age sects.

There is little that is deadly serious in Humphries beyond the exposure of "swinging England" and "Ockerism." The satire of English and Australian stereotypes is as unjust as all satire, but like all satire contains home truths. Humphries like Fielding delights in showing the essential comedy of the innocent's confrontation with the world and ultimate victory ironically is granted to the innocent after suffering much pain at the hands of the world, the flesh and the devil. Many stupidities of the 60s are beautifully speared in the Bazza script.

Desani attempts through his comedy a kind of resolution of opposites, a plea for the universal to unite East and West. Desani spent a good part of his life in England, becoming a kind of "English" Indian like the great Bengalis of the early 20th cuntury--Aurobindo and Manmohan Ghose and the Dattas. In opposition to Kipling *and* Forster, Desani seems to say that West and East can and should meet. Meanwhile Bazza and the British remain in perpetual mutual puzzlement.

## NOTES

1. Barry Humphries, *The Complete Barry Humphries* (London: Methuen, 1988).
2. Molly Ramanujan, *G.V. Desani* (New Delhi: Arnold-Heinemann, 1984), p. 19.
3. G.V. Desani, *All About H. Hatterr* (London: The Bodley Head, 1970). This is the revised edition of the novel first published in 1948.

# Malouf's *An Imaginary Life*

VERONICA BRADY

Religion, it seems, is a scandal that refuses to go away, even in the most secular of societies. As Victor Turner observes, it cannot be dispelled by magical incantation but cannot be reduced either to nonsense by positivist or linguistic philosophy.[1] The impulse continues and must be acknowledged and lived through, especially perhaps in a secular society since it has to do with negative or midliminal experience of the kind which provoked Wittgenstein's famous aphorism, "whereof we cannot speak, thereof we must remain silent," experiences as common to the unbeliever as to the believer.

In India, or at least in traditional India, this kind of awareness is taken for granted, perhaps necessarily so, if it is the case that religion begins with thinking about the universe. Interestingly, however, it is beginning to manifest itself also in Australian literature, as well as in our music and painting--think, for instance, of Fairweather, Boyd and, to a lesser extent, Nolan. Patrick White is probably the best known of such writers, concerned, indeed preoccupied, with the question of the divine. But so, too, are many others, Randolph Stow, David Malouf, Tim Winton, and, differently but just as intensely if more ambiguously, women writers like Beverly Farmer, Helen Garner, Jessica Anderson and, amongst the poets, Antigone Kefala. Indeed, their situation as women which sets them somewhat outside the structures of power, and with it, of what belief there is, often gives their work an affinity with Eastern as distinct from Western religious thinking. For them as women, life full of a sense of this ambiguity; of the redoublings and reflections, of the play between self and other, loss and longing which is characteristic of Hinduism and, to a lesser extent, of Buddhism. In this essay, however, I want to look at the work of David Malouf and in particular at *An Imaginary Life*, a novella which seems to me to be closer than any other Australian work I know to Hindu thought, in particular to its non-dualistic, non-judgemental and multivalent sense of reality.

From the beginning of his career, Malouf's imagination appears to have been fascinated by religion, by the multiple possibilities of divinity, though also with their loss and, mostly, disguising this sense of loss with the pose of an ironic agnosticism. The poem "Mythologies," for instance, opens:

> In the old days it was easy:
> enough to recognize
> a god or two benignly
> winking above the sill, barely surprise
> if a bull you stroked
> with blue eyes and a love curl
> between his horns tried it
> on or a swan came thwacking
> your thighs.

But its conclusion is desolate enough:

> Old charms laid out
> in the sun catch nothing
> but a headcold or a bad case of sunburn. For both
> of which we have remedies:

This desolation, ironically concealed yet perhaps therefore the more intense, arises from a sense that if the gods do not exist, then there is no real truth to be had, for it is their power which gives language its power, making words more a kind of charm than a sense of information.

Malouf's permanent concern with language springs perhaps from this intuition, from their desire to rescue words from its exile amongst abstractions and restore words to their proper relation to the living world of things as well as of people. It is because of this exile, he implies, that:

> Legends nowadays are hard to get started
> and the gods aren't easy
> to believe in, let alone
> offend.[3]

A world which is nameless is also speechless and the comment, "Nature alas/leaves much to be desired" occurs, significantly therefore, in a poem entitled "A Critique of Pure Reason."[4] Mere reason cannot bring Nature back to life. What is needed is a new sensitivity, an openness to the mysterious multiplicity of being, to the music of things which celebrated, for instance, in "Harmonica Mundi," which begins:

> Here, take a tuning fork, throw it
> down and hear the planet
> hum: A natural. Vibrations scatter
> from Mont Blanc towards
> the limits, a tinkling
> of ice at either pole.[5]

Things for Malouf demand speech, indeed signify speech. But it is the speech of what is other, not just what is familiar. This strangeness, implicit in the familiar, is what is pointed to in "Off the Map," the speech of

> --black piers, bright water--silos
> moonstruck, pointing nowhere
> like saints practising stillness
> in the ripple of grain.

The words which finally matter are about this kind of "nowhere," to be found in the most ordinary places, in the mystery, for example, of:

> . . . new streets that shine
> in the eyes of farmboys, cities . . .
> alive only at nightfall
> that span a continent. Nameless. Not to be found by day on any map.[6]

This is the place which the poet, Ovid, is searching in *An Imaginary Life*, "the very edge of things, where nothing begins."[7] Religious thought both of the West and of the East is also preoccupied with it. Indeed, it is in a sense its goal, since it is the place of encounter between self and Other, the Other which is not entirely outside the self yet also not entirely within it but which flows backwards and forward between the two, demanding recognition yet easily denied or ignored. Malouf is clear, however. The presences which meet us here are what we have dreamed of "in our deepest lives and they are ourselves." (28)

As he develops it, this sense of depth is closer to Eastern than Western thought since the Otherness he perceives is not absolute and self is neither separate nor fixed but caught up in the flow of being, concerned as fluid, indefinable, even illusory:

> It is as if each creature had the power to dream itself out of one existence into a new one, a step higher in the ladder of things. Having conceived in our sleep the idea of a further being. Our bodies find, slowly, painfully, the physical process that will allow them to break their bonds and leap up to it. (29)

But, initially at least, this emphasis falls on the human side of the equation. As we shall see, *An Imaginary Life* begins sceptically, in the mind of a worldly-wise poet. But in his poetry also, the focus at first seems to be more psychological than religious. The longing is to rescue what is unconscious and unspoken in order to speak it into consciousness, but also, paradoxically, to rescue consciousness from its exile in a world in which

> We turn aside from miracles
> to the plain facts of a case, having put ourselves
> in service to *this* and *that*, the denominative
> clowns who are double agents in an affair
> more actual fabulous of *is* and *were*.

This speaking thus moves away from certainty, involving the kind of loss which the opening of the poem from which we have just quoted suggests:

> The new day finds us here. We have come down
> from the high lands of sleep in the company
> of dreams, shy beasts whose scene is still upon us
> invisibly we herd them, feel the heart of

their breath.[8]

This could, of course, be read as the secular irony of self-awareness expressed in Lacan's aphorisms; "I think where I am not because I am where I do not think, and I am where I am the plaything of my thought. I think of what I am where I do not think to live."[9] But that, of course also involves an awareness of loss. As Lacan also puts it, "I am someone who has lost something." For Malouf, it seems, this "something," for all his agnosticism--perhaps even because of it--has to do with what he calls "the gods," part literary conceit yet also part object his desire. His longing is for some kind of revelation, and what is revealed is something. As Etienne Gilson writes:

> It is quite impossible to come to the act-of-being by an intellectual intuition which grasps it directly, and grasps nothing more. To think is to conceive. But the proper object of a concept is always an *essence* or something presenting itself to thought as an essence, in brief, an object.[10]

So Malouf continues to carry on what Sartre called "la grande affaire," the "scandal" of theological survival even in a secular age, the scandal evident in a writer like him, willing in Wallace Stevens's words:

> to be stripped of every fiction save one.
> The fiction of an absolute.[11]

So we come to *An Imaginary Life*, the clearest but also perhaps the most lyrical expression of this "reality hunger" in Malouf's work, at one and the same time personal and yet also strangely impersonal. It may be, as Malouf says, that it is

> Out of the dark
> we bring these fictions forth to explain ourselves
> before bicycles and clocks. The dynasties
> are marked out on our palm.[12]

But it is also the case, that for him, as we have seen, self is also somehow other, in Lacan's sense, in the sense of Rimbaud's famous "Je est un autre." His main character, Ovid, is a poet, as he is, though dead, it is true, two thousand years ago, also living in exile,[13] a self and not-self, caught up in the endless process of transformation and transmigration which the original Ovid described in his *Metamorphoses* and which the novel clearly argues for also. Dead yet in a fictional sense still alive, fictional and non-fictional, speaking in equivocal language which has been composėd for him by another, this character addresses the reader as someone living in another century, which is, of course, our century, writing a letter, which he says he will never send but, which is sent for him by the text, writing:

> to you, unknown friend, who do not exist at the time of my writing and whose face, whose form even, I cannot imagine. Can one imagine the form of a god? For that surely is what you must be at your great distance from us--the god who has begun to stir in our depths, to gather his being out of us, and will, at the other end of the great cycle that has rocked our world with its quakings, have evolved at last and come into being. (18)

Most Western readers find this fascinating but puzzling, bound, as we are, into unitary notions of time, space and self and into the logic of non-contradiction. But the sense of self as multiple, as process rather than entity "like smoke/drifting up at dawn," as Malouf puts it in the poem "A Poet Among Others,"[14] is familiar to Eastern thought, in general, and to the Hindu tradition in particular. The very notion central to that tradition, "That Thou Art," the identification of the divine and the soul--the elision of subject-object absorbed into some larger reality, is implicit here, though it is true, in a highly ambiguous way. But Vedantic thought is no stranger, of course, to ambiguity. Revelation is always also concealment as Krishna's words in the *Gita* imply:

> Foolish people despise me
> When taking a human body
> They ignore my high being
> As the great Lord of beings. (*Gita*, 9, 11)

What is revealed at the end of *An Imaginary Life* is similarly ambivalent, different in kind from the clarity of the Judaeo-Christian and Islamic tradition. Not that the goal is purely subjective, and is not that even in the *Upanishads*. The solitary self is lost, led astray by illusion--as Ovid is initially. Rather, the goal is oneness, unity with the all-pervadingness of being, the unity, which Malouf finely expresses in the poem, "A Poet Among Others":

> . . . holding
> to the isness of
> things: a blade of rye, a moment spiralling
> up from the stubble field on a lark's wing . . .
> to enter the whole day's blue, a waterdrop filled with the light of conscious.[15]

At the beginning, then, Ovid is in exile, banished by the Emperor to the frontiers of the Roman Empire, the fringes of the known world, and exiled from all that he, sophisticated, an acclaimed and witty writer, and a nobleman and heir to his father's estates regards as civilization. But as the story unfolds, it is clear that his real exile is something else, more profound yet also more remediable. Even at home in Rome he was in exile, alienated from being itself, "distracted from distraction by distraction," a prey to illusion. Not that he understood it then. Rather he rejoiced in his situation, rejoicing in a "sophisticated impudence" which seemed to him "an enlightenment so great that there was no longer any need for belief." (25) True, he was even then faintly troubled by the sense of divinity: "the gods are not quite dead was my news from the universe." (25) Mostly, however, he turned that news to his own sceptical ends:

> But they too have ceased to be serious. They have entered the age of play. They have abandoned the holy places and taken up residence in fables that require only our amused detachment from disbelief. They would be embarrassed by anything so glum and humourless as our grandfathers' piety. We are free at last to believe in ourselves. (26)

This is the classic stage of enslavement to illusion, of course. But the novella's action moves away from it towards liberation and moves, significantly, by means of grace. The bliss Ovid finally achieves is revealed, not achieved by his own efforts, though as in classic Hindu teaching this revelation is highly ambiguous, as much discovery of the divinity within himself as of that which is.

In order to make this discovery, however, he has to make a journey within himself, as in the classic way of Sankara, and to discover there another mode of being, another language, the language of the universe, of being itself. The stages are quite clear. First of all, on the frontier, living amongst the "barbarians," Ovid is taken away from his own certainties and from the power which his skill with language gives him. As he reflects, his exile also means loneliness, isolation from language:

> They are not uncivil. But no one in Tomis speaks my tongue, and for nearly a year now I have heard no word of my own language. I am rendered dumb. (17)

Life is thus stripped to its simplest terms. But in the silence he begins to listen to others and to the world and learn another language, that of objects, not only because he is only able to communicate with others by their means, using them as signs, but also because he begins to be aware of them as fellow creatures:

> I never had much contact with the creatures before this, not even with dogs or cats. Now I find something oddly companionable about them. Like me, they too cannot speak. They move about in the cracks, in the gaps in our lives, and are harmless. Even the spiders, poor creatures. Do they have a language of their own. I wonder, if so I might try to learn it. (20)

He is beginning here to see that what formerly gave him so much pride, so much self assurance, was and is in fact a kind of loss. Then he was unable to speak this larger range of being which he is discovering here and in sleep, in

> what the simple daylight blinds me that the dark side of every object here, and even more, the landscape itself when night shadows flow over it, is a vast page whose tongue I am unable to decipher, whose message to me I am unable to interpret. (17)

But now he is beginning to learn what he calls in one of his poems "the body's syntax"[16] and to listen to "a new style of preaching" which tells him that

> there's another . . .
> world to be grasped,
> if only for dizzy seconds, of jumping
> free of the "not yet proved."[17]

Nevertheless it is not yet a language he can use. It remains somehow separate even from his own body which tags along, to see what goes/what goes in time.[18] What he is groping towards at this stage only seems to increase this alienation from himself and from others. The language he knows and even the language he is learning seems also part of this separation since it is a repressive gesture. "Latin is a language for distinction, every ending defines and divides." (98) What he is seeking is one rather "whose every syllable is a gesture of reconciliation." (98)

It is here that the figure of the Child, introduced at the very beginning of the story becomes crucial, becoming in effect, a kind of avatar, a "down coming" or manifestation which draws him out of the impasse of self, leading him from illusion to enlightenment.

This is not a common reading of the Child, and his function, of course. To the extent that any attempt is made to decipher it, *An Imaginary Life* is usually read psychologically, mostly in terms of a development from Lacan's "Mirror Stage" towards the Symbolic. Descriptions of the Child's appearance, apparently out of the depth of the self, like the one early on in the story, lend credence to this kind of reading:

> And something came out of the depths of my sleep towards the point where we stood facing one another, like a reflection rising to the surface of a mirror. It was there, outside me, a stranger and something in me that was its reflection had come up to meet it. (24-25)

But to anyone familiar with the Hindu doctrine of the Avatar this might also be read as the beginning of the divine manifestation which is to call Ovid from illusion to liberation, from darkness to light. As Geoffrey Parrinder summarizes the various aspects of this doctrine,[20] the Avatar represents a visible and fleshly descent of the divine to the animal or human plane. The intimacy of this encounter with a presence which seems to come out of the depths of the self is described in Ramaniya's commentary on the lines in the *Gita* in which the devotee is exhorted to show love to God. God, he says, needs his worshipper as the devotee also needs him:

> Who approaches me as his ultimate goal cannot maintain himself in existence without me, so I too cannot maintain myself without him. Thus he is my very soul. . . . Unable to endure separation from him, I cause him to possess me.[19]

Those of us brought up within the Christian tradition have no doubt missed this implication of Ovid's encounter with this figure from the depths of himself; because our theology emphasizes the others of divinity and the dialectical nature of grace. But the apparition here, is not of this kind, being non-dualistic. In a sense it might even be seen as an illusion, as Sankara does in his commentary on Bhavage Bhavage Bhavage the crucial passage in the *Gita* (4, 6-8) which deals with the coming of the Avatar:

> Though I am unborn, though by nature my power of vision is undecaying, yet ruling over by nature, the *maya* of Vishnu . . . by which deluded the whole world knows not Vasudeva, its own self--I appear to be born and embodied, through my own *maya*, and not, in reality, unlike others.[20]

But he comes, for purposes of enlightenment, for the "preservation of earthly Brahman of spiritual life upon earth."[21] Even at this stage of the action, there is at least a hint of this in Ovid's encounter which precedes this scene with the strange centaur-like creatures which precedes his dream:

> One of those creatures, out of the shadowy forces that blocked out the whole horizon above me, came slowly, putting its hooves down gently in the dust, towards me, and halted just a foot away, so that I felt its breath, its warmth, and thought I heard on the flow of its breath a sound whose syllables I could interpret.[22]

An Entrance--Avatar of this kind, according to the commentators, can be produced in human or animal forms. Here, this, it seems, is a "power-entrance" rather than the "Own Form Entrance" of the subsequent dream which we have been discussing in which the Avatar takes human form, even the form of the self. According to Ramanuja the Lord often manifests himself out of compassion, taking the form, as it seems he does here, which will best make him understandable:

> This essential form of his most compassionate Lord by his mere will individualizes as a shape human or divine or otherwise, so as to render it suitable to the apprehension of the devotee and thus satisfy him.[23]

True, here it is not so much a matter of satisfaction as of disturbance, but this disturbance is the first step toward the enlightenment, to the discovery of the paradoxical unity Ramanuja describes when he writes: "the Brahman to be reached by the meditating devotee must be something different from him."[24] God, soul and world form a unity; soul and word are the body of God but they are real also even though they depend on God and are nothing apart from him.

In the novella, in the strange and savage presence of the horses here Ovid recognizes an aspect of himself, hearing a "sound whose syllables I could interpret." Moreover what he recognized is music, more rhythm than words the tune, a Hindu thought, would say of his own divinity. Moreover, this insight comes out of the detachment forced on him; "having no language of my own now, I had begun to listen for another meaning." (24) In traditional teaching, the Avatar comes with work to do, and the Child's task here is clearly to lead Ovid to salvation, to the enlightenment of the final moments of his story. True, at this stage he is not sufficiently detached to go further. But Ovid understands at least that this meaning and the further glimpse he is given of his goal in the dream from which he awakens crying out, uttering a word in a language he did not understand, is the goal of his existence:

> I have since tried to remember that word, but the sound has sunk back into my sleep. If I could recall that sound, and speak that word again, I think I would know what it is that I

> have named, what it is that I have encountered with it is out there that is waiting to receive me. (25)

The action thus moves towards this reality, away from the fragmentation of his former life towards unity, towards the open flow of life.

The first stage is negative, unmasking the culturally defined illusions, the actions, institutions, words and poses which have separated him from this flow. He realizes that where he has lived, Italy, is "a created place." Even its gods have been made and shaped by human hand and are the creation of human need. But here he must confront "what earth was in its original bleakness" (28) "a place of utter desolation, the beginning." (30) In its sheer unmade and unmaking force this power is embodied in Hindu thought in the figure of Kali. Yet as in Hindu thought, this is a necessary stage. Existence is cyclical and must pass through the darkness if it is to come to the light.

*An Imaginary Life* also envisages time in this cyclical fashion. Ovid introduces himself, for instance, as someone who lives "between two cycles of time, the millenium of the old gods, that shudders to its ends, and a new era that will come to its crisis at some far point in the future." (19) The Child's coming, too, is part of this process. Appearing first to Ovid when he is a child, he is bound, Ovid realizes, to come again. As Parrinder remarks:

> The Avatars do not just drop into the human "scene" . . . without roots in anything that came before or relationship to what comes after. Each Avatar . . . appears "whenever there is a decline of righteousness." He maintains harmony. He is in a succession, of those who have gone before. He is in turn succeeded, and since early days there has been a looking forward to the Avatar to come.[25]

Beginning with this belief, Ovid's story concludes, as we shall see, with a return which is also a going away--Avatars finally die, as Krishna did, fatally wounded by an arrow, or as Rama walked into a river, both dying when their purpose was accomplished.

> The end of the mortal episode must be completed, for if it is real it is only occasional. God is not always visible though he

> constantly maintains the world by his power.[26]

Hence, there is an elegiac as well as a triumphant note to the story's conclusion. If, as the *Gita* puts it, all the beings spring from the Lord and all the universe is strung upon him like jewels upon a thread, then at the end of an age all things will pass back into the Lord's material nature:

> By applying my own nature
> I send out again and again
> All this helpless host of beings. (*Gita*, 9, 8)

Nevertheless this cycle is ultimately benign, as Ovid realizes early on in his desolation

> and yet even here [in the frozen landscape of winter] there are stirrings of new life. The first seeds are there to be separated and nurtured, and led on their long path to perfection. (30)

Someone familiar with the *Gita* might hear an echo here of Krishna's words to Arjuna that he is Lord of all, and seed of all that is. (*Gita*, 10, 20-42) She might also find it significant that Ovid's movement towards enlightenment begins amongst simple shepherd people--Krishna, it will be remembered, also disguised himself as a shepherd and lived amongst simple people. Here, too, Ovid lives amongst simple people and learns from them a sense of wonder. Glimpsing in their presence the unity of human life with the life of all other creatures, he then recognizes the frivolity and uselessness of his former life. Whatever else they may do, these people remind him of his own situation as a luminary, in passage away from a life based on social and cultural distinctions, cognitively defined, logically articulated and endowed with legal rights and obligations[27] towards another kind of reality. Living in community with them therefore marks an important step towards liberation, towards the awareness of the cosmos not as organized hierarchically but rather as the common life which exists beyond all categories of manifestation or explanation, transcending divisible time and space and beyond words, a life in which people, objects and relationships are endlessly transformed into one another.[28]

The key to this liberation, however, lies, as it always has done--Ovid first glimpsed him in his own childhood with the Child. The central episode of this section is thus the search for the Child, in the guise of the wild boy brought up by wolves who has been glimpsed by hunters in the forest. An Avatar, of course, can manifest himself in any form and, as we have seen, usually chooses the form best suited to people's understanding. The form here is therefore at first a savage one, corresponding to the "wolf man" within, who lives "secretly among us" whom Ovid recognizes in the Child, captured from the wilds and brought in to be adapted to the ways of man, (10) and in himself. Just as important, however, is the sense of wonder his presence generates:

> Where does the boy come from? Who were his parents? How did he get here? How can he have survived, naked in all seasons, with no one to feed him or nurse him? (48)

One is reminded here of Ramanuja's commentary on Arjuna's question to Krishna in *Gita* (4), "How can I understand that it was you who taught this yoga in the beginning?" This question, Ramanuja argues, was put purposely to evoke or provoke thought about the Avatars; whether they were real or imaginary, under what circumstances they might manifest themselves, what the nature of the body they assumed might be and so on.[29]

Evidently, the Child here is something of a miracle. His gaze, Ovid reflects,

> is something I could not have imagined. I have seen nothing like it before, except from the eyes of my Child, so many years ago. I have invented nothing like it in my poems, that were full of strange creatures caught between man and some higher or lower creature, in a moment of painful transformation. It exceeds my imagination. (50)

Nor is it clear where he has come from--the times of the Avatars are not fixed in classic teaching but "whensoever night declines" then the Lord manifests himself.[30] His gaze here suggests the power he brings to bear on the need he perceives,

> Whatever conception they choose to seek me, I manifest

> myself to them in that mode . . . I suit myself in such a manner that I am to them not only a visible demonstration, but that they may enjoy me by every one of their sense faculties, and in all diverse ways.[31]

So the poet of the *Metamorphoses* who has figured forth so many strange beings encounters here a presence beyond his comprehension, terrible as well as compelling. The Child, then, has to do with the holy, with the "mysterium tremendum et fascinans" which exceeds human comprehension. In his presence, Ovid is at times afraid, therefore glimpsing:

> Some animal presence we do not know and have never seen. What if he were in communion with that, or had the power of assuming the form of a creature whose shape, whose horror, we can only imagine, and have no magic and placate? (66)

At other times, the Child calls upon "a tenderness" within him, "an immense pity, a need to free him into some clearer body, that is [Ovid says] like a pain in my own." (77) But the Child is in no sense a projection of need, much less of desire. Godlike, he creates both the kindness and the terror he calls forth and threatens at times, like the wolf in Ovid's earlier dream, "to consume the whole pool of my being." (77)

But the fear this threat occasions is, in effect, a holy fear. Creator, preserver and destroyer, the Avatar is self and not self, but also the central goal of the self. As one of the Vedas puts it:

> There is no equality in experience between the Lord and the self; for the Lord is all-knowing, all powerful and absolute; while the self is of little understanding, of little power and absolutely dependent.[32]

What matters is knowledge, knowledge of this truth which is manifest here, of the eternal nature of the soul and its identification with the divine.[33] This, for Hindu belief, is worth far more than cult or morality.

So, too, here. The final stage of *An Imaginary Life* is taken up with this search for truth, a search which arises, characteristically, out of Ovid's preoccupation with language. Having captured the

Child, he decides to teach him his language. But the Child is not to be coopted in this way. The Avatar's task is instruction, to teach *dharma* for this life. Instead of bringing comfort, he begins disturbance, exposing illusion. He catches a fever, for instance, threatening the whole village with infection and death, testing their attitude to immortality in terms of the search for truth. But the threat he poses to Ovid's self-assurance is more important. Teaching the Child to speak his language, he gradually comes to realize that it is he who is the learner and the Child the teacher.

> When I try to articulate what I know, I stumble suddenly on what, till that moment, I did not know. There are times when it comes strangely that *he* is the teacher, and that whatever comes new to the occasion is being led, slowly, painfully, out of me. (95)

How all this had begun to happen, he reflects, is a mystery. But if one sees the Child as the Avatar, the manifestation of the divine in human form, it is not--provided, of course, one believes in the divine. The central question, to which Ovid implicitly gives a positive answer, is whether or not one is prepared to accept within the self the presence of another who may in fact seem to be an alien, someone who, as the Child dies here. Self is no longer something accidental, a mask to put on or a part to be acted out. It is rather a matter of deadly earnest, of entering the dimensions of self in which truth at last is to be brought to birth.

Nevertheless, this process of learning does not begin immediately with the Child's capture--there is too much self-will perhaps in that. It begins rather when the poet begins to sense "some process of reaching up out of himself" (79) and when untying the bonds, by which he has secured the Child's presence, realizing that they are no longer necessary, he also understands that his life is now inexorably tied to the Child's, to that "timeless place" within him from which the Child is also coming to him. (82) But here, he recognizes what he has long lost or forgotten in himself an old simplicity but also the old cruelty which made him leave home to go his own way, killing his brother and his father, in wish if not in deed.

To know oneself is to know evil as well as good. As in the *Gita* Krishna declares his teaching and exposes evil so here, Ovid is led to self-knowledge and then, beyond this, to know how much he does not know. Now with the Child, he begins to understand that he does not know "who he is or what his fate is to be." (89) "The unmanifested goal (as Krishna tells Arjuna) is hard to reach for embodied beings" since it is "not this, not this" nothing which can be put into words. The way to it, however, leads through practical knowledge, the experience deeper than any theory which is now leading him to the discovery of "things [which] happen, deep in our lives," usually not spoken of and hidden even from ourselves but which "do not leave us," (88) remaining to become the occasion of true self-knowledge.

This, as the *Gita* teaches, demands demotion, the gift of oneself. So Ovid gives what he most values, his language, devoting himself to teaching it to the Child. But devotion brings its reward:

> If one gives me with devotion
> Leaf or flower, fruit or water,
> From that earnest soul I relish
> Such an offering of devotion. (*Gita,* 9, 26)

Ovid in the past had been a master of words. But now becoming their servant, learning to listen as well as to speak, he learns a deeper and richer language. Earlier, he had glimpsed this possibility, stopped in his tracks out walking one day by "a little puff of scarlet amongst the wild corn." (30) Revelation comes in many forms and here it comes in the form of "a little wild poppy, of a red so sudden it made my blood stop." (31) But what it brought with it is the wonder of the earth, of being itself, in its colour, energy and fertility, putting him in touch with a spring within himself, and giving him access to a kind of password "that would release me from my own life." (32) To reach it, however, he had to learn to be silent, to let the gods name him. That happened years ago. Only now with the Child does he begin to discover its true meaning, to comprehend the real message of the words he wrote then, "You will be separated from yourself and yet be alive." (33) Now, however, he understands that it means: "I too must be transformed." (33)

According to the *Gita* the revelation of the Lord brings divine speech to human beings. The task of the devotee is to respond, to give himself to this revelation. Ovid's dedication to the Child becomes a matter of listening to him rather than to himself, tasting the new life he has to offer, in the spirit of Krishna's words to his disciples,

> Abandoning all duties
> Come to me for refuge,
> From every evil I will save you, do not sorrow. (*Gita,* 18, 60)

In this case the evil is the possession of one's own gifts. So Ovid begins to realize that language is not his own but given to him out of the gracious compassing of the gods in order to lead him to enlightenment:

> This . . . is how it is done. We give the gods a name and they quicken in us, they rise in their glory and power out of minds, they move forth and act in the world beyond, changing us and it. So it is that the beings we are in process of becoming will be drawn out of us. We have only to find the name and let its illumination fill us. (32)

Pious repetition of "the Name" is true religion for some branches of Hinduism. There are two forms of the Absolute, Tulasi taught, the personal and the impersonal, but the Name is greater than both, for it makes them both known. Although the Absolute, the Lord, dwells in all hearts, people are sad. It is only when his Name is uttered that he becomes manifest and they are able to rejoice. But for this so here Ovid's task is to listen and gradually to learn the Name. So he must learn to submit to instruction:

> We are moving in opposite directions, I and the Child, though on the same path. He has not yet captured his individual soul out of the universe about him. His self is outside him his energy distributed among the beasts and buds whose life he shares, among leaves, water, grasses, clouds, thunder--whose existence he can be at home in because they hold, each of them, some particle of his spirit. (96)

He has been enclosed himself, but the Child leads him into the fullness of being.

The fact that the one who knows all manifests himself as a Child is important here, because it keeps alive the great paradox that that which *Is* is also that which *Is Not*. As the *Rig-Veda* declares:

> Purusha is all this, that has been and will be . . .
> A quarter of him in all beings,
> Three quarters are the immortal in heaven . . .
> With three quarters Purusha rose upward
> One quarter came to be here again.[34]

The Lord's presence in this hidden form is the "greatest secret/Of them all, the highest message" of which the *Gita* speaks, the message that "by me you are much beloved." (*Gita*, 18, 64) The task, Ovid begins to understand, is thus to learn to accept, to let enlightenment come upon him, to give up writing and let himself be written.

> . . . this is the way. Slowly I begin the final metamorphosis. I must drive out my old self and let the universe in. The creatures will come creeping back . . . re-entering their old lives, deep in our consciousness and, after them, the plants, also themselves then we shall begin to take back into ourselves the lakes, the rivers, the oceans of the earth, its plains. its forested crags with their leaps of snow. Then little by little, the firmament. The spirit of things will migrate back into us. We shall be whole. (96)

Physical incidents like the Child's illness, the crisis in the village that follows during the long winter when the headman's son also falls ill, no longer seem to matter. Everything in the story is now moving towards its culmination, the spring time in which Ovid follows the Child across the frontier into a "life that stretched beyond the limits of measurable time . . . a space that has no physical dimensions." (144) At the same time, the novel insists on the sheer reality of what is happening. "No more dreams. We have passed beyond them into the last reality." (141) Those who would cling to matter of fact, to the mere evidence of the sense, are the ones who are deluded. What is glimpsed here is fullness. As Ovid watches, the Child is finally transfigured before him. It is, the poet realizes, his own nature as a god that his body is straining towards." (150) But he also draws the watcher with him, to become one with him, paradoxically, at the moment which he seems to move away into this godhead. "Some new energy is in him. He is lighter. He moves faster over the earth." (118)

Language begins to give way here. The reality being revealed is continuous, while language, and the systems of thought that depend upon it are discontinuous. As so often, the revelation arrives[35] here with blinding force which disables reason and the senses. The description is full of images of light, of dazzle and glitter, of light shining on pebbles and of flowing movement and of flowing stream. But there is a certain terror as well. This is a new birth, and a new, more powerful manifestation of being. The springtime of the earth also marks perhaps the beginning of some possibly more terrible, certainly more intense, being:

> A membrane strains and strains, growing transparent, till the creature who is stirring and waking in there is visible in all its parts, forcing its own envelope of being towards the breaking point till with its folded wings already secure in the knowledge of flight, and of all the motions of the air, it flutters free. (147)

When Krishna revealed his supreme form to Duryodhana, he, too, was terrible and terrified all the assembled Kings, making the earth tremble. But afterwards, he withdrew that wonderful form and went out arm in arm with his friends.[38] So here, Ovid, drawn into the experience of rebirth, feeling the breaking that is going on around him as if it were "occurring at the very end of [his] nerves," (141) also feels a new intimacy with the Child. Even as he moves away from him, he is also "feeding me now out of his world as I once fed him out of ours." (148)

Thus he has been brought at the last to the "place I dreamed of so often, back there in Tomis, but could never find in all my wanderings in sleep--the point on the earth's surface where I disappear." (150) Here letting go of himself, he discovers his true self "ascend[ing], of lower[ing] myself, grain by grain, into the hands of the gods" (150) discovering the godhead in himself which is one with all things as the Child goes before him "his whole body strain[ing] towards some distance that I cannot grasp," (140) drawing him into "some life that I have not taken into account and which he will be free to enter only when our journey together is done." (149-50)

The gods come out of their compassion to rescue human beings from evil and illusion. But they withdraw their presence when they have enabled their devotees to realize the divinity within them. It is only then the Child moves away, that Ovid finally achieves illumination. The last glimpse of the Child is a kind of hierophany:

> He is walking on the water's light and as I watch, he takes the first step off it, moving slowly away now into the deepest distance, above the earth, above the water, on air. (152)

Distinctions of here and there, like those between this and that, give way. But so, too, do distinctions between human and divine, himself and the Child:

> The fullness is in [his] moving away from me, in his stepping so lightly, so joyfully, naked, into his own distance at last as he fades in and out of the dazzle of light off the water. (152)

This fullness is now also his own: "the Child is there." (151) But so, too, at the end Ovid is able equally to say, "I am there." (152) Time is now no longer operative either: "I am three years old. I am sixty, I am six." (152) "Put your thoughts on me," the *Gita* commands and "be absorbed in Me."[36] So now the poet is merged into divinity, into the supreme bliss of eternity. "It is summer. It is spring. I am immeasurably, unbearably happy." (152)

This may seem a strange novel, then, to come from an Australian writer. But its strangeness has made it very attractive to many readers. The important thing about any work is surely that it wins the adherence of consciousness, touches upon that impulse to transcendence which, so religious belief would have it, each of us has to find and fulfil within ourselves. Whether or not they will be able to perceive the ways in which *An Imaginary Life* accords with traditional Hindu teaching, of course, is another, and probably less important, matter. Nevertheless, Indian readers may find it significant that, written by a Westerner, this novel lends itself to the kind of interpretation we have been giving it. Ramanuja's conclusion to his commentary or the Vedanta Sutra sums up this interpretation:

> We know from Scripture that there is a Supreme Person whose nature is absolute bliss and goodness, who is fundamentally antagonistic to all evil, who is the cause of the origination, sustenation and dissolution of the world; who differs in nature from all other beings, who is all-knowing, who by his mere thought and will accomplishes all his purposes; who is an ocean of kindness as it were for all who depend on him; who is all merciful; who is immeasurably raised above all possibility of anyone being equal or superior to him; whose name is the Highest Brahman.[37]

The Child is, I have been arguing, the Avatar of this Supreme Person, manifesting himself in order to reveal to Ovid the illusion in which he has been living and open out to him the full range of divinity, its terror and well as its bliss, within him. In this way, as Ramanuja comments, the Lord "frees [him] from the influence of Nescience . . . and allows [him] to attain to that supreme bliss which consists in the direct intuition of his own true nature."[38] The revelation which came to him first in dream as another "like a reflection rising to the surface of a mirror" (24) proves itself finally as the fullness of his own truth. Nor is it all the Lords's gift. Ovid has responded also according to his own gift, his dharma, forgetting his own purposes, moving simply for the joy of his discovery. He has "given the gods a name" and they have quickened him rising "in their glory and power and majesty" out of his mind, going forth from there "to act in the world beyond, changing us and it." (32) The conclusion, as Ramanuja says, is liberation:

> We need not fear that the Supreme Lord, when once having taken to himself the devotee whom he greatly loves, will turn him back to samsare (transmigration). For he himself has said, "To the wise man I am very dear, and he is dear to me."[39]

Western scepticism may find this a hard saying, but, as we said initially, the religious impulse continues, even in sceptical Australia. What else, Ovid asks as his story nears its conclusion, should our lives be but, troubled by this impulse, "a continual series of beginnings, of painful settings out into the unknown, pushing off from the edges of consciousness into the mystery of what we have not yet become?" (135) As he comes to understand, "We have only to find the name and let its illumination find us." (32) *An Imaginary Life*, then, represents an attempt to find this name and let this illumination find us. The "scandal" remains.

## NOTES

1. Victor Turner, *Revelation and Divination in Adembu Ritual* (Ithaca: Cornell University Press, 1975), p. 15.
2. Pietro Spinucci, *Un Poeta Australiano, David Malouf,* Bulzoni, 1983, WO-2. Henceforth Spinucci.
3. "The Little Aenerd," *Ibid.*, p. 88.
4. *Ibid.*, p. 120.
5. *Ibid.*, p. 122.
6. *Ibid.*, pp. 62-64.
7. David Malouf, *An Imaginary Life* (London: Chatto and Windus, 1978), p. 27.
8. Spinucci, pp. 132-34.
9. Jacques Lacan, quoted in Sherry Turkle, "Why Are You Here?" *London Review of Books*, 5 January 1989, p. 3 .
10. Turner, p. 18.
11. Quoted in John Dominic Crossan, *In Parables.*
12. "Ode One," Spinucci, p. 134.
13. Malouf at that stage spent most of his time in Italy, living in a village in Tuscany, not in Australia.
14. Spinucci, p. 176.
15. *Ibid,* p. 178.
16. "Ode One," p.134.
17. "A Critique of Pure Reason," p. 120.
18. "Wild Lemons," p. 60.
19. Geoffrey Parrinder, *Avatar and Incarnation: A Comparison of Indian and Christian Belief.* Hereafter Parrinder.
20. *Ibid.*, p. 50.
21. *Ibid.*, p. 51.
22. *Ibid.*, p. 59.
23. *Ibid.*, p. 54.
24. *Ibid.*
25. *Ibid.*, p. 123.

26. *Ibid.*, p. 122.
27. Turner, p. 22.
28. *Ibid.*
29. Parrinder, p. 56.
30. *Ibid.*
31. *Ibid.*, p. 58.
32. *Ibid.*, p. 53.
33. *Ibid.*, p. 67.
34. *Ibid.*, p. 16.
35. Turner, p. 19
36. Parrinder, p. 41.
37. *Ibid.*, p. 35.
38. *Ibid.*
39. *Ibid.*

# Arun Kolatkar's *Jejuri:* Quest as Stasis

SUDESH MISHRA

*We must be still and still moving. . . .*
*In my end is my beginning.*

T.S. Eliot

"*Jejuri* is a non-event," said Arun Kolatkar as we lunched on a wet and funereal afternoon in July at the Wayside Inn, a modest eating-house frequented by the Bombay literati. He was responding to a tentative comment I had made concerning the eventlessness of his literary jaunt to Jejuri, geographically located some thirty miles from Poona in western Maharashtra. Earlier on he had described the physical journey as an assignment; Kolatkar had been commissioned to select a potential site for (what else!) a movie in the vicinity of Jejuri.

Kolatkar's comments indicate that the poem cannot be profitably seen to belong to the traditional *récit de voyage*.[1] The circumstantial ordinariness, some would claim bathos, underlying the actual journey to the holy site is reproduced by the text. The physical journey becomes transcribed into a literary pilgrimage in which not much occurs. Structurally, *Jejuri* is divided into distinct scenes and events which are arranged in seemingly unconnected visual "stills."[2] These "stills" or "frames" give the poem its static quality and perform a similar--although not exactly the same--function in relation to the poem as the episodic plot does in relation to the picaresque novel. Like the picaresque mode, *Jejuri* is organized around juxtaposed fragments consisting of witty asides, interpolations, divagations, parentheses, "extrospective" monologues,[3] and so on. Again, in *Jejuri*, as is common to the picaresque mode, "nothing strictly speaking happens."[4] The poem, if I may borrow the words of Stuart Miller, "merely records fragmented happening after fragmented happening."[5] In Kolatkar's poem, however, there is a diminished sense of movement within individual episodes, which is understandable since the medium of poetry, in comparison with the medium of fiction, is greatly restricted in its narrative scope and freedom. Furthermore, in contrast to the observer-participant of Kolatkar's poem, the picaro is often viewed in terms of his, occasionally her, adaptability to a predominantly corrupt social milieu. Society traditionally compels the picaro--habitually a rogue and social outcast from a lowly background--to travel from place to place, from master to master, in search of social and economic stability.[6] The episodic movements of this anti-hero are potentially comic and, as a first-person narrator, his observations are redolent with ironic possibilities. During the course of his travels the picaro is invariably confronted with a number of moral issues to which, more often than not, he responds negatively. The picaro's wavering moods and changeability of character are meant to serve as commentary on the relative merits or demerits (mostly the latter) of the society through which he moves.

*Jejuri*, then, appears to have an affinity with the picaresque mode. The poem has a peripatetic anti-hero[7] acting as the author's ironic mouthpiece;[8] its structure is largely episodic; nothing really happens in the poem; it displays the same sparseness of language and fidelity to petty detail; the tone is primarily cynical; and decadence and anarchy are prevalent in the projected social world. Yet, *Jejuri* is not strictly a "picaresque poem," an epithet one might reasonably apply to, say, Byron's *Don Juan* or Pushkin's *Eugene Onegin*. In the poem there is no identifiable first-person narrator; moral issues do not eventuate because the protagonist undertakes the journey with a predetermined viewpoint (which is neither moral nor immoral); the itinerant hero is not exactly a social reject; and the poem is generally quasi-autobiographical and not pseudo-autobiographical.

In a brilliant study called *Travel Literature and the Evolution of the Novel*, Percy G. Adams has singled out seven types of quests that occur in the bourgeois novel and the *recit de voyage*, and which may be extended to include the medium of poetry. These quests revolve around the following issues: "religion, war, a golden or social utopia, exploration, monetary gain, a person, and knowledge of the world or oneself."[9] Some commentators--and in particular Guy Amirthanayagam[10]--consider *Jejuri* a poem of pilgrimage, although it is generally noted that the pilgrim is an urbanized sceptic, which, according to Adams's classification, would posit it in the sub-genre of the religious quest. Pilgrimage essentially implies a ritual-quest undertaken in expiation and/or thanksgiving to one's chosen deity.[11] It could also be, as F.W. Clothey puts it, "the acting out of a religious person's life."[12] He adds:

> In pilgrimage, the religious participant journeys, literally and symbolically, to a sacred center in such a way that the pilgrim is enabled to affirm his or her own identity especially as a member of a specific religious tradition; at the same time, the pilgrim is afforded a new perception of self and context.[13]

The archetypal interiorized quest is structured around four visible movements or stages: the primary, the intermediate, the secondary and the tertiary. The primary phase involves a departure or descent into an unknown or nether region. This is followed by the intermediate stage where the often solitary questor encounters persons, creatures and things, or sees objects, sights and visions which image his or her inner predicament. This inner predicament frequently takes the form of an internal struggle between two antithetical forces which, for the modernists, represent the unresolved conflict between the Freudian *id* and *ego*, the Dionysian and Apollonian principles. The secondary stage is epiphanic insofar as the questor undergoes experiences that involve a profound self-revelation, whereby he gains insights into his relationship with a previously incomprehensible universe. And the conclusive or tertiary stage records the ascent or return of the enlightened questor to a symbolic area of light. (This four-fold pattern is also in Hinduism; consider the four *asramas* or stages of enlightenment: (1) *brahmacarya*, the period of instruction and discipline; (2) *grahasthya*, the life of family man and committed worker; (3) *vanaprasthya*, gradual retreat and loosening of attachments; and (4) *sannayasa*, spiritual contemplation in a hermitage.) Obviously the foregoing model is fairly restrictive and cannot be uncritically applied. It is however possible to isolate a sufficient number of great literary works as justification for the model. Some well-known examples would be Wordsworth's "Resolution and Independence" and "The Prelude," Coleridge's "Rime of the Ancient Mariner," Browning's "Childe Roland," Conrad's *Heart of Darkness* and Golding's *Lord of the Flies*. The list, it will be noticed, includes Romantic as well as modernist texts, and rightly so inasmuch as the model is relevant to both periods and movements. On what grounds then does modernism claim discontinuity with Romanticism in its treatment of the internalized quest? Modernist criticism contends that in the Romantic quest there is ultimately a resolution or epiphany which is often by implication affirmative. In the modernist quest, on the other hand, there is either no apocalyptic moment or, when there is, it is by implication negative and destructive. This, they contend, is the fundamental difference between, say, Wordsworth's handling of the quest motif and Kafka's or Beckett's or Conrad's.

Before discussing *Jejuri* in relation to the picaresque mode, the pilgrimage and the internalized quest, it is imperative that I briefly discuss how the quest motif operates in the Indian context. The quest theme is of course central to the two great Sanskrit epics, *The Ramayana* and *The Mahabharata*. The former, for instance, is structured around the protagonist Rama's search for his abducted wife Sita, while the latter, which consists of roughly one hundred thousand verse-stanzas, has countless digressive episodes (other than the spinal episode involving the Pandavas's struggle to regain their usurped kingdom) that deal with pilgrimages, journeys and quests of sorts. The Indian romance is essentially made up of the same ingredients as the Western romance. A *kshatriya* (member of the warrior caste) is often the hero and resembles the knight of the medieval Western romance; he has to confront similar adversaries--*raksasas* (demons), evil serpents, etc.--who stand between him and the object of his desire. The magical and the supernatural are likewise a part of Sanskrit literature. An example would be Kalidasa's play *Vikramovvasiya*. The play focuses on the theme of the King Pururavas's love for the divine nymph Urvashi. The opening act dramatizes the king's chivalric deed of rescuing his future consort from the clutches of the demon Keshin who is trying to abduct her. The fourth act introduces the fantastical when Urvashi, chafed because Pururavas has looked upon a fairy-girl, strides off into the forest and inadvertently enters a sanctified grove prohibited to women. She is immediately changed into a jungle-creeper for her transgression. The bereaved king scours the forest for her and finally meets up with the transformed Urvashi. He then invokes the power of a magical stone which returns Urvashi to her original human form.

In any cross-cultural analysis it is easy to overlook the differences inherent within the studied traditions for the few similarities one invariably encounters. The Indian romance, it needs to be stressed, varies widely both within the Indian literary tradition and in relation to the Western romance. Yet, the basic structural devices used by the writers of romance in both traditions appear to transcend cultural boundaries. At this juncture a brief enquiry into the institution--and it is an institution--of the Hindu pilgrimage would be profitable. *Tirtha-yatra* is the Sanskrit expression for pilgrimage and literally means, as Surinder Bhardwaj says, "undertaking journey to river fords."[14] Etymologically, this compound word has accumulated wide denotative and connotative meanings and may refer to many sorts of pilgrimages. The Hindu pilgrimage--for the pilgrims at least--is an intensely sacrosanct affair. A pilgrim may embark on a journey to a holy site, often a shrine of some god or goddess, for a number of reasons; he or she may be seeking the following: purgation or redemption from past misdeeds, self-realization through penance, cure for some bodily affliction, exorcism of an evil spirit, religious merit through *darsana* (sight of a demiurge), success in harvest or a daughter's marriage or a business transaction, and so on. Often the fulfilment of a wish is followed by a second journey where the pilgrim shows his or her gratitude by presenting oblations to the deity in question. But the journey, as Bhardwaj explains, may not be necessarily physical. There is a very strong connotative slant within the pilgrimage tradition in Hinduism:

> *A yogi*, for example, may physically stay put and yet, through a specific type of meditation, may "perform a pilgrimage" to the seven "Shrines." Here both the "pilgrimage" and "Shrine" are to be understood in their generalized meaning. Pilgrimage here means to "partake of" and the "shrine" implies a certain quality such as "truth." We may further clarify this metonymy by referring to a verse from *Skandapurana* (a religious treatise): "Truth, forgiveness, control of senses, kindness to all living beings and simplicity are *tirthas*." Thus, *tirtha-yatra* not only means the physical act of visiting the holy places but implies mental and moral discipline.[15]

Bhardwaj's allusion to the *Skandapurana* suggests the centrality of the figurative pilgrimage in the religious scriptures and literatures (often the two are inseparable) of India. The *Aranyakaparvan* of *The Mahabharata*, if I may cite another instance, deals specifically with *tirtha-yatras*, both literally and figuratively. In fact the pilgrimage is considered indispensable to the structural pattern of the great epic. *The Mahabharata* has often been regarded as one grand circular (in the clockwise direction) pilgrimage of the Indian subcontinent.[16]

*Jejuri*, I believe, does not snugly fit into any of the quest types hitherto outlined. It approaches closest to the modernist quest as it occurs in Beckett's *Waiting for Godot*, where there is neither affirmation nor denial, only a forlorn sense of anticipation in an atmosphere of perpetual stasis. Yet, I must again gainsay myself, for--even though *Jejuri* manages to achieve a certain level of stasis--the poem's mood is far from being irrevocably bleak and despondent. If anything the poem crystallizes a non-analytical existentialist celebration of the given moment; what S.K. Desai has called the poem's "ISNESS."[17] Moreover, *Jejuri* is not subject to the nihilistic humour of Beckett, nor does it ever pretend to entertain abstract philosophical issues *apropos* the meaning or the meaninglessness of human existence. It has a lightness of tone, a "surface" quality and a certain picaresque levity which has caused some critics, Chirantan Kulshrestha for instance, to downgrade Kolatkar's achievement.[18] *Jejuri*, I propose, is a *tour de force* within the genre of the quest and may be considered a sophisticated parody of the *récit de voyage*. It seems to be a reactionary extension of the modernist quest and, insofar as the continuing evolutions of the *récit de voyage* is concerned, supersedes such works as *Heart of Darkness, The Waste Land* and *Waiting for Godot*. The next section will be devoted to an analysis of the poem against the backdrop of all that has been said so far.

## The Hero, His Journey and the Dramatic Narrative

Adams has listed the three stages of the typical romance as defined by Kathryn Hume: "first, the Hero's Departure following the call to adventure, supernatural aid, and crossing the threshold; second, the Initiation--the great middle of the story--with its road of trials, its temptresses and temptors, its atonement with the Father; and finally, the Return of the Hero as Master of Two Worlds."[19]

Although in *Jejuri* there is a setting forth, a destination reached and an implied return, the poem fails to subscribe to Hume's highly conventional model.

The initial phase of the Hero's Call to Adventure, which Adams describes as taking "the form of voyages to the unknown, the lure of excitement in adventure, the fascination of travel,"[20] is a non-factor in terms of both the actual and the literary journey to Jejuri. First, the destination is popular and well-known; secondly, the protagonist is *assigned* to Jejuri and does not go there for the love of adventure and travel; thirdly, there are no roads fraught with serious antagonists or temptors and temptresses; and, fourthly, since the hero's personal value-systems are never threatened, the question of atonement and expiation does not arise. There is an implied return of course, but as a consequence of the protagonist's deliberately non-attached attitude which obstructs interaction between the personal-subjective and the impersonal-objective stances, he fails (predictably) to emerge from the journey with a knowledge of Two Worlds. In fact, the wheel imagery in the final section of "The Railway Station" implies a symbolic, uneventful return to the point of departure. And, finally, the poem cannot be treated as a conventional pilgrimage, Hindu or otherwise, since the protagonist does not undertake the journey with any ostensible religious motive or eschatalogical expectation.

I have previously noted that *Jejuri* uses a framing device which may be roughly analogous to the episodic plot used in picaresque literature. The text of the poem consists of apparently autonomous units or frames which S.C. Harrex has identified as the montage technique.[21] The *visual* gets consequently privileged over the *aural*. A lot can be said for Harrex's analysis since Kolatkar is vocationally a graphic artist and, as I have pointed out before, he had a film-maker's motive for going to Jejuri. The emphasis on exact photographic detail and the cinematographic interacting of individual frames is therefore a natural and inescapable feature of the poem. The framing technique may be employed to launch a protagonist in such a way that he becomes the pivotal centre for actions, ideas, and all sorts of parentheses and interpolations. The opening frame of *Jejuri* introduces the observer-participant, the "you," headed for Jejuri in a bus carrying "live, ready to eat" pilgrims. The precise identity of "you" is not clear. He appears to straddle the boundless authority of a third-person omniscient narrator and the restricted, questionable authority of the first-person "I." The distancing pronoun is maintained for most of the poem and affords Kolatkar adequate scope to relate his experiences (or the lack of them) as observer-participant with ironic immediacy. In Conrad's *Heart of Darkness,* Marlow re-experiences his journey to the Congo as he retells it; and his insights into the darkness blighting the human heart is drawn from this process of dynamic recollection. Unlike Marlow, Kolatkar's central persona, displaying certain Prufrockesque traits,[22] provides commentary as he undertakes the "pilgrimage," but his extroverted cynicism shuts him off from the influences as well as the impositions of his milieu. He emerges from the journey without any revealing insights into the human condition, nor does he grow morally or spiritually as a character. However, in the course of reading the poem, we gradually become aware of a second, author-sanctioned presence who stands apart, in the manner of a film critic, from the projected scene. He is the non-participating narrator overlooking the participating observer--the latter, as Amirthanayagam points out, may even be the reader.[23] Evidence for such a reading is afforded by the second frame entitled "The Priest." In the poem a *purohit* (officiating priest) awaits the arrival of the state transport bus carrying *jajmans* (pilgrim clients) and the protagonist who is travelling with them. Clearly, it cannot be the observer-participant who relates the anxious behaviour of the expectant priest since he is still some minutes away from Jejuri: "Is the bus a little late?/The priest wonders." We can logically infer that a second, superintending personality exists who narrates, observes, comments, often foreshadowing and anticipating the journeying hero, but who does not physically participate in the pilgrimage to the holy shrine. An acceptance of such a reading may appear to support and consolidate Desai's assertion that *Jejuri* discloses a "unity of consciousness" in a manner similar to *The Waste Land* or *Ulysses.*[24] But "unity of consciousness" is too convenient; and whilst it may account for the more introspective and psychological styles of Eliot and Joyce, it explains little about the extrospective method employed by Kolatkar. In *Jejuri* there is structural unity certainly, but it depends largely on the juxtaposition of separate, autonomous frames set against a background which chronologically progresses from morning to nightfall.

Thus *Jejuri* has two observing personalities: one is the projected participant who enacts the journey, the other is the overseer-narrator who commands a broad vision in the mode of the omniscient speaker in fiction. Both voices lean towards irony and are ideologically compatible. From the very outset the participating hero, whom critics have identified as "Manohar"[25] named in the eponymous frame,--though one is not completely certain whether the text allows for this identification--assumes an intransigently sceptical attitude thereby nullifying the possibility of a conventional pilgrimage. It is not as if we receive intimations of a serious, temporarily cynical, seeker who will be transformed by his experience. The scepticism is too profoundly embedded in the text to lend weight to such expectations. Moreover, the self-assured, non-diffident stance of the protagonist (as opposed to the nervous and indecisive Prufrock of Eliot's poem) is reinforced by the superintending narrator, which does lead us to suspect that no real moments of spiritual turmoil or moral questioning will be inscribed in the poem. Most of this we gather from the opening frame where the itinerant hero begins to record the platitudinous details of the bus trip with a self-relish that combines visual irony and non-didactic humour:

> The tarpaulin flaps are buttoned down
> on the window of the state transport bus
> all the way up to Jejuri
>
> A cold wind keeps whipping
> and slapping a corner of the tarpaulin
> at your elbow.
>
> You look down the roaring road.
> You search for signs of daybreak in
> what little light spills out of the bus.
>
> Your own divided face in a pair of glasses
> on an old man's nose
> is all the countryside you get to see.
>
> You seem to move continually forward
> towards a destination
> just beyond the caste mark between his eyebrows.[26]

The bus is going "up" to Jejuri and the morning is suggestively dawning, but these signs fail to betoken spiritual ascent since the various bathetic details (flapping of tarpaulin, state transport bus, the failure to see the countryside) in conjunction with tonal irony and witty inversions undermine the overt indicators of an earnest pilgrimage. The tradition represented by the "caste mark" of a fellow, presumably authentic, pilgrim is exactly *what is not* the sceptic's destination. It is also rewarding to speculate on the hero's comments about his own divided face mirrored "in a pair of glasses/ on an old man's nose." Is he imagistically alluding to the dual voice of the participating observer and the non-participating narrator that is being used in *Jejuri*? One isn't certain, mainly because the poet often tends to play impishly without expectations, raising and then undercutting them. But, one must remember that Kolatkar has recourse to the burlesque mode in his treatment of the hieratic quest.

It would be thus erroneous to read *Jejuri* as a poem that displays a superficial (lighthearted, comic, speciously ironic) mask beneath which there is denser (moral, philosophical, recondite, psychological, social) stuff that could be unearthed if one were sufficiently sagacious. There are ironic observations certainly; and irony, in spite of Desai's assertion to the contrary,[27] is the prime catalyst of satire which, in turn, implies criticism of individual and/ or society; however, Kolatkar's brand of irony, when and where deployed, is generally casual, by-the-way, with more levity to it than gravity. I am not suggesting that *Jejuri* lacks the kind of seriousness one associates with significant works of literature. *Jejuri* is serious because both the participant and the non-participant narrator are committed to an attitude, even if it is one leavened with wry, though not pugnacious, cynicism. And to assume an attitude is to occupy a position from where one can perceive and comment on, perhaps even judge, the object under perception. The protagonist is indeed a sceptic which implies his emotional dislocation from the surroundings of Jejuri. The adopted ethical stance, in other words, neither evolves nor fractures, mainly because it has been resolutely fixed and determined prior to the journey's beginning. Also, the extrospective method obstructs access into the inner world of the itinerant hero; while most of the tonal irony is neutralized by the sustained undertone of comedy. A certain measure of criticism is nevertheless intended. Criticism is implicit in the assumed stance.

What Kolatkar accomplishes in *Jejuri* is the subversion of our expectations of quest literature. The surface quality of the poem, the undermining of seriousness and the stance of the caviller pilgrim are deliberate ploys he uses to *put one over us*. Most great quest texts deal with the hieratic quest; their purpose is to offer vatic pronouncements on human existence. The issues and themes that concern them are "serious" ones, and include war, death, life-after, evil, morality, love, charity, valor, tragedy, sorrow, loyalty, paradise, benevolence, sacrifice and the purpose of existence. If one were to adopt Bloom's thesis, then, the interiorization of the quest in the nineteenth century brought to the genre an intensified seriousness, whereby the journey motif became invested with a multiplicity of meaning, ranging from the personal-symbolic to the impersonal-anagogic. The post-Romantic quest thus becomes a metaphor for an internal, spiritual journey into the consciousness or psyche of an individual, a society or an epoch. *Jejuri* reverses the trend; the journey is wholly exteriorized, aspiritual. Harrex calls this method "extrospection," though the context in which he uses it is marginally different from mine:

> [Kolatkar's] primary concern in *Jejuri* is to present place as object, object as object, and to objectify the spirit of place, the spirit residing in an object: in this sense, the subjective self is also an "object." Thus extrospection does not entail the elimination of subjectivity, of personal or first-person protagonist consciousness, for the unifying factor in *Jejuri* is the poet's thinking pair of eyes. His conscious and sensory relationship to place, people, lower life from all the way down to stone, his occasional projection into another "I" consciousness (as in "A Song for a Vaghya" and "A Song for [*sic*] Murli"), further help to unify the sequence. But extrospection dominates, and some of its best effects are achieved through a technique of imagism which is strikingly analogous to that of the visual artist in the media of both paint and film.[21]

Extrospection, as Harrex is undoubtedly suggesting, does not necessarily entail the reversion to a Hindu or medieval European formula of the *récite de voyage*. There is, in Kolatkar's poem, no allegoric scheme or acquiescence to an external divinity. Also, as

Harrex has noted, Kolatkar's objective correlatives are not, as in the case of Eliot, self-reflexive; in other words, the projected "objects" fail to entertain any correlation with the interiorized, emotional self. Subjectivity itself is objectified to the degree that one cannot easily determine the stances, attitudes and moods of the two predominant voices. *Jejuri*, then, is hardly a quest poem in the conventional sense. There is indeed no real hint of a "quest," no definite movement through an intricate medieval maze or labyrinth towards an even nebulously defined moral centre. Kolatkar's poem offers a strange version of the *récite de voyage* insofar as it renders static a genre traditionally considered dynamic.

In travel literature a character's entry into his chief location of trial and experience is through difficult initial stages. In *Heart of Darkness*, for instance, Marlow is faced with a number of obstacles--human, geographical and otherwise--before he succeeds in commanding an expedition to the portentous inner station run by the amoral Kurtz. The hero of Kolatkar's poem has no obstacles to overcome. He casually boards a public bus (crowded, hackneyed) that goes regularly to Jejuri, a pilgrimage site which is both tourist and accessible. The bus journey is trite and eventless, even from the standpoint of a tourist: "Your divided face in a pair of glasses/ on an old man's nose/is all the countryside you get to see." Another bathetic deflation of the quest paradigm concerns the poem's inward and outward movement, suggested respectively by the opening and concluding frames. Traditionally, in quest literature, the inward movement is towards an area of darkness and the outward movement is towards an area of light. *Heart of Darkness* and *The Divine Comedy* adhere to this scheme. In *Jejuri* the reverse is true since the initial movement is accompanied by the break of dawn and the outward movement by the setting of the sun. But, unlike (say) *Lord of the Flies*, the reversal of the pattern is not meant to be symbolic. Kolatkar tempts us to read it as such, only to subvert our expectations of the symbol-laden modernist journey into the nature of the human heart.

The protagonist, I have remarked earlier, is briefly absent in "The Priest," but subsequently re-emerges as observer in "Heart of Ruin." It is also true that the attitudes of the participating hero and the non-participating narrator are often seen to coalesce. In "Heart of Ruin" the comic-ironic description of the dilapidated shrine of the god Maruti illustrates the hero's dispassionate attitude and his deliberate, almost premeditated, decision to peel off from the observed instances their figurative layers; to keep, in other words, the external externalized:

> The roof comes down on Maruti's head
> Nobody seems to mind.
>
> Least of all Maruti himself.
> May be he likes a temple better this way.
>
> A mongrel bitch has found a place
> for herself and her puppies
>
> in the heart of ruin.
> May be she likes a temple better this way.
>
> The bitch looks out at you guardedly
> past a doorway cluttered with broken tiles.
>
> The parish puppies tumble over her.
> May be they like a temple better this way.
>
> The black eared puppy has gone a little too far.
> A tile clicks under its foot.
>
> It's enough to strike terror in the heart
> of a dung beetle
>
> and send him running for cover
> to the safety of the broken collection box
>
> that never did get a chance to get out
> from under the crushing weight of the roof beam.

The *familiarized* details do momentarily penetrate the observer's analytical faculty since he comments: "No more a place of worship this place/is nothing more than the house of god." This is one of those rare occasions when Kolatkar *assesses* the recorded scene by temporarily jettisoning his stance of the disinterested chronicler. In some measure the couplet affirms Nature's capacity to re-assert itself over the apocryphal creations of man. Embedded in it as well, one suspects, is Kolatkar's approval of the utilitarian purpose fulfilled by the rubbed shrine, a purpose it had failed to serve in its original form. Yet, the narrator subverts even this attempt at constructive analysis by shrewdly implying the anagrammatic relationship that exists between the words "god" and "dog," and which he later makes explicit in "A Song for a Vaghya": "God is the word/ and I know it backwards." The hero's comments, taken in this context, do not suggest a learning experience; they simply reinforce the blasphemously superior position of the experienced traveller he has occupied from the beginning. The protagonist, then, cannot be considered a picaresque novice for whom the journey is an edifying undertaking insofar as he "controls the fictional narrative, moves through space, and grows with that movement or is exposed by it." Kolatkar's hero is a man of the world--journalist, graphic artist, photographer, traveller--who has previously undergone similar experiences, embarked on similar journeys.

I have said before that there is no real sense of kinetic progression in *Jejuri*. The shifts in scene and location are implied by the transition rom one frame to another. "The Doorstep" seems "banal and flat," it is because the text in its muted visual and tonal effects *celebrates* the flatness and banality of the journey:

> That's no doorstep.
> It's a pillar on its side.
> Yes.
> That's what it is.

This particular frame fails to transcend the projected "literal" image because the observer, and implicitly Kolatkar, is unable to see any meaning beyond the visual, or, to use the argot of the Russian Formalists, the text fails to function as an active defamiliarizer.

Although he resembles the anti-hero in many ways, the protagonist is not really a picaroon. However, the objective world that we perceive largely though his eyes is unmistakably picaresque. First, the depicted empirical world, as in the picaresque mode, is chaotic and disordered not to mention ruinous.[29] A graphically witty example of this thread of ruin and disintegration which runs through the poem is afforded by "The Door": "Since one hinge broke/the heavy medieval door/hangs on one hinge alone." Likewise the subsequence called "The Railway Station" furnishes a conceit-laden account of the disorder and chaos which prevails in the manifestly Smolletesque world of *Jejuri*. Take the opening, delightfully flippant, sub-frame called "the indicator":

a wooden saint
in need of paint

the indicator
has turned inward
ten times over

swallowed the names
of all the railway
stations it knows

removed its hands
from its face
and put them away
in its pockets

if it knows when
the next train's due
it gives no clue

the clock face adds
its numerals

the total is zero.

Secondly, the milieu of *Jejuri* is stocked with the same diversity of characters and types one finds in the picaresque universe. Included amongst these are priests, a guide, dogs, tigers, a butterfly, an old woman, a station master, cocks and hens, a booking clerk, a temple rat, a dung beetle and the solitary calf. It is an imagist's concern for precision of detail, where even the partly and the trivial has a part, that leads Kolatkar to assemble such a motley crowd in his poem. Moving among them is the self-assured, camera-eyed protagonist.

One consequence of sustained irony is the literature of burlesque. *Jejuri*, in the manner of *Ulysses*, *The Waste Land* and sections of Pound's *Cantos*, is to some degree a parody of bygone literary styles and attitudes. The suffusion of irony, the alternating frames, the curious set of "presences" (ranging from priest to dung beetle), the extrospective method and the use of a banal and deflatory style bestows on the poem a refreshing, mock-heroic quality. In the mode of Kenneth Slessor's "Captain Dobbin," *Jejuri* puts on the appearance of an epic poem in order to undermine the "glamour" and the seriousness of that genre. Kolatkar's accent falls on the hackneyed and not the heroic, the mundane and not the ideal, which invariably suggests that his poetic discourse is more phatic than vatic. Neither is there in *Jejuri*, as is true for *The Waste Land*, a powerfully felt and damaging indictment by the poet of his environment, people and civilization. The reverse is true. The authorially-sanctioned protagonist, in his own unexhibitionist fashion, revels in every sight he beholds, animal or person he encounters. Surely this is because Kolatkar, unlike Eliot, is loath to cast backward glances at a wholesome past. His existentialism leads him to mistrust such projections and instead encourages a commitment to the here and now. Desai has perceptibly identified this ideological discrepancy between Eliot and Kolatkar:

> In Kolatkar's consciousness there is [the] kind of sensibility where the past does not dominate the present, where the present is all that matters. Eliot's mind is full of history, myth, legend and strong emotional attitudes, whereas Kolatkar's mind is free from knowledge which is always of the past, but fully engaged in the present with an implied conviction that simple, direct engagement with the present is a way to truth.[30]

One is not too sure whether Kolatkar believes that an "engagement with the present is a way to *truth*." What is true, however, is the poem's lively preoccupation with the immediate, the extent of which leaves neither the time nor the desire for priestly speculation. In fact, as is evident in the sub-frame called "the station master," Kolatkar makes friendly mockery of writers who engage in conscious philosophizing:

> The two headed station master
> belongs to a sect

that rejects every timetable
not published in the year the track was laid
as apocryphal but interprets the first timetable
with a freedom that allows him to read
every subsequent timetable between
the lines of its text he keeps looking anxiously at the setting sun
as if the sunset were a part of a secret ritual
and didn't want anything to go wrong with it
at the last minute
finally he nods like a stroke
between a yes and a no
and says
*all timetables ever published*
*along with all timetables yet to be published*
*are simultaneously valid*
*at any given time on any given track*
*insofar as all the timetables were inherent*
*in the one printed*
*when the track was laid.*

Eliot is ingeniously transformed into a ridiculous station master who does everything but tell the protagonist the time of the next train's arrival. The station master's incompetence is suggestive of a facetious bureaucrat (a bank clerk?) who complicates simple issues, which is the above poem, as is the case in "Burnt Norton" from *The Four Quartets*, has to do with notions of time. Kolatkar's dislike for hieratic pronouncements and abstract statements is highlighted in the cited passage. The simple pragmatics of a traveller endeavouring to catch a train home are lost on the station master because of his obsession with the validity of past, present and future timetables. A juxtaposition of the germane passage from "Burnt Norton" with the highlighted lines from "the station master" will illustrate the subtlety and brilliance of Kolatkar's parody:

Time present and time past
Are both perhaps present in time future
And time future contained in time past.
If all time is eternally present
All time is unredeemable.[31]

The subliminal power of the original is suitably counterbalanced by the bathetic virtuosity of Kolatkar's burlesque.

So far my comments have foreshadowed a more explicit discussion of Kolatkar's use of the dramatic narrative. The first two of the much-quoted poems on Chaitanya will best illustrate his flexibility while shedding light on the complexity of his approach. In the first poem the problems associated with a dual narrative viewpoint (for the reader, anyhow) is further compounded by the dramatization of Chaitanya, a distinguished Bengali saint who, as M.K. Naik has noted, is reputed to have sojourned in Jejuri around 1510:[32]

> come off it
> said chaitanya to a stone
> in stone language
>
> wipe the red paint off your face
> i don't think the colours suits you
> i mean what's wrong
> with just being a plain stone
> i'll still bring you flowers
> you like the flowers of zendu
> don't you
> i like them too

Here the monologuist is manifestly Chaitanya; but it is a harmlessly irreverent monologue dramatically recapitulated by the non-participating narrator acting (one suspects) in conjunction with a conspicuously absent protagonist. This particular frame once again demonstrates Kolatkar's readiness to undercut the high seriousness represented by the "stone" in its figurative and religious incarnation. Through his saintly mouthpiece Kolatkar asserts the essential *stoniness* of the stone, its natural place in a natural milieu, and opposes the religious connotations it carries in the eyes of the homage-paying devotees. The colloquial tone and the desublimated language underscores the main features of Kolatkar's caricature and negates the high religiosity of Hinduism by supplanting it with a casual, light-hearted animism, which itself is not meant to be taken in earnest. Likewise the first stanza of the second poem engages Chaitanya as the speaking persona: "sweet as grapes/are the stones of Jejuri/said chitanya"; but the second and final stanzas betray the presence of an observer who responds:

he popped a stone
in his mouth
and spat out gods.

The observer--who is either the protagonist or the non-participating narrator or both--intrudes because he wishes to comment ironically on the effects of Chaitanya's sanctified approval of the stones of Jejuri. The saint's words, according to the poem, led to the wholesale consecration of the site and sprouted countless gods who are worshipped in the various manifestations of insentient Nature. Unlike the first Chaitanya poem, the irony of the second is too pungent to be entirely comic. An onomatopoeic verb like "spat" does not altogether diminish seriousness. It may in fact betray it. Chaitanya's actions have, in other words, fallen under authorial scrutiny.

I have said before that the hero begins his journey in a sceptical frame of mind and what he sees only reconfirms his predetermined scepticism. As a consequence the poem neglects to provide visible signs of moral development and there are no foregrounded incidents that could be said to represent moments of exhilaration and epiphany. An exception to this pattern of emotionally staticity would be the frame entitled "An Old Woman," in which Kolatkar's supremely dispassionate hero gets buttonholed by an elderly female mendicant. The incident takes on a tragic dimension as both the poet and his protagonist try but fail to suppress the emotions generated in them by the poignancy of the encounter. The protagonist attempts to shake off the pleading woman, but is arrested by her pitiable words and the sheer helplessness of her gaze:

You turn around and face her
with an air of finality.
You want to end the farce.

When you hear her say,
"What else can an old woman do
on hills as wretched as these?"

You look right at the sky.
Clear through the bullet holes
She has for her eyes.
And as you look on,
the cracks that begin around her eyes
spread beyond her skin.
And the hills crack.
And the temples crack.
And the sky falls.
with a plateglass clatter
around the shatter proof crone
who stands alone.
And you are reduced
to so much small change
in her hand.

What attracts in the poem is the experience the self-assured hero undergoes in his largely non-verbal exchange with the old woman. There is the familiar casualness of tone and diction, and a levity of style that one might call Kolatkarese, but on this occasion these are deployed for non-ironic reasons since the encounter, for the protagonist, amounts to something of an intense spiritual realization and communion. Significantly, his realization that the infirm and impoverished woman is essentially alone in an uncaring world is conveyed through imagery of a disintegrating universe. The event is significant because it is the protagonist who experiences the universe fragmenting around him. What "cracks" then, though it is only a transient chink, is the dispassionate mask of the participating observer. The alms-giving hence becomes more than an ethical or pecuniary gesture; it implies the hero's recognition of the remarkable fortitude displayed by the old woman in a world which must seem to her as callously unsympathetic. The protagonist's reduction "to so much small changes/in her hand" is clearly an admission of his gesture's paltriness in the face of the mendicant's stoicism and indomitable courage. For a brief second, the hero achieves an insight into the precariousness of human existence and the essential tragedy of individual human lives. Immediately afterwards, however, he re-assumes his dispassionate pose, thereby once again shutting himself off from the impinging external world. There are no further intimations of growth or vision in the poem as a consequence.

If "An Old Woman" has a concealed moral dimension to it, then the digressive parable "Ajamil and the Tigers" would qualify as patently didactic. The poem may strike the reader as a fantastic piece of whimsy, posited somewhat arbitrarily in the *Jejuri* sequence. The apparent illogic of the inclusion might, however, disappear if one noted that *Jejuri* employs an excursive technique, that the entire poem is a pseudo-pilgrimage (and parables are a fundamental component of pilgrimage literature) and that the poem in question enacts the "springing up" of the legend suggested in the frame which precedes it. The connection between the hero and the protagonist is ambiguous. It is possible that he unites with the non-participating narrator to relate the story. However, it is clear that the tale is external to him (insofar as it is a story within a story) and does not imply any ideological shift in his perception. In other words, the moral behind the tale is to be read within the autonomous frame and not outside of it.

Sometimes between specific frames Kolatkar has recourse to a device that Shklovsky has called "linking," meaning that in a work of discontinuous narrative two or more episodes are literally strung together. Instances of linking can be found in the frames "A Scratch" and "Ajamil and the Tigers," "A Low Temple" and "The Pattern" and, perhaps most graphically, in "The Priest's Son" and "The Butterfly." In "The Priest's Son" the protagonist searches for a butterfly that is being pointed out to him by his guide, the boy of the title: "look/there's a butterfly/there." His sighting of it results in a subsequent poem which considers the butterfly in greater detaii. The butterfly-image inconclusively "ends" "The Priest's Son" but spills into the next frame, thus forging a vivid imagistic link between the two parts.

To return to the narrative voice. In *Jejuri* there are instances I have not adduced where the non-participating narrator allows the narrative voice to fork out into dialogues between characters ( "The Blue Horse") or else leaves the handling of the monologue to characters other than the hero--"A Song for a Vaghya," "A Song for a Murli," "A Little Pile of Stones," "Yeshwant Rao" and "Makarand" are examples. The last of these is an accomplished poem; its speaker is the sceptical, reluctant, apologetic Makarand, an appropriate companion to the protagonist:

Take my shirt off
and go in there to do pooja.
No thanks.

Not me.
But you go right ahead
if that's what you want to do.

Give me the matchbox
before you go,
will you?

I will be out in the courtyard
where no one will mind
if I smoke.

I have chosen to focus on the structural arrangement, the use of framing strategies and the dramatized narrative movement in my discussion of *Jejuri* largely because these help us to understand the way in which the poem works as an exteriorized quest, wherein the reader is shifted from frame to frame by the itinerant hero and the non-participating narrator as part of an essentially ocular experience. It is evident that this exteriorization is a consequence of the hero's self-assurance, his perceptional fixity (as opposed to the picaro's perceptional dynamism), a sceptic's unyielding will, ironic extroversion and an obvious lack of the pilgrim's faith, curiosity and passion for religious enquiry. Such a muted stance places him squarely in a position alongside the reader insofar as both have to be simultaneously involved and uninvolved. Kolatkar's hero is involved because he participates in the journey, but his inherent existentialism disallows the passionate engagement of a true believer. Analogously, the reader's involvement is assumed in the reading and understanding of the text, while judicious non-involvement is required in the process of evaluation and commentary. I have mentioned that the hero's stance is muted; it is in the sense that we are not given an organic (growing, changing, rounded) figure who is memorable. Consequently, Brijraj Singh's comment that "Kolatkar's creation of his protagonist's character is one of his greatest triumphs" may be a misreading for the hero's personality hardly emerges with any vividness. Save on one occasion, recognition, growth, knowledge and epiphany are never a part of his experience of *Jejuri*. No gnostic questor like Childe Roland, his personality neither evolves (as does Lazaro's in *Lazarillo de Tormes*) nor regresses (as does Kurtz's in *Heart of Darkness*). On the whole it is static. To be more exact: the protagonist of *Jejuri* is reminiscent of a non-self-doubting Prufrockian anti-hero who is the one constant in the alternating frames of a quasi-comic montage. Unlike the true questor he is consigned to the restrictive and decadent microcosm of Jejuri. As a result his journey never takes on the rhapsodical quality of an odyssey in the manner of, say, *The Waste Land*. Neither does it take the form of a real pilgrimage, Hindu or Western, literal or metaphoric. The protagonist has no mission in the moral or spiritual sense, nor does he--even fortuitously--at any stage approach the threshold of psychic revelation. There is, to argue against Harrex, no climatic resolution to speak of.[33]

*Jejuri* leaves us with an unprecedented concept of the quest as stasis, where nothing *serious* really happens and where the hero, even when faced with situations that tax his patience, willingly surrenders himself, with the wry humour of the existentialist traveller, to the moment's absurdity:

> slaughter a goat before the clock
> smash a coconut on the railway track
> smear the indicator with the blood of a cock
> bathe the station master in milk
> and promise you will give
> a solid gold toy train to the booking clerk
> if only someone would tell you
> when the next train is due.

In the context, Kolatkar has advanced beyond the modernists in his treatment of the quest motif. To begin with: his poem is not patterned on the interiorized quest; unlike *Heart of Darkness*, *The Trial* or *The Waste Land*. *Jejuri* has little use for extended, larger-than-life journeys into the intricate labyrinth of the human psyche. There are no apocalyptic moments (negative or positive) worth speaking of, no internal struggles or crises where a character has to make decisions which would affect his personal life, the course of future events or even the complexion of entire societies. Further, there are no moral dilemmas or spiritual quandaries to confront and resolve, largely because the predetermined, self-assured stance ensures that the protagonist is shielded from anarchic external forces. Unlike Eliot in *The Four Quartets*, Kolatkar does not undertake the journey to assert his place in a specific religion, community or tradition. His identity is never threatened which nullified any need for self-affirmation. If Beckett advances beyond Eliot, Conrad and Kafka in his discovery of existentialist despair in the futile anticipation of spiritual illumination rather than in the moment of illumination *per se*, then Kolatkar, in his innovative use of the exteriorized quest, proceeds beyond Beckett by subverting the very *idea* of a quest. And since the protagonist embarks on the journey with a degree of foreknowledge and positivism, he neutralizes the morbid despair that arises from questing after existential solutions. If there is no quest, then the protagonist is confident of his position in the universe, and if the universe itself is anarchic, then he can neither seek nor learn anything from it. The human will and the human wit, in *Jejuri* at least, emerges triumphant. Whether this prank of grinning existentialism, the mortal laugh hurled at the gaping Void, is in the end absurdly positive or hysterically negative is another matter altogether.

## NOTES

1. I have borrowed the term from Percy G. Adams who in *Travel Literature* and *The Evolution of the Novel* (Kentucky: The University Press of Kentucky, 1983), refers to travel literature as *recite de voyage*.
2. S.C. Harrex, "A Critical Approach to Indo-English Poetry," *Only Connect*, eds. G. Amirthanayagam and S.C. Harrex (Adelaide: CRNLE, 1981). Harrex offers an excellent analysis of the visual method in *Jejuri*.
3. The term, as I shall elaborate later, has been coined by Harrex to describe the outward-looking or reflectionary style of Kolatkar as contrasted with the more inward-looking or self-reflexive style of the modernists. See Harrex, p. 170.
4. Stuart Miller, *The Picaresque Novel* (Cleveland: The Press of Case Western Reserve University, 1967), p. 12.
5. *Loc. cit.*

6. This is not always the case. The picaresque hero may not *intentionally* look for social and economic stability; however, the overall movement of the picaresque plot does usually direct the picaroon towards these goals.
7. To avoid awkwardness I shall henceforth call the protagonist "hero."
8. The picaro is the author's ironic mouthpiece to the extent that his satirical observations, if any, are condoned by the writer. This does not mean that the author identifies with his protagonist. On the contrary, as Robert Alter observes, he usually "maintains a careful satiric distance between himself and his protagonist." See Robert Alter, *Rogue's Progress* (Massachusetts: Harvard University Press, 1964), p. 13.
9. Adams, p. 153.
10. G. Amirthanayagam, "Kolatkar's *Jejuri:* A Pilgrimage into the Past and the Present," *Only Connect*, pp. 177-85.
11. Donald R. Howard, *Writers and Pilgrims* (Berkeley: University of California Press, 1980), p. 11.
12. F.W. Clothey, "Pilgrimage," *Abingdon Dictionary of Living Religions*, ed. Keith Crim (Tennessee: Abingdon Nashville, 1981), p. 568.
13. *Loc. cit.*
14. Surinder Bhardwaj, *Hindu Places of Pilgrimage* (Berkeley: University of California Press, 1973), p. 2.
15. *Loc. cit.*
16. *Ibid.*, p. 43.
17. S.K. Desai, "Arun Kolatkar's *Jejuri:* A House of God," *The Literary Criterion*, Vol. XV, No. 1, 1980, p. 53.
18. Chirantan Kulshrestha, "English Verse in India: Some Obstinate Questions," *Contemporary Indian English Verse*, ed. Chirantan Kulshrestha (New Delhi: Arnold-Heinemann, 1980), pp. 13-14.
19. Adams, p. 204.
20. *Ibid.*, p. 151.
21. Harrex, pp. 170-71.
22. M.K. Naik in *Dimensions of Indian English Literature* (New Delhi: Sterling, 1984) has identified Kolatkar's protagonist with Eliot's Prufrock. See p. 26.
23. Amirthanayagam, p. 177.
24. Desai, p. 49.

25. "Manohar" provides additional evidence supporting my contention that there is a non-participating narrator overlooking the hero. If Manohar is the hero then it has to be someone else who objectively describes his actions in the eponymous frame.
26. Arun Kolatkar, *Jejuri* (Bombay: Clearing House, 1977).
27. Desai claims that in *Jejuri* "irony is often used as a strategy of maintaining objectivity and neutrality of vision, and should not be mistaken for satire or 'criticism of life'." See Desai, p. 51.
28. Harrex, p. 170.
29. Miller says that the "picaresque plot expresses an intuition that the world is without order, is chaotic." See Miller, p. 9.
30. Desai, p. 50.
31. T.S. Eliot, *Selected Poems* (London: Faber and Faber, 1983), p. 189.
32. Naik, p. 29.
33. S.C. Harrex, "'Obstinately Minor': Poetry from India," *South Asian New Series*, Vol. 3, No. 2, 1980, p. 66.

# Nissim Ezekiel: Inlets to an Indian Sensibility

WALTER TONETTO AND ENRIQUE MARTINEZ

I wax old as a garment;
as a vesture I am changed.
In this I accept the condition of humanity.
Ezekiel

Nissim Ezekiel's poetry seeks a social *engagement* in human terms, and not in abstract heartless cannonades that belong to the polemical vein. At first this assertion may appear confounded by the poet's formal and rigid rhythmic patterns, but the apparent contradictions between the form and the issue of the poetic movement account for an ambiguity in the reader's response. This ambiguity is, one suspects, under the reign of our accustomed practices of responding to formal structures, rather than a response to an actual absence of poetic clarities in the text itself.

We will, I hope, be able to demonstrate that though there is here no simple demarcation between form and content, the poetic issue breaks free almost as if in spite of formal constraints. This will give pause to ponder the arising incongruity, and perhaps indicate the zeal and effectiveness of this kind of poetry, existing almost in spite of itself. The fustian bravadoes of an Aurobindo Ghose and a Toru Dutt are rejected by Ezekiel with a decidedly rational temper in his censure of forms which ramble without striking, so he believes, for the authentic utterance. This drives us, even for a moment, towards initiatory, perhaps rhetorical, questions, which--in order to remain that to the reader, and to be active as undercurrents throughout--are perplexities not directly answered. What then constitutes--if we have to be awkward--Indic English, and to what degree does the work of Ezekiel contribute to, or partake of, it; or what, more broadly viewed, warrants universal interest in writers of English from India--if it is geographic placement that must accompany our readings? The first duty of a writer is of course to give expression to his own country and her spirit, and then--if he will reach that far--of his country which has become the world. The physical geography will not matter in the end. The American David Ray's magnificent *The Maharani's New Wall and Other Poems* (1989) is a paradigm; the writer's home is America, his language English, yet his collection palps the delicate spirit of India with a capacity that would put him, *culturally* (and of course poetically), amongst the foremost Indic writers.

Returning to the shallow pool of aboriginal. It is a symptom of our misapprehensions when Yeats's letter to Rothenstein--pronouncing that "Tagore does not know English, no Indian knows English"--is by some still taken seriously, and not as the petulant outburst of offended sensibility that it evidently was. Indeed, the flogged horse of such ruminations is dead, and will not revive by continued flagellation. (If Yeats were indeed merited in his remark--Tilottama Rajan reminds us--then he himself did not *know* English, since his mother-tongue was Gaelic). And need we stress it: the crux of Yeats's speculations was ever the engagement with *thought*.

What offering, then, can Indian poets writing in English make not only to their country, but to the world? We must remember that the bulk of contemporary writing in the so-called English-speaking world is a patch of fads and fashions that enervate the direction and the incognito genius of the language, and earns no more distinguished, ragged epaulettes for overseeing the direction of idiomatic manners which in truth are never confined to the expressions and desires of one tribe. For example, what more poised and tenderly compassionate poem is there in the English language than Vikram Seth's *The Accountant's House*, distilling its contemplative moment without crushing the bitter grape of life against the palate of language?

In an approach curiously analogous to Ernest Fenellosa's commentaries on syntactic discords in English (via his ruminations on Chinese), C.D. Narasimhaiah has commented on the damage to the young Indian mind by structures of English-teaching that ignore the complexities of Indian life, in particular its metaphysical inclinations, suggesting there are vistas which are debarred to the Western mind that takes its accents from a different attitude and an often spiritually vacant or defiant temper. Modern Western poets, indeed, are frequently more concerned with patrolling and magnifying their intellectual precincts than with looking at the world. Even the poet Auden, echoes of whom will be found in Ezekiel's verse, lacks for all *his engagement* with social issues a poetry of the heart. Hence the locale and colour of writing are appealing sidelights to the main show, which is the value and strength of poetic movement. A commotion away from questions of value has in the Western world had the consequence of weakening the purposive word, and the desired relaxation of rhythmic forms (increasing the range of utterance) has led to a flaccid and uninspired poetry of machinated bits of data. The poet laureate of our Age would already be an American supercomputer, *if* the programmers (in a befitting irony) had had less regard for the inducements of programs whose direct spin-off are shekels.

Embracing the commonplace is a skirting dangerously close to an evaporation of lyric possibilities, but it is Ezekiel's essential honesty that paradoxically often keeps the poetry integral and rich. Many contemporary Indian poets of distinction eschew the lyrical in order to draw social concerns to greater prominence. Grierson's advice about the modern tendency, that it "eliminates any conscious reference to a literary background altogether, to give poetry a setting not of literature and tradition but of nature and reality," finds its arguably strongest exponents in India. Only some living Indian poets will maintain Pound's credo in Mauberley "to resuscitate the dead art of poetry," "to maintain the sublime." How is it with Ezekiel? An early poem of his, the 1965 *Enterprise*--exploring the spirit of modernity--is a suitable starting-point. A company set out on a pilgrimage (which is also an exploration), charting the habits of all creatures in its movement towards an objective that causes weary puzzlement at the end. The exploratory instinct is broken, and in the ensuing inability to pray, the residual spirit is thrown back on a sense of home which finally sustains the grace to go on with life. Five years later, the poem *Philosophy* embarks on a kindred theme of exploration, and though the place this time is crypted in as much uncertainty as that of the pilgrims of the earlier poem, there is a *physical* sense here despite its placement "away from all existence." It is not a place staked out by compass and chart, for it follows the flow of a subtler current:

There is a place to which I often go,

Not by planning to, but by a flow
Away from all existence, to a cold
Lucidity, whose will is uncontrolled
Here, the mills of God are never slow.

Two things are crucial here: the spontaneity of a flow and its conveyance to a *cold* lucidity. "Lucidity," somewhat more intense than "clarity," unmistakably bespeaks the rationality when in juxtaposition with "cold." Its ecstasy is akin to Pater's "hard, gemlike flame." To Wittgenstein's austere beauty of rationality is rendered what is considered its due, but it also indicates that the prime mover behind such acquiescences is that unfathomable flow of life, the intuition, which even here regulates the direction. One wonders if from here on the age-old contention between philosophy and poetry will dissolve in mutual amities which contain the bounding steeds of Harit which head for the torrent of pure poetry, or if it may lead to a *sol negris*, a black sun, freezing rhythm to a mechanical and structured re-enactment. Across Ezekiel's work, there stretches from time to time the shadow that brings a solar eclipse of poetic certainties, a failing of the easy canter, for the rational purposes--sounding out the truth of things--will often put blinkers on the steed that carries them towards discovery, which then appears in a light of limitation. "I, too, reject that clarity of sight/ What cannot be explained, do not explain." Here the poet as *kavi*, seer, is frozen to a dialectic that is foreign to his sensitivities. The meanderings of "darkest myths" bring up "a final formula of light," tantamount to "clarity of sight," but the jump to linguistic interaction is not justified or negotiated poetically. This is the paradox of Wittgensteinean doubt--curiously espoused here by Ezekiel--and poised forever against the realities of living. Wittgenstein's recalcitrance to discourse on the inexplicable is the foe of all things poetical, cutting out the tongue and declaring it void of wisdom. Perhaps Jayanta Mahapatra's *Logic* responds limpidly to such enormity by "clasping geometric hands together" in a prayer of sorts; his *Indian Summer* shows to what coils the poet's hands must fold: "dreaming still, unexhausted/by the deep roar of funeral pyres" explores the sky with tongues of fire, while the ash fertilizes the earth underneath: Nature explaining herself, and the world *feels* the truth--though it might take poets to *know* Her speech. Mahapatra's poem possesses a *subhasitas* (felicity) which rolls counter to the perceived intentions of its title and presumably to what most Western sensibilities would claim as their own.

Jyotsna Agnihotri's *Introduction*--to present a final instance--appeals to the mean of living with a directness and clarity of utterances that are completely disarming, and might not sit well amongst the thwarted clarities of life in the dominant English-speaking countries. And again Mahapatra, whose *A Missing Person* puts the knowledge, intended for those of Wittgenstein's ilk, inside the very flame:

In her hands she holds
the oil lamp
whose drunken yellow flames
know where her lonely body hides.

That this is a prototypal "Indian" poem becomes apparent when we remember that Soma and Agni (the Lord of Fire) are *padavih kavinam*, the instigators of the poetics, the *Kavya;* but even without such reminder, the poignant embodiment of knowledge speaks for itself.

## I. Why read Ezekiel?

Why read Ezekiel? Is not his work uneven, marred by an occasional glaring loss of formal control? He lacks Ramanujan's strong Indian ethos (expatriate though Ramanujan be), Parthasarthy's sculptural scrupulousness (pithy though Ezekiel himself would be), Daruwalla's impressionism and P. Lal's evocativeness. Yet within the economy of Ezekiel's language there spins a commitment to humanity that keeps the reading alive, nurturing it from deep sources.

What are Ezekiel's virtues? His rhyme is seldom complex, and lacks the supple autonomy of blank verse, yet it has substance, harking back to a distinguished tradition:

The people walk, and eat. The waves
Rise and fall like nightmare graves
That cannot hold their dead. The sky
Is smaller than this open eye.

It is impossible not to note the metaphysical intensity in the oblique expression, and the Dadaist array of imagery succumbing to its sweeping force. Ezekiel's existential doubts notwithstanding, he creates early on an inspirational Trinity of "Philosophy, Poverty and Poetry," *(Background, Casually)* which shares his basement tenement (a further oblique referent to his perception of self) in his London years away from India. Compellingly resembling the Trimurti, Poetry is the creative, Philosophy the sustaining, and Poverty the destructive force. In the poetic manner, such division is of course never as simple as it seems--since even Brahma, Vishnu and Shiva's roles intersect, for each puissance stresses only its principal function. Ezekiel, again, shifts emphases according to need, while implicitly acknowledging how each interlocks with the others. Poverty is necessary for poetry, for its hunger gives a keen sensation of life, and is not blinded by life's self-seeking and affluent ceremonies. But a poetry without philosophy is like living with meaning in the more prosaic interstices that divide the poetic moment. What binds the three for a time in the poet's life is a *genius loci*, which is at once dreaded and welcome. Thus his lodgings take on an undefinable and highly suggestive hunch for the sacred:

> Arranged and rearranged,
> the room is always the same.

This place shapes future vision, and its door is always aslant; yet the speaker finds it impossible to leave the room. It is the same room as in *London*:

> a permanent and proud
> metaphor of struggle

and only towards the end does a resolution evolve

> I want to leave that room . . .
> and go into something
> so public and anonymous.

But with the foreign country, in an exile of learning familiar to many upper-class Indians since British dominion, there came an equal share of disenchantment. A Western world that moves with a distinctly faster pace, Ezekiel's "London seasons" passed him by, on a journey of inwardness that observed little of the outside world. The poet sings a song of experience, and it metaphorizes in a directness of voice that is rarely filtered or masked, and in a detachment that together give his verse an authentic and comelling ring:

> The song of my experience sung,
> I knew that all was yet to sing.
> My ancestors, among the castes,
> Were aliens crushing seed for bread
> (The Hoarded bullock made his rounds)

Is the "all" of the cited, final stanza of a background (contrary to the title, not casually evoked at all) not also the inclusiveness of the above similitude of "sky" and "eye"? The homonym in the latter is the ambiguity of the former, for both affirm the sense of self, its unboundedness, while at the same time dissolving it within the context of language and living. Rajgopal Parthasarathy's *Exile* casts light on the positives that come with (though frequently after) exile and confinement:

> You learn roots are deep,
> That language is a tree, loses colour
> under another sky.

Perhaps depth is also distance, since heaven is far removed from the modern mind, whose tree of language is not the most successful scion from the rootstock of the Aswattha. Ezekiel's metaphoric struggle is arguably strongest in his early verse. *The Unfinished Man*, his maiden collection--for all its echoes of Auden--has signal resemblances with his Australian contemporary, the poet Alec Hope. *Night of the Scorpion*, appearing five years later in *The Exact Name*, remains perhaps unparalleled in the simplicity of its narratival flow, restoring the vigour of the overused epithet "haunted." *Hymns in Darkness*,[1] and *Latter-Day Psalms*,[2] then, mark the turn towards a pithy vein, a sometimes compressed, imagist utterance. *Poster Poems* (from *Hymns*), if not his finest aphoristic poem, has a starkness and opening linearity that speaks with greater candour than folios of more accomplished verse:

> I signed the manifesto.
> I paid the subscription.
> I worked on the committee.
> I attended the part.
> It made no difference.
> The common language
>   hid my absence.

"Common language" is the various strand of activities and objects that circumscribe our modes of living; every movement, every thought, reflected in the iridescence of language, falls under the rubric of categories which contain it; the monotony of the "I"--wedded to activities and to objects or functions--highlights the despair of speech to which we are forever in thrall. But with the sharp stops and the final line's glitch to escape its telling, the articulatory aspect shines in a push towards a higher expressiveness via the commonplace; if it is only a straining, as there is no sounded and humanly audible language beyond language, its earnestness nevertheless remains apparent. Thus when the penultimate line runs on into the final, truncate statement, it is also, somewhat strangely, a caesura, for all is this one common tongue which gives life and expression to the object of the world. Thus the terse "London"--again--expresses this *ennui* with more impatience, sounding a programmatic note:

> I want to leave that room,
> the paraphernalia,
>
> the fuss, the chatter,
> the whole bag of tricks,
>
> and go into something
> so public and anonymous.

*There* is the rub: the movement into what is both public and anonymous, foreshadowed already in his *Morning Prayer*, when he was still an unfinished man. *In Warning: Two Sonnets*, Ezekiel, never putting on a mask, dons the enigmatic attribute; and though amid the clowning, say, of his *Very Indian Poems in English*, or the *causerie* of verse arranged from government reports or letters, the buckling aphoristic stance is his most signal weapon to fend off an ingrown casualness of living. *The Poster Poems* gives a firm expression of his espousal of the public spirit, whereas the *Egoist's Prayers*, a few pages later, is flat from the outset, and does not rise to any heights by attempting to make the common man a worthy subject-matter. Turn it which way you will: poetry always needs wings for flight, and invariably looks haggard and forlorn if a mere waving of arms tries to attain altitude. The famed Australian poet Chris Wallace-Crabbe, waving as Ezekiel does in these moments, has theorized the tug issuing from the common, vulgar expression and the demands of the sublime; wishing in the course to express the language of the tribe but jumping in his zeal from a promontory of Mount Helicon, he has repeatedly landed on a rather more Stygian barge--that cannot be bound for the shores of the living. Even uncouth Caliban is alive and finds our ear because his language is vital, though perhaps never well.

The will towards a language and speech that have meaning, that do not bend under the weight of a removed and seemingly forever ulterior metaphoric, has in the post-war years led to the supposition that poetry--an incarnate carcass--had nothing left to say, and some poets celebrated a spontaneous muteness. The spontaneity of poetic speech naturally releases also the gift of silence. But this reticence belonged, in essence, also to Hofmannsthal's famous Chandos-letter that attempt to express the inexpressible. Ezekiel's *For Satish Gujral* is for this reason one of his most enagaging poems, negotiating the modernist crux with remarkable adroitness:

Deaf artists all,
all of us who martyr the meaning
  in the flux
  to lonely
and heated visions whoring
  after truth.
*Mea culpa*. Punish me.
It is the task
  of love
  and imagination

to hear what can't be heard
when everybody speaks.

Ezekiel rarely varies his line-length; that it should happen here demonstrates one or two things about the autonomous movement of such tensions as there are. The poet as clown and the artist who cannot hear the world, are variations on the theme of obliqueness. Success in poetry, as Dickinson observed with genius, lies in circuit, and at no time more so than today. But this is not Ezekiel's point here. The meretricious pursuit of the sublime--if it proceeds from an attitude, and not an inner conviction;--if by probing, it impales, standing over and not under things, may bring visions which are not the magnificent harbingers that enter when the nature is calm and steady, receptive for growth, but feverish, self-spun gauze that turns into a spider's webs before our eyes.

But when fragmentation beckons, Ezekiel becomes a taskmaster and speaks for the silence amid the babel of the poets and the tribe. For all the revisionary titles of his two most recent collections, *Hymns in Darkness* and *Latter-Day Psalms*, Ezekiel's undergirding spirituality lights up his wavering and impatient ambivalences. While *The Tribute to the Upanishads* was a flailing tribute--rehashing the lore of the Kena Upanishad--his *Hymns in Darkness* redeem the failure by poignant silences that are the only valid tributes to the spirit. Kalidasa's ghost, in the swinging of breasts and buttocks, hovers hereabouts, voided of the master's sensuousness, as the pipette drips the distillate of what makes man human from a shored river of words. *Poem No. 10* presents alternative picture of a man, yet none of these are judged to fit that thing which they describe, which is a man; and *Poem No. 13*, building on these quiet-keyed assertions of the suite, concludes in unremarkable, but moving lines;

I saw him cheerful
in the universal darkness
as I stood grimly
in my little light.

That this cheerfulness is a Nietzschean bravado in a different key, belying some of the submerged and valorized uncertainties, does little to spoil the sharpness of the evocation. And *Poem No.14*'s final couplet, "I heard him out/in black wordlessness"--catching the spirit of Celan's "the dethroned, inwarded"--encrypts wistful allusions to the hidden journey of light. With *Poem No. 12*'s wayward and playful

> The Darkness has its secrets
> which light does not know

the philosophico-poetical intransigence finds retrospective placement as a kind of Mephistophelian wager that senses the very foibles it would hold up for praise.

Running through Ezekiel's verse from his first beginnings to his present state of poetic maturity, his pedigree of religious affinities--though not always attained of a resonance (as Birje Patil has already pointed out), and proceeding tongue-in-cheek--indicate the above confidences, but it is the Silence the *Pashyanthi*, the seen but not formulated Word as formulated in the *Kavya*, which is present like a tremor that one feels but cannot trace. This invisible shuffle of the earth at times saves the facile statement from decay: "The fog in the head and the sense of success" from *Hangover* is one such movement, reminiscent of Eliot.

It becomes noteworthy--even if never memorable--when we recognize that the *Para Vak*, the Ultimate word, the Silence beyond silence, never gives birth to the deformed offspring of flippancy, which though belonging to the same tree issues rather from a gnarled and already misshapen branch of mental habit or expression. It is for this reason that some modes of irony, praised and adored by the supposed intelligentsia of criticism, raise the most serious difficulties for maintaining the harmony of the sensibility. It is too often a blade that, while cutting flesh, slices into the cutter's own hand. It is the modern age which craves, of course, this ambivalent posture of the destructive self-destruction, thrust up like a mirror to catch the reflections of our living. Salving the occasionally destructive turn of irony, Ezekiel's instincts are directed towards fruitful postures in the *Nudes of 1978*, celebrating a nuptials of spirit and flesh:

> I listened to the darkness breathing:
> your body had an inner light
> for me to contemplate. I knew

each part but now I saw
the sacramental pattern, soul
inviolate within all that
pure flowing from its source.

Nothing here reminds one of the startling remark in his *Hymns* that "The Enemy is God," or of his uninspired "Tribute to the Upanishads," although his *Psalms*--as indicated before--are aphoristic and world-wide in poignant persiflage almost of Khalil Gibran's profundities. His verses see-saw between seriousness in the gesture of affirming physical life--opposing action to meditation--yet not quite winning through to his valued altruistic credo. The subtle lesson of the *Srimad Bhagavad Gita*, stressing that meditation and action are not opposite, is never embodied. At this point the question materializes as to what kind of *engagement* may be discovered in Ezekiel.

## II. Literature as *engagement*

Ezekiel's concern seems to lie in the necessity for clarity in a world of ideas and contradictory conceptions; his *engagement* is not one of ideology but of consciousness. The poetic will seizes matters of social concern without making them subservient to intellectual strategies. Social commentary is authenticated through factual rendition; this is Ezekiel's method (though one inextricable from his personal convictions), and we need to accept it *on its own terms* in order to enter his world. One of the first things we notice is that the timbre of his verse uncovers the traps conjured by ideology. The result is an affective poetry of statement. Witness the directness of *Minority Poem:*

It's not mythology
or the marriage customs
that you need to know,

It's the will to pass
through the eye of a needle
to self-forgetfulness.

The guests depart, dissatisfied;

they will never give up
their mantras, old or new.

Ezekiel complains about the absence of a real public, and not only in India. As he himself admits in an interview, he does not write as an Indian, yet after studying abroad he returns to India, and makes it his home. His poetry declares a movement away from a world of ideas, anchored though his poetical impulse be to past experiences; it remains even after his early, more lyrical and "self-possessed" poems a poetry of statement and purpose. Yet there is an apparent dichotomy alive as well, a prophetic tension in which light and darkness occasionally merge to give an impression of the flow of time:

Except the Lord build the ho
use--and not even always then--
they labour in vain that build
it. Yet, it is better to build
than to abstain from building,
and no labour is altogether
in vain. It is not vain to rise
up early, to sit up late,
to eat the bread of sorrow.

Here Ezekiel, reworking the Psalms in his own, latter-day versions, appropriates the prophetic vein of Gibran and stands it on its head, yet there is no anaemia or attrition of meaningful comment, but a surprising obliqueness that stales with its residual, and consciously "marginalized," stance. Such "commentary," guardedly avoiding the sublimity it nevertheless retraces by implication, is perilously close to common speech, and appears as possessing little besides its reportorial virtues. But limitation of expression is perhaps countermanded by reference to tradition, and to careless handling of ritual; to constitute a world that is, again by implication, not as good as sublime pronouncements would have wished, or were ever able to attain beyond what are, from the vantage of needs and the reality of living, often indeed *sublime failures*. The ironies, whatever they be in this revisionary ethos, stand almost too denuded to allow for an indulgence in the kind of abstractions literary devices would seem to invite. The call for action, for taking religious inspiration not as an elixir but at most as a *spur* to the actualities of action, defeats even the blithe and noble sentiments of the *Karma-Yogin* as enunciated in the Vedas, counselling to action, a call always proceeding mysteriously, and from high altitudes and the mouth of a declared prophet.

It is within the setting of this call for action where Ezekiel's *engagement* should be defined. In a battle reminiscent of the theorizing of *Beyond Good and Evil,* Ezekiel engages his poetic soul without pleading a truce:

> I shall not expect goodness
> and mercy all the days of
> my life, even if I dwell
> in the house of the Lord.

The intent is to metamorphose, to purge the old conditioning. Yet even here--unless we take the words to mean more than what they so blatantly express-we will slight a deeper conflict of the mind. For in one sense, Ezekiel might be retracing his steps from the desert regions inhabited by Nietzsche, and for all the sternness of tone, there is an unusual sense of humility arising from the recognition of contraries and the free-play of his own individuality; to these the poet swears complete allegiance. That such confidences move beyond a narrow solipsism, assures their universal appeal.

It is from this perspective of extreme awareness (since the emphasis in the first line is on "expect")--of a perpetual questioning, in other words--that the poet moulds the imagery of the surrounding world. But awareness not only lightens the ambient world; the inner mind of the poet is also under examination. When the poetry thus refers to events in the world at large, its charge will be subjective, its movement occasionally derivative, and the rhythms and technicalities subject to the strictures of the current fads in criticism. Yet with Basho, the great Japanese poet of the 17th century, we have the idea that fashionableness in literary matters is to be welcomed--and by implication even sought by the poet--provided sincerity is constant throughout:

> Indians are a friendly people, anyway,
> she said, "So they are," I agree,
> "so they are." She stares at me

dubiously, I listen to the buzzing air.

Perhaps she thinks it best
not to argue. I think so too.

What on a first reading reveals a reprimand of social mores not devoid, some would like to think, of cultural acrimonies, emerges later as the sole criterion of simple sincerity, and not as some peremptory ostentation. When studying Anglo-Indian poetry, we indeed chart our analyses not by remaining true to the serpentines of the expression, but rebound from a malformed sense of *Indianness* which is rarely reading more than the track of extremity to which alone belongs our consideration. Nationality is never a passport to identity. More importantly, and in this poem, the conflict created by the apparent fruitlessness of remarks that are uttered in the presence of a thing of such consequence as poverty, mute any reply, and jostles the heart with silences. Hence two *kinds* of poverty, share the privilege of expression within the intangibles of the poetical; one to do with the outer world, the other--arguably a thing of wealth, if it didn't imply a poignant transcendence of it--clinging to the inner life.

But there is a stronger push towards removing ignorance at a very basic level, towards tempering the stultifying beliefs of some classes in India. Ezekiel tries his "bare bone" poetry on the rituals and customs of his country. This has been attempted in various forms by the majority of contemporary Anglo-Indian writers. Ezekiel's approach, however, is conversant with the more direct and refined syntax of the modernists; he has not recanted the teachings and struggles of early century London, but has instead endeavoured to adopt some of their more demanding qualities. Echoes of prewar T.S. Eliot and Auden, and a regard for the consciences which Pound admired in Chinese and Japanese poetry (to which Pound could seldom conform outside his work of translation), are confirmation of an education in the neo-classical English tradition--but also of a kinship for themes universally relevant. Ezekiel's tone surrenders at times some of the mournful earnestness to which the previous comparisons might have directed our thought, and though never eschewing the possibility for dramatic turns, he magnifies to a farcical degree the extent of the *poetic* substance of his experiences:

Still later,
we lay on the floor mattress in the kitchen of my wife's
family apartment and though it was past midnight, she
kept saying let's do it darling let's do it darling
so we did it.

More than ten years passed before she told me that
she remembered being very disappointed. Is that all
there is to it? she had wondered. Back from London
eighteen months earlier, I was horribly out of practice.

There is accommodation within these lines for the arousal of diverse feelings; the trial of the gun-powder of emotions is shown, and though the commissioning hand reaches down with a lucifer match, it is not lit. The past is the past, after all, and a hand moves in at a crucial moment to deflect the turn towards the fire of a hedonism burning in the still more distant recollection of the speaker. The thought is mordant, but the ironic is foreclosed by a candour tugging towards the sad face of learning that remains a cloistered scowl, and remains defiantly unfledged and inaccessible even when showing its face:

During our first serious marriage quarrel she said Why did
you take my virginity from me? I would gladly have
returned it, but not one of the books I had read instructed
me how.

There moves also of course a derision of the triviality of social conventions here. Yet it is not attended by irony, which notions of guilt--absent in the poem--might evoke in the reader. Social critique has slunk past the usual boundaries of aversion to offer us a deep histogram of a relationship. There is an avoidance of philosophical considerations--yet the unfeigned philosophy of life brings not scintillating but gentle suspense to the moment, bestowing a gravity to the improbables of the obvious. Such candour prepares in the end for the relinquishing of masks we may have unconsciously shared with the author:

There was no dowry because they knew I was "modern"

> and claimed to be modern too. Her father asked me how
> much jewellery I expected him to give away with his daughter
> When I said I didn't know, he laughed it off.

Some say that the underlying *laissez faire* in Indian society promotes evils like poverty and oppression. Ezekiel also moves against this perennial acquiescence:

> All of us are sick, Sir,
> not just the eldest daughter,
> no, nor the younger one.
> It's not the son, not the son,
> It's all of us who need you, Sir
> Psy--chi--a--trist! . . .
>
> Time is ripe for Sai Baba.
> Time is ripe for Muktananda.
> Let father go to Rajneesh Ashram.
> Let mother go to Gita classes.
> What we need is meditation.
> Need to find our roots, Sir.
> All of us are sick, Sir.

India remains a very fertile ground for social movements and leftist political options; her level of poverty ranks among the world's largest. Marxist approaches have gained many acolytes, yet the perplexities of India belong not to the category of ideologies but to ones of belief--to faith and its counterparts: superstition and blind faith. (We speak loosely here, mindful of Aurobindo's assertion in his *Essays on Yoga* that *blind faith* is a contradiction in terms). Ezekiel directs his observations at the actions (or inactions) of Indian society, parodying the pathetic ceremoniousness of urban life; direct *engagement* with suffering, as in the early *A Morning Walk*--with its "Barbaric city sick with slums"--is rare in him.

Although a poet writes in essence because he is a poet--not because poetry is a medium conveying ideas--poetry is nevertheless the optimal medium for summoning the most refined thinkers of any country, and possesses the attribute of provoking hermetic images, which are usually abutting with scriptural tiers. The task here of *resocializing* religion sometimes smudges the stamp of rectitude to the blur of self-righteousness, but some success at least is achieved.

In *The truth about the floods,* we are taken on an excursion through villages ravaged by floods. The simple language, the matter-of-factness and the dramatic irony of repetition in "I wasn't a government official" are the sole literary devices in this exposition. The reality is obvious, and the language is a landscape of poverty, fear and despondency; it telegraphs us closer to the bare reality of the suffering. The result is no maudlin sigh-tempest but a clarity illumining with a transcendence firmly rooted to the soil of its *earthly* concerns: "My husband has been washed away"-- "We took shelter on tree tops."

Here the *engagement* is none other than the report of calamity and the evidencing of consequent miseries. Yet the poetry conjures up a network of resonant silences, denouncing an oppression deeper than that inflicted by acts of God, silently studying the long-winded quacking of bureaucrats: its arraignment is deeper than vociferous protestations could hope to accomplish. Like the sage Narada's *Bhakti Sutras* epitomize the lover of God as one who like a deaf-mute raises arms and twists the mouth in eloquent demonstration of his ineffable devotion, the charged silences spill over into other areas almost unopposed, for the Ignorance finds it difficult to grapple with the "unsighted" adversary.

Then there are the more personal poems, in which the relationship between the poet and his vision form a new creation--a living imagination--and a new picture of mankind. These pictures, as in *Poverty Poem 2,* have their own stress of emotion, without which they would risk disintegration. The speechless is moved to speech, the sick to joyfulness:

> I offered a coin
> he took it
> without a glance at me
> nor made the slightest gesture
> in acknowledgement.

The absolute right of receiving assistance is the right to live, incontestable. It is the *truth* of hunger which comes bluntly and grazes the skin of the poem to make customary responses like "ungrateful" or "impassive" appear raw and specious; for there is candour and genuine regard for life in the silences of the beneficiary.

We have seen that what Ezekiel proposes is something other than mere *protest*, which is altogether too *loud* to convey his concern. The relevance of his poetry lies in the depiction of the mundane, the physical reality which is inescapable. The rest is vision, arising from a zealous adherence to the cold facility of the world *as it is;* "What cannot be explained, do not explain," the poet, as we saw, said earlier--though there is disbelief in the poet's gift of simple wings to take him aloft from the Wittgensteinean compound.

We can expect little that strikes a false colour in Ezekiel's landscapes and few undercurrents or overtones, apart from what critics have chosen to call irony but which, under scrutiny, come to denote something intangible, but certainly more substantial. That Ezekiel chooses to state and re-state the case of misery, the lack of understanding and the ignorance undressed and sans masque (with the warming wind of village ritual and motion) keeps the studied largesse of irony at bay. Even if some wisp of irony is detected by the reader (each of whom, for his own reasons, is the final judge), it would be distorting to say that it has become the final purpose of the poem. Here we have to agree with the remarks of Perry in his review of Vilas Sarang's *Indian English Poetry since 1950: An Anthology*, where the case against the labelling of a school of Indian ironic poetry supposedly headed by Nissim Ezekiel is supported by pointing out that the poet's attitude might be the best response to the *tradition-bound* pressures of the audience.

Ezekiel's detail, without stating all, reaches somewhat deeper than the perhaps more outwardly appealing minutiae of, say, Ramanujan's *Obituary*, for Ezekiel merges disparate acts in a single sequence of thought. Observation is Ezekiel's first inclination; following which a fancy for slight abstractions within the material of the poem extends the meaning of the objects depicted: a pretence not yet turned into disguise:

> accompanied by a woman
> whose love is partly doubt

But the most successful abstractions in Ezekiel's work are the ones which imbibe the central metaphor of the poem and lace it with a highly ethical message emanating from the piece and reminiscent of scriptural intent:

There's only this:
  a tarred road
  under a mild sun
  after rain,
  glowing;

  wet, green leaves
  patterned flat
  on the pavement
  around dog-shit;

  one ragged slipper
  near an open gutter,
  three crows
  pecking away at it.

And breasts, thigh, buttocks
  swinging
  now towards
  now away from him.

Morality springs from what has customarily been considered immoral;--no doubt a contradiction in terms but also the seed-bed of poetic growth. The mood of this poem recalls Ezekiel's desperation elsewhere at his restraints in talking, unlike the Sanskrit poets, of the body's forms; and yet it is very similar to Sri Sankaracharya's chant guiding people away from the futility of a sensuous life: *Bhaja Govinda Mudhamate.* ("Praise the Lord, stupid . . . do not keep on looking at the breasts of women. . . !") A lucidity reminiscent of the writings of saints pervades a poetry which claims no transcendence. The clue to this question might, again, be found in the poem *Philosophy;* "A place to which I often go. . . . Here the Mills of God are never slow," and "The mundane language of the senses sings" to become "An argument against the nakedness/That dies of cold to find the truth it brings." The intellectual insight takes its rightful place in an awareness of worldly experience. There exists a curious detachment from the hedonistic in his poetry, despite the dubious wisdom of his first publishing his *Psalms* in the bawdy magazine *Debonair:*

> I hate it,
> however great the image,
> Praise the form,
> praise the modelling,
> praise the dynamic movement
> and the complex synthesis
> of muscular tensions:
> the woman plainly needs
> her common arms and legs.

One recalls that Shakespeare's lady (when she walks) *treads* on the ground; familiarity with the mundane and methodical scepticism are the major emissaries of an attitude of talking to the common man in simple-hearted language equally grasped by Wallace Stevens's "pensive man." Certainly Ezekiel's vision of India is one which profits from all the advantages of social status and a foreign education. But for all his solipsism, his imagination always returns to the real world. There are themes which carry the weight of diurnal relevances; *Entertainment* is one such poem:

> The monkey-show is on:
> patient girl on haunches
> holds the strings
> a baby in her arms.
> Two tiny monkeys
> in red and purple pantaloons
> prepare to dance . . .
>
> Anticipating time for payment,
> the crowd dissolves.
> Some, in shame, part
> with the smallest coin they have.
> The show moves on.

Ezekiel could have entered into the intricacies of the performance and the tricks of the animals, but he confines himself to a depiction of the scene as simply a passing event in suburban life. Emphasis is on the matter-of-factness of the spectators and (ironically) on the seemingly casual titling of the piece. What Ezekiel describes here is by Western standards only a pitiable scenario; perhaps the only Westerner able to respond in an *Indian* way to the monkey tricks might be the child who has not yet succumbed to the silent persuaders of the television circus.

A wealth of possible metaphors (which inevitably emerge from these scenes) is relinquished in this poem. An indifference to the flights into the loftier zones of intellect is at work, where concepts and ideas are played with for their own sake. When the common man leaves at last the monkey-show of poverty, a little money also exits the pocket of those among the humbled audience who cannot manage a timely escape from shame; a stress falls on the parting, and with the escaping breath we too are held to unspoken exigencies of grace.

It is difficult to attempt a critical placement of Ezekiel's poetry; there is so much of it that defies commentary, escaping--like Impressionism in painting--the religious, metaphysical and scientific covert objectives; or else, like the Dadaism of Magritte (who is erroneously considered a Surrealist), connoting an insistence that his poems (Magritte's *trompe l'oeil*) are the real things they describe, and mean nothing beyond that point.

Entertainment draws us further back, to Rilke and Apollinaire's *Saltimbanques* (and further back to Picassso's *Les Saltimbanques*) in the picture of pathos; where the boy of Rilke's poem transcends the adversities of his milieu by a paradoxical smile, Ezekiel's offers no transcendence and gives no features to the performers; all is mute acquiescence--with the barb still lodged in the skin. The affinities to the visual arts are obvious since Ezekiel's finest poems--for all their abstract moment--have a pictorial heart.

The instant of the pauper's frail and unequally poised and tenuous prospect for benefit, arresting the trickery and the entertainment, juxtaposing the moment of revelry with the immense question of survival, reveals the poet in ragged garments, a Christ-figure; and even though he be swaddled in the cerements of his craft (never quite abounding the accoutrements of sorrowful humanity), such writing raises its author from the flawed horizon of our present-day world towards the sublimity of silence.

## NOTES

1. Nissim Ezekiel, *Hymns in Darkness* (Delhi: OUP, 1976).
2. Nissim Ezekiel, *Latter-Day Psalms* (Delhi: OUP, 1982).